TASTE OF ROMANIA

Hippocrene is NUMBER ONE in

International Cookbooks

Africa and Oceania
Best of Regional African Cooking
Egyptian Cooking
Good Food from Australia
Traditional South African Cookery
Taste of Eritrea

Asia and Near East
Best of Goan Cooking
Best of Kashmiri Cooking
The Joy of Chinese Cooking
The Art of South Indian Cooking
The Art of Persian Cooking
The Art of Israeli Cooking
The Art of Turkish Cooking
The Art of Uzbek Cooking

Mediterranean
Best of Greek Cuisine
Taste of Malta
A Spanish Family Cookbook
Tastes of North Africa

Western Europe
Art of Dutch Cooking
Best of Austrian Cuisine
A Belgian Cookbook
Cooking in the French Fashion
(bilingual)
Celtic Cookbook
English Royal Cookbook
The Swiss Cookbook
Traditional Recipes from Old
    England
The Art of Irish Cooking
Traditional Food from Scotland
Traditional Food from Wales
The Scottish-Irish Pub and Hearth
    Cookbook
A Treasury of Italian Cuisine
(bilingual)

Scandinavia
Best of Scandinavian Cooking
The Best of Finnish Cooking
The Best of Smorgasbord Cooking
Good Food from Sweden

Central Europe
Best of Albanian Cooking
All Along the Danube
Bavarian Cooking
Traditional Bulgarian Cooking
The Best of Czech Cooking
The Best of Slovak Cooking
The Art of Hungarian Cooking
Art of Lithuanian Cooking
Polish Heritage Cookery
The Best of Polish Cooking
Old Warsaw Cookbook
Old Polish Traditions
Treasury of Polish Cuisine (bilingual)
Poland's Gourmet Cuisine
Taste of Romania

Eastern Europe
The Cuisine of Armenia
The Best of Russian Cooking
Traditional Russian Cuisine (bilingual)
The Best of Ukrainian Cuisine

Americas
Cooking the Caribbean Way
Mayan Cooking
The Honey Cookbook
The Art of Brazilian Cookery
The Art of South American Cookery
Old Havana Cookbook (bilingual)

TASTE OF ROMANIA

Its Cookery and Glimpses of Its History, Folklore, Art, Literature, and Poetry

NICOLAE KLEPPER

I sincerely wish, one day my daughter, Caroline, will have this book and make a very happy family.

Feb. 2000

HIPPOCRENE
New York

For information, address:
HIPPOCRENE BOOKS, INC.
171 Madison Avenue
New York, NY 10016

Cataloging-in-Publication data available from the Library of Congress

ISBN 0-7818-0766-2

Printed in the United States of America.

DEDICATION

To my mother, Irina, whose gift to me of her old Romanian cookbook got me started on writing this book; and to my wife, Ann, for her patience with my endless talk about the book and her harsh but invaluable critiques.

ACKNOWLEDGMENTS

*I*t would just take too much space if I were to list everyone who has contributed to this work and helped me in so many ways. I would like, however, to make special mention of a few, and ask those that I may have overlooked to forgive me.

In the United States, special thanks to the Romanian Cultural Center in New York and especially to Michaela Ionescu for her encouragement and her help with research material. I am also especially grateful to Simion Alb, director of the Romanian National Tourist Office in New York, who has done so much to help make my research trip to Romania a success.

Before publication of *A Taste of Romania*, I spent four weeks in Romania doing research and collecting additional recipes to complete the book. It was a productive trip, and a great experience. Contrary to the astonishingly negative press in America, I found this diverse and beautiful country a delight. And, in spite of their present difficult economic struggle out of communism and into capitalism and democracy, I found the people warm, hospitable, and very helpful.

In Romania, I would like to thank all the cooks and chefs who contributed their interesting and tasty specialties to the book. Their names are listed with their recipes.

In the city of Braşov, I will always remember Violetta and Constantin Tudose, friends of the family, whom I met for the first time and with whom I spent two days, for their warmth and hospitality. They even called the police to look for me when I was late from my wanderings around the town. Violetta is an exceptionally good cook and hostess, who did some unforgettable Romanian home cooking for me.

In Suceava, where I stayed five days to visit the famous Painted Monasteries, I would like to thank Mr. and Mrs. Nadejdea Giosu, owners of the delightful small Hotel Balada, for the personal attention, help with my research, and especially for care while I was grounded with tonsillitis and bronchitis. They even convinced a busy doctor to make a house call; their homemade soups and nourishing meals got me back on my feet in two days.

In Iaşi, a special thanks to Dr. Kurt W. Treptow, director of the Center for Romanian Studies, and his lovely wife, Laura. Kurt, who has published, among other works, an extremely well written and interesting 600-page *History of Romania*, proofread my chapter on "The Heritage of Romania and Its People." He was also instrumental in obtaining access to special research rooms at the Library of the University of Iaşi. In addition to that he was of great help in

7

arranging my accommodations in Iaşi and making his office and staff available to me. To Laura I owe the translation of a poem included in this book.

In Bucharest, I am indebted to Nicky Nicolaescu, country manager for GE, who gave me much invaluable advice on my travels throughout Romania, and through a friend of his found me a cozy, comfortable apartment in the heart of the city, a welcome change from three weeks in hotels.

And finally, back in the United States, I must add to this list Henry and Alfie Butun, good friends, without whom this book would probably never have been published. They are the couple I mentioned in the PREFACE, who one day, over dinner, asked me: "Why don't you write a cookbook?"

CONTENTS

PREFACE

I was twelve years old when my parents left Romania, and took me with them to live in America. It was about the time when Nazi Germany began its incursions into neighboring countries, Neville Chamberlain was still "appeasing" the Axis Powers, and Franklin D. Roosevelt was preparing to campaign for his third term of office. We settled in New York. I went to school, quickly learned the language, became a New Yorker, joined the American Armed Forces, went to the University, married, had kids, a career—and generally gave little thought to my country of birth; that is, until fifty odd years later, when, during an innocent dinner conversation with friends, the seeds of an idea began to germinate. I was going to write a book. Here is how it happened.

I was serving in the American Armed Forces in Italy when my parents bought a summer cottage on a beautiful lake in Connecticut, near New York—pier, float, and boat included. They surprised me with it when I came back home. I couldn't wait to make use of the place, so the next summer school vacation I invited Frank, one of my university classmates, to join me for two weeks of swimming, boating, and fun—just the two of us—no parents around. We had a great time, but there was one problem—we had to eat, and neither of us had the slightest notion about cooking, nor did we have enough money to eat out. After a few disastrous culinary experiments, we concluded that of the two, my cooking was slightly more digestible, so we made a pact: I was to be the cook and he, the dishwasher, and that was the start of a lifelong interest in cooking. By the time the two weeks ended, we were actually enjoying some of my meals, and not too soon.

I married a lovely girl—a lot of fun, intelligent, a good hostess, and a good social worker, but a terrible cook. She had no interest in anything remotely associated with food preparation. We set up household, and made the same pact as I had made with Frank in Connecticut—I did the cooking and she did the cleaning up. My success ratio kept increasing, and so did my interest.

Hearing about my newly acquired interest, my mother gave me her old Romanian cookbook, which she had received as a wedding gift, in the early

1920s. Its covers had been lost long ago, and its pages were brittle and yellowing. Never one to like spending time in the kitchen, she must have brought this book with her to New York as a last resort in the event of hardships. As I write this book, she is going on 94. To this day, every time she visits and I prepare a special meal for us, she always says, "This you did not learn from your mother." What she doesn't know is that I used to spend a lot of my after-school time in the kitchen. You see, we were lucky to have domestic help in those days, and I had a crush on Ilona. She let me watch while she prepared various delicacies for us, and I also got to scrape and lick the bottom of the pots. I must have picked up some hints along the way.

Much has happened in my life since those early days. I remarried twice, and raised families. My career gave me the opportunity to live in many parts of the United States, and then abroad, in France, Holland, England, Switzerland, Algeria, and Saudi Arabia. Wherever I lived and traveled, I took a special interest in the local cuisine. I tasted specialties, collected regional cookbooks, and tried out recipes. Mother's cookbook traveled with me, neglected, collecting dust.

I no longer do all the cooking, but I still enjoy preparing special recipes for dinner guests. It was during one of these dinners that the inspiration came to me. My wife, Ann, and I had two couples for dinner. Ann took care of the appetizer, smoked salmon, and the dessert, mousse-au-chocolat, which, by-the-way, she makes better than any I have ever tasted in France. I prepared a Gigot Rôti au Gratin de Monsieur Henny (Monsieur Henny's Roast Lamb with Gratin of Potato, Onion, and Tomato) from one of my favorite French cookbooks, Bistro Cooking by Patricia Wells. The dinner was a success, and the guests were raving about the lamb roast when one of them said to me "Why don't you write a cookbook?"

I made some comment about the fact that there were thousands of cookbooks out there—and then suddenly I knew what I was going to do. It all came together like in a flash. I remembered Mother's old cookbook, and thought about my lifetime interest in cooking. What if I were to write a book containing a selection of the best in Romanian recipes, and then add some historical and cultural facts? I could tell others about Romania, while, at the same time, have fun rediscovering my native country, a country with a long and colorful history; one rich in beauty, resources, tradition, folklore, and culinary diversity, yet so little known in Western Europe and America.

And so I started to work on *Taste of Romania*. Have a good time reading about Romania, as well as preparing and tasting its great cuisine.

INTRODUCTION

TASTE OF ROMANIA is a book combining over 140 tasty traditional recipes with compelling examples of Romania's folklore, humor, poetry, and proverbs. It will also take you on a brief historical journey across the 4000-year-old history of its people and their Roman ancestry.

There was a time, before the Second World War and before the many hardships that Romanians suffered under oppressive and misguided regimes, when Romania was a pleasant country to live in and a place to eat well. Before the Second World War, Romania had a modern rail system, a highly developed tourist industry with modern hotels, beautiful beaches, excellent ski resorts, and busy industrial ports. One could drive across the country and enjoy seemingly endless wheat and corn fields. Once Romania was a supplier of petroleum and the bread-basket of Europe. The cities' shops were full of shoppers buying goods from all over the world. Restaurants, cafes and pastry shops were packed. Since the revolution of 1989, there has been much effort to improve conditions. However, the ravages of the recent past, and the rapid change to a market-oriented economy have left the country polluted, impoverished, and disoriented.

The Romanian is of a naturally fun loving nature, warm, hospitable, playful, with an innate sense of humor, and enjoys the pleasure of eating well. Unfortunately not many young Romanians remember the "good old days." Although today stores again are filled with goods, the average Romanian lacks the purchasing power to avail himself of basic food products, and has to struggle just to survive. Today one must eat to live and not live to eat.

At the writing of this book, six years have passed since the revolution which brought to an end thirty years of communism, and one can already see some improvement in living conditions. Only five months before the publication of *Taste of Romania*, the first democratically conducted election brought in a new president and new government, dedicated to encouraging investment and tourism, raising salary levels, and improving living conditions. Hopefully, it will not be too long before Romanians will again be able to enjoy the pleasures of their gastronomy too.

In Romania, hospitality and religion are closely tied to the meal. It is not incidental that such words as ospitalitate (hospitality), oaspete (guest), ospeţie (feast), in Romanian are related to ospăţ, meaning "big dinner." Most Romanians belong to the Eastern Orthodox Church. Special dishes are prepared on religious holidays. Chrismas is when Romanians, irrespective of where they live, partake in an old ceremony starting with the slaughter of a pig. The pig is roasted, and special dishes are prepared from all parts of the animal, including sausages, black pudding toba (chopped meat from the head, tongue, and heart, stuffed in the skin of the stomach), ham, ribs, smoked bacon, and pig's trotters. At Easter, after several weeks of fasting, feasts are prepared from lamb, and always include hand-painted Easter eggs and sweet cream cheese cake.

What is Romania's cuisine? It is the product of a series of historical, geographical, and religious influences. The result is a rich variety of specialties, from the tasty, hearty, and nutritious dishes of the peasant and shepherd to the gastronomic, French influenced delicacies of the 19th century nobility.

Little is known about the culinary habits of the Romanian's ancestors, the Getae. A Thracian tribe, they lived in the region of Romania for over two thousand years before the Romans turned it into a Roman province, which they called Dacia. We do know that toward the end of the seventh century BC, the Getae exchanged grain, cattle, fish, and honey with the Greeks for oil and wine. They were blessed with fertile plains where they grew good crops of cereals. They raised cattle at the foot of the Carpathian mountains. Their forests were an abundant source of a great variety of game animals and birds; and the Black Sea, lakes, and rivers provided them with fish.

We also know that Roman soldiers stationed in Dacia ate a staple dish, the pulmentum, a sort of mush made from grain. Much later, during the 16th and 17th centuries, the Turks introduced corn brought from the New World by the Venetian merchants to Eastern Europe. The Northern Italians and the Romanians planted the corn and began to make the pulmentum from corn meal. This became the Italian polenta and the Romanian mămăligă. This is the only dish that can be traced directly back to the Romans. It remains to this day both a tasty and nutritious part of the daily diet in villages, and at the same time is featured on the most sophisticated of menus.

During the centuries of Turkish domination over Romania, the boieri, a landed nobility, rose to power. They enslaved the peasants and put them to work in the fields. The great expanses of land north of the Danube, the bărăgan, supplied all of Europe with grain until the First World War, and still produce vast quantities of wheat and corn. In the area Jews were traders. Gypsies who wandered around the country in search of work, became skilled at making, lining, and repairing enameled copper kitchen pots, as well as making wooden spoons. The boieri began to use Gypsies as kitchen helpers and cooks in their mansions, and from their nomadic life-style, the Gypsies brought with them the skills of grilling meat over charcoal. To this day, a favorite specialty in Romanian restaurants is steak grilled over charcoal, usually seasoned with garlic, vinegar, and parsley, and served, sizzling, on wooden platters.

Conversion of the ancient Dacians to Christianity began around 350AD, and by the end of the first millennium AD, Dacian Christians adopted Byzantine Orthodox rites. The Eastern Orthodox Church has remained the principal church in Romania. Many beautiful old monasteries dating back to the 15th and 16th centuries are today a major artistic and tourist attraction. Monks usually did their seminary studies in Greece, and brought back with them a taste for Greek cooking. They adapted recipes to locally available ingredients. Monasteries were known for their delicious meals and soon their cuisine found its way into the Romanian cookery.

Another source of Romanian specialties was the ever present street vendor. Most were from surrounding countries and prepared foods typical of their homelands. Romanians became accustomed to tasting many varieties of food in this way, and adapted some of these dishes. The Russian invaders, the German and Hungarian ethnic groups in Transylvania, and the Turks, all made their imprint on the Romanian cuisine.

By the mid-nineteenth century, it became fashionable for the ruling families and nobility of Romania to send their children to Paris for education and "proper up-bringing." As a result, the Greek and Slavic influences in Romania made way for more Western habits. French became the language of the "upper-classes," and Western, especially French, cuisine was introduced. French chefs came to Bucharest and opened restaurants, cafes, and pastry stores. Bucharest became known as "little Paris." By the turn of the century, native Romanian dishes, Eastern and the Western influences all were blended, so much so that origins were lost and a true Romanian cuisine emerged.

Across centuries, from generation to generation, Romanian peasants created and passed on folk tales, proverbs, and fables— full of humor, philosophy, and wisdom. In sections between the recipes, a few examples of these folk literary delights are included, as well as a sampling of Romania's poetry; and finally, there is a brief look at Romania's 4000-year historical heritage.

ART, LITERATURE, AND COOKERY

Cookery can be said to be one of the highest forms of art, as it affects all of our senses: sight, smell, taste, touch, and even hearing. Certainly an artistically arranged dish is an object of beauty and a pleasure to more than the taste buds—the aroma emanating from the kitchen, the taste of a well prepared dish, the touch of fresh bread, and the sizzling sound of a freshly charcoal-grilled steak—or the gurgling sound of the Cabernet Sauvignon being poured by the sommelier—all provide delight.

It is probably also the reason why well-known writers and artists were also interested in cookery. Some, like Claude Monet, just enjoyed entertaining his friends, and served them meals that became renowned, from recipes collected all over the world by his wife Claire Joyes Monet. Toulouse-Lautrec loved cooking as much as he did painting. Cézanne prepared his own favorite recipes such as bouillabaisse and salted cod soup, and Alexandre Dumas (father) spent the last 10 years of his life writing a monumental cookery encyclopedia, Le Dictionnaire de la Cuisine.

In Romania, too, we find many famous literary men also preoccupied with cookery. The first professional cookery book in Romania was published in

Madmoiselle Pogany *by Constantin Brancusi.*

INTRODUCTION

1841 in Iași by two writers, leaders of the Romanian Enlightenment, Costache Negruzzi and Mihail Kogălniceanu. It contained some 200 recipes. Towards the end of the 19th century, many of these literary giants were known for their cookery. However, they say that it was rather due to economic considerations, as they were not able to earn a living by writing alone. The great Romanian playwright, journalist and humorist Ion Luca Caragiale owned at times a café, a theater, and a beer hall in Bucharest, named Academia Bene Babenti. Journalist and humorist Alexandru Teodoreanu was also known as a leading gourmet, a hotel manager, and a poet. He wrote many articles and essays on food and wine.

Finally, here is a thought for you to ponder: Charles Baudelaire, the French poet and critic of literature, painting and music, was well known for his *joie de vivre*. He enjoyed good food as much as good sex, and it is said that he once told one of his friends: "If you have no lover, take a cookbook to bed instead."

PRONUNCIATION

ENGLISH	ROMANIAN	FRENCH
Ago	Ă(ə)	Le
Lesson	Â,Î(Œ)	Seul
Ship	Ş(ʃ)	Chat
Gets	Ţ(ts)	Tzigane
Chew	Ci('tʃi)	Tchin-tchin

ENGLISH-ROMANIAN-FRENCH DICTIONARY

ENGLISH	ROMANIAN	FRENCH
Apricot	Caisă	Abricot
Artichoke	Anghinară	Artichaut
Bacon	Slănină	Bacon(Lard)
Baker	Brutar	Boulanger
Baked	Copt	Au Four
Basil	Busuioc	Basilic
Barley	Arpăcaş	Orge
Bay Leaf	Foaie de Dafin	Feuille de Laurier
Boiled	Fiert	Bouilli
Boletus	Mănătârcă	Bolet
Braised	Fiert Înăbuşit	Braisé
Braised Meat	Stufat	Estoufade
Bread	Pâine	Pain
Butter	Unt	Beurre
Capers	Capere	Câpres
Caraway	Chimen	Carvi
Carp	Crap	Carp(Carpeau)
Carrot	Morcov	Carotte
Celeriac	Ţelină	Céleri-rave
Cheese	Brânză	Fromage
Cheesecloth	Tifon	Étamine
Chervil	Haţmaţuchi(Asmaţui)	Cerfeuil
Chives	Arpagic	Ciboulettes
Chop, Cutlet	Cotlet	Côtelette
Cinnamon	Scorţişoară	Cannelle
Cloves	Cuişoare	Girofle
Cod	Cod	Morue.Cabillaud
Coffee	Cafea	Café
Colander (strainer)	Strecurătoare	Passoire
Corn Flour (maize)	Mălai	Farine de Mals
Crayfish	Raci	Langoustes
Cream Cheese	Brânză Grasă de Vaci	Fromage Frais
Cumin	Chimion	Cumin
Dill	Mărar	Fenouil
Dumpling(s)	Găluşcă(şte)	Boulette(s)
Eel	Ţipar	Anguille
Egg(s)	Ou(ă)	Œuf(s)
Egg Yolk	Gălbenuş	Jaune d'Oeuf

Egg White	Albuş	Blanc d'Oeuf
Ewe	Oaie	Brebis
Farmers Cheese	Brânză de Vacă	Fromage Blanc
Fennel	Molotru	Aneth
Fish	Peşte	Poisson
Flank Steak	Fleică	Bavette
Flour	Făină	Farine
Fried	Prăjit	Frite
Fritter(s)	Gogoaşă(Gogoşi)	Beignet(s)
Garlic	Usturoi	Ail
Garlic Sauce	Mujdei	Sauce à l'Ail
Ginger	Ghimber	Gingembre
Goat(male)	Ţap	Chèvre
Goat(female)	Capră	Chèvre
Grilled on charcoal	Pe Grătar	Grillé sur charbon de bois
Ham	Şuncă	Jambon
Hard boiled	Răscopt	Dur
Herring	Scrumbie	Hareng
Horseradish	Hrean	Raifort
Ice Cream	Îngheţată	Glace
Kid	Căpricioară	Chevreau
Kidneys	Rinichi	Rognons
Lake Bream	Bremă	Brème
Lamb	Miel	Agneau
Leek	Praz	Poireau
Leg of Lamb	Pulpă de Miel	Gigot d'Agneau
Lemon	Lămâie	Citron
Lobster	Homar	Homard
Lovage	Leuştean	Livèche
Marjoram	Măghiran	Marjolaine
Medium(cooked)	Potrivit	A Point
Morel	Sbârciog	Morille
Mutton	Berbec	Mouton
Nettle	Urzici	Ortie
Nobleman	Boier	Noble
Nutmeg	Nucşoară (Nucă Tămâioasă)	Noix de Muscade
Oil(Cooking)	Ulei	Huille

Okra	Bamă	Okra
Olives	Măsline	Olives
Olive Oil	Untdelemn	Huile d'Olive
On Skewer	Frigărui	Brochettes
Oregano	Sovârf	Origan
Orange	Portocală	Orange
Pancakes	Clătite	Crêpes
Paprika	Boia	Paprika
Parsley	Pătrunjel	Persil
Parsnip	Păstârnac	Panais
Pepper	Piper	Poivre
Perch	Şalâu(Biban)	Perche
Pie	Turtă	Tarte
Pike	Ştiucă	Brochet
Poached meat or fowl	Rasol	Viande ou volaille pochée
Polenta	Mămăligă	Polenta
Pot Roast	Friptură la Tavă	Rôti á la Poêle
Pumpkin	Bostan(Dovleac)	Potiron
Quince	Gutuie	Coing
Ragout	Tocană(meat) Plachie(fish)	Ragoût
Rare(cooking)	Cu Puţin Sânge	Saignant
Roast	Friptură	Rôti
Roasted	Prăjit la Cuptor	Rôti
Roll	Chiflă	Petit Pain
Rosemary	Rozmarin	Romarin
Ruler(Prince)	Voivodă	Chef d'Etat
Saffron	Şofran	Safran
Sage	Salvie	Sauge
Salmon	Somon	Saumon
Salt	Sare	Sel
Sardine	Sardele	Sardines
Semolina	Griş	Semoule
Shallot(Eschalot)	Ceapă de Apă	Echalote
Shrimp	Crevete	Crevettes
Sieve	Sită	Tamis
Sirloin	Muşchi	Faux Fillet
Sole	Calcan	Sole
Soup	Supă	Soup

Soup soured with Borş	Borş	Soup aigri avec Borş
Soup soured with lemon or sauerkraut	Ciorbă Ciorbă	Soup aigri avec citron ou choucroute
Soured(Sour) Cream	Smântână	Crème Fraîche
Sterlet	Cegă	Esturgeon
Sturgeon	Nisetru(Sturion) (Morun)	Esturgeon
Suckling Pig	Purcel de Lapte	Cochon de Lait
Sugar	Zahăr	Sucre
Tarragon	Tarhon	Estragon
Tea	Ceai	Thé
Tenderloin(Fillet)	Muşchi Fillet	Fillet de Boeuf
Thyme	Cimbru	Thym
Trout	Păstrăv	Tuite
Tuna	Ton	Thon
Very Rare(Cooking)	În Sânge	Bleu
Walnut Sauce	Scordolea	Sauce de Noix
Watercress	Măcriş(Ştevie)	Cresson
Well Done(Cooking)	Bine Prăjit	Bien Cuit
Whey	Zer	Petit-lait
Whipped Cream	Frişcă	Crème Chantilly
Wood Stick used to stir Polenta	Melesteu(Făcăleţ)	Baton pour remuer la Polenta

DICŢIONAR ROMÂN-ENGLEZ-FRANCEZ

ROMÂNEŞTE	ENGLEZEŞTE	FRANŢUZEŞTE
Albuş	Egg White	Blanc d'Oeuf
Anghinară	Artichoke	Artichaut
Arpăcaş	Barley	Orge
Arpagic	Chives	Ciboulettes
Bamă	Okra	Okra
Berbec	Mutton	Mouton
Bine Prăjit	Well Done(Cooking)	Bien Cuit
Boia	Paprika	Paprika
Boier	Nobleman	Noble
Borş	Soup soured with Borş	Soupe aigri avec Borş
Bostan(Dovleac)	Pumpkin	Potiron
Brânză	Cheese	Fromage

Brânză de Vacă	Farmers Cheese	Fromage Blanc
Brânză Grasă de Vacă	Cream Cheese	Fromage Frais
Bremă	Lake Bream	Brème
Brutar	Baker	Boulanger
Busuioc	Basil	Basilic
Cafea	Coffee	Café
Caisă	Apricot	Abricot
Calcan	Sole	Sole
Capere	Capers	Câpres
Capră	Goat(female)	Chèvre
Căpricioară	Kid	Chevreau
Ceai	Tea	Thé
Ceapă	Onion	Onion
Ceapă de Apă	Shallot(Eschalot)	Echalote
Cegă	Sterlet	Esurgeon
Chiflă	Roll	Petit Fain
Cimbru	Thyme	Thym
Chimen	Caraway	Carvi
Chimion	Cumin	Cumin
Ciorbă	Soup soured with lemon or sauerkraut	Soupe aigri avec citron ou choucroute
Clătite	Pancakes	Crêpes
Cod	Cod	Morue/Cabillaud
Copt	Baked	Au Four
Cotlet	Chop, Cutlet	Côtelette
Crap	Carp	Carp(Carpeau)
Creveți	Shrimp	Crevettes
Cu Puțin Sânge	Rare(cooking)	Saignant
Cuișoare	Cloves	Girofle
Făină	Flour	Farine
Fiert	Boiled	Bouilli
Fiert Înăbușit	Braised	Braisé
Fleică	Flank Steak	Bavette
Foaie de Dafin	Bay Leaf	Feuille de Laurier
Frigărui	On Skewer	Brochettes
Friptură	Roast	Rôti
Friptură la Tavă	Pot Roast	Rôti à la Poêle
Frișcă	Whipped Cream	Crème Chantilly
Gălbenuș	Egg Yolk	Jaune d'Oeuf

Găluşcă(şte)	Dumpling(s)	Boulette(s)
Ghimber	Ginger	Gingembre
Gogoaşă(Gogoşi)	Fritter(s)	Beignet(s)
Griş	Semolina	Semoule
Gutuie	Quince	Coing
Haţmaţuchi(Asmaţui)	Chervil	Cerfeuil
Homar	Lobster	Homard
Hrean	Horseradish	Raifort
Înghețată	Ice Cream	Glace
În Sânge	Very Rare(Cooking)	Bleu
Lămâie	Lemon	Citron
Leuştean	Lovage	Livèche
Măcriş(Ştevie)	Watercress	Cresson
Măghiran	Marjoram	Marjolaine
Mălai	Corn Flour (Maize)	Farine de Maïs
Mămăligă	Polenta	Polenta
Mănătârcă	Boletus	Bolet
Mărar	Dill	Fenouil
Măsline	Olives	Olives
Melesteu(Făcăleţ)	Wood Stick used to stir Polenta	Baton pour remuer la Polenta
Miel	Lamb	Agneau
Molotru	Fennel	Aneth
Morcov	Carrot	Carotte
Mujdei	Garlic Sauce	Sauce à l'Ail
Muşchi	Sirloin	Faux Fillet
Muşchi Fillet	Tenderloin(Fillet)	Fillet de Boeuf
Nisetru (Sturion) (Morun)	Sturgeon	Esturgeon
Nucşoară (Nucă Tămîioasă)	Nutmeg	Noix de Muscade
Ou(ă)	Egg(s)	Œuf(s)
Oaie	Ewe	Brebis
Păstârnac	Parsnip	Panais
Păstrăv	Trout	Truite
Pătrunjel	Parsley	Persil
Pe Grătar	Grilled on charcoal	Grillé sur charbon de bois
Peşte	Fish	Poisson
Pâine	Bread	Pain

Piper	Pepper	Poivre
Plachie	Ragout(fish)	Ragoût(poisson)
Portocală	Orange	Orange
Potrivit	Medium(Cooked)	A Point
Prăjit	Fried	Frite
Prăjit la Cuptor	Roasted	Rôti
Praz	Leek	Poireau
Pulpă de Miel	Leg of Lamb	Gigot d'Agneau
Purcel de Lapte	Suckling Pig	Cochon de Lait
Raci	Crayfish	Langoustes
Rasol	Poached meat or fowl	Viande ou volaille pochée
Răscopt	Hard Boiled	Dur
Rinichi	Kidneys	Rognons
Rozmarin	Rosemary	Romarin
Şalâu(Biban)	Perch	Perche
Salvie	Sage	Sauge
Sardele	Sardines	Sardines
Sare	Salt	Sel
Sbârciog	Morel	Morille
Scordolea	Walnut Sauce	Sauce au Noix
Scorţişoară	Cinnamon	Cannelle
Scrumbie	Herring	Hareng
Sită	Sieve	Tamis
Slănină	Bacon	Bacon(Lard)
Smântână	Soured(Sour) Cream	Crème Fraîche
Şofran	Saffron	Safran
Somon	Salmon	Saumon
Sovârf	Oregano	Origan
Ştiucă	Pike	Brochet
Strecurătoare	Colander (strainer)	Passoire
Stufat	Braised Meat	Estoufade
Şuncă	Ham	Jambon
Supă	Soup	Soupe
Ţap	Goat(Male)	Chèvre
Tarhon	Tarragon	Estragon
Ţelină	Celeriac	Céleri-rave
Tifon	Cheesecloth	Étamine
Ţipar	Eel	Anguille

TASTE OF ROMANIA

Tocană	Ragout	Ragoût
Ton	Tuna	Thon
Ulei	Oil(Cooking)	Huille
Unt	Butter	Beurre
Untdelemn	Olive Oil	Huille d'Olive
Urzici	Nettle	Ortie
Usturoi	Garlic	Ail
Zahăr	Sugar	Sucre
Zer	Whey	Petit-lait

AMERICAN-BRITISH DICTIONARY

For our British readers who may not be familiar with some of the American expressions used in this book, here is a handy list of equivalents:

AMERICAN	BRITISH
BEEF FLANK STEAK FILLETS	GOOSE SKIRT
BEEF FORESHANK	SHIN
CAN	TIN
CENTER CUT PORK LOIN	PORK FILLET
CORN MEAL	MAIZE-FLOUR
EGGPLANT	AUBERGINE
FISH MARKET	FISH MONGER
GROUND	MINCED
OMELET	OMELETTE
PORK SHOULDER BUTT	SHOULDER BLADE
REFRIGERATOR	FRIDGE
SCALLIONS	SPRING ONIONS
SHALLOTS	ESCHALOTS
SOUR CREAM	SOURED CREAM
STRIPS OF BACON	RASHERS
TENDERLOIN	FILLET STEAK
ZUCCHINI	COURGETTE

OVEN TEMPERATURE SETTINGS CHART

Fahrenheit Degrees	Centigrade Degrees		British Gas	French
230	110			3
240	116	Very Slow	¼	Doux
290	143	Slow	1	Moyen
355	179	Moderate	4	Bon Four
375	190			5
380	193		5	
400	205	Medium Hot	6	
425	218		7	6
428	220	Hot		Chaud
470	243	Very Hot	9	Vif
500	260			7
525	274			8
550	288			9

CONVERSION METHOD

FAHRENHEIT (°F) INTO CENTIGRADE (°C):

Subtract 32, multiply by 5, and divide by 9.
Example: 400 - 32 = 368
          368 x 5 = 1840
          1840/9 = 204.45 (205)

CENTIGRADE (°C) INTO FAHRENHEIT (°F):

Multiply by 9, divide by 5, and add 32.
Example: 179 x 9 = 1611
          1611 / 5 = 322.2
          322.2+ 32 = 354.2 (355)

CONVERSION TABLE

LIQUID MEASURES:

AMERICAN	AMERICAN fl oz	BRITISH	BRITISH fl oz	METRIC
1.00 fl oz	——	——	1.04	29.60 ml
0.96 fl oz	——	——	1.00	28.50 ml
1.00 pt	16.00	——	16.50	470.00 ml
——	19.00	1.00 pt	20.00	570.00 ml
1.00 qt	32.00	——	33.00	950.00 ml
——	38.50	1.00 qt	40.00	1.10 l
——	33.50	——	35.00	1.00 l
1.00 cup	8.00	——	8.33	235.00 ml
——	9.50	1.00 cup	10.00	285.00 ml

SOLID MEASURES:

BRITISH	METRIC
1 oz	28.4 gr
¼ lbs. (4 oz)	113.5 gr
½ lbs. (8 oz)	226.8 gr
¾ lbs. (12 oz)	340.2 gr
1 lbs. (16 oz)	454.4 gr

METRIC	BRITISH
10 gr	0.4 oz
50 gr	1.8 oz
100 gr	3.5 oz
500 gr (½ kg)	17.6 oz (1 lbs. 2 oz)
1000 gr (1 kg)	35.2 oz (2 lbs. 3 oz)

MEZELURI AND OTHER APPETIZERS

ROMANIAN COLD AND HOT APPETIZER TABLE
Mezeluri

Originating from the Turkish meze, the Romanian mezeluri, a variety of cold and hot appetizer dishes, is a popular starter, and can be as simple or as elaborate as you wish. It is usually accompanied by a cold glass of ţuică.* Here are some more suggestions of what to include:

Cold dishes
Eggplant salad (see p. 49)
Pickled vegetables (see p. 34)
Grilled pepper salad (see p. 52)
Greek olives
Caşcaval and Telemea cheeses**
Black caviar

Hot dishes
Little grilled sausages (see p. 171)
Meatballs with tomato sauce (see p. 175)
Breaded calves brains (see p. 44)

---

* Ţuică is a Romanian plum brandy, a pure, three times distilled, fiery drink, aged in oak barrels. Unfortunately, these days the only good quality, aged ţuică is home-made, in Romanian villages. Most of the commercial products available are just alcohol with a ţuică flavoring added.

** Caşcaval cheese—a hard ewe's milk cheese, belonging to the same family as the Italian Caciocavallo. It can be substituted with other ewe cheeses such as the Italian Pecorinos, or the Greek Kaseri or Kefalotiri.Telemea cheese—a pure white ewe's milk curd cheese, dry-salted, usually stored in a whey and salt brine. Often, cumin seeds are added for extra flavor. It can be substituted by a Greek Feta cheese.

STUFFED MUSHROOMS
Ciuperci Umplute

2 tbsp. butter
16 large mushrooms
2 tbsp. oil
4 oz. scallions, chopped
2 tsp. bread crumbs
1 tsp. fresh gound black pepper
2 tbsp. fresh parsley, chopped
1 tbsp. fresh dilll, chopped
2 tsp. salt
½ cup caşcaval cheese, grated*
¼ cup dry white wine

Serves 4
Preparation time: 15 min., Cooking time: 40 min.

❑ Preheat oven to 350°F.
❑ Butter an oven dish.
❑ Wash mushrooms, Remove stems and save. Place mushroom caps in oven dish. Put a pat of butter in each cap. Bake uncovered 10-15 min.
❑ Chop mushroom stems.
❑ In a skillet, heat oil over medium-high heat. Sauté scallion about 3 min., stirring continually. Add chopped stems and bread crumbs. Continue to cook another 2-3 min. until scallion has softened. Add pepper, 1 tbsp. parsley, and dill. Mix well, then add salt. Remove from heat and cool.
❑ Remove mushroom caps from oven and let cool a few minutes, then fill caps with mushroom and onion stuffing.
❑ Sprinkle with grated cheese. Bake another 20-25 min.
❑ Remove from oven, sprinkle with wine and some of the juices in the oven dish. Place stuffed mushrooms on a plate. Pour the rest of the juices from the oven dish over them, and let cool.

Keep in refrigerator until ready to serve cold, as an appetizer, or as part of a ROMANIAN COLD AND HOT APPETIZER TABLE (see p. 32).

---

* You can substitute caşcaval with such ewe milk cheeses as the Italian Pecorinos or Toscanellos, or the Greek Kaseri or Kefalotiri. Grated Swiss cheese will also work.

PICKLED VEGETABLES

Murături

¾ lbs. cauliflower (florets)
¾ lbs. carrots, cut into 2 in. sticks or slices
2 oz. red pepper, cut into long strips
2 oz. green pepper, cut into long strips
¼ lbs. red cabbage, cut into small wedges
2 oz. radishes, whole with skin
6 slices hot pepper
6 sprigs fresh fennel
3 bay leaves
3 garlic cloves, peeled, whole
4 tsp. salt
24 black peppercorns, whole
¾ cup tarragon vinegar
3 cups water

Serves 8-9
Preparation time: 30 min.

❑ Prepare three wide-necked sterilized glass jars (see p. 281 for sterilizing method) for making pickles. For this recipe, three 14 oz. jars are used.
❑ Divide vegetables equally between jars, layering them attractively by color with herbs and spices. Fill jars to capacity.
❑ Bring 3 cups of water to a vigorous boil over high heat. Add salt and vinegar. Pour boiling liquid over the vegetables, filling the jars to capacity. Cover and seal.
❑ Keep at room temperature overnight. Then place in refrigerator or cool place at least 48 hours before serving.

Murături are crisp, tasty, and refreshing. They can be served as part of Romanian mezeluri starters, or to nibble, with a glass of ţuică before eating a good bowl of ciorbă.

PORK AND RICE SAUSAGES—BOLTA RECE

Chişcă Moldovenească cu Orez (Caltaboşi)

Iaşi was just a village at the beginning of the 15th century when it became the capital of the province of Moldavia. It remained its capital until 1859. Since the 17th century, it has been a great cultural center. Romania's first university was founded in Iaşi, and the first printing press was established here. The first plays in the Romanian language were presented here, and many of Romania's best writers, poets, playwrights, and painters were either born or settled in Iaşi. The first Romanian cookbook written in this city in 1841 was by two well known writers, Costache Negruzzi and Mihail Kogălniceanu.

On a little street up on a hill, called Strada Rece, a modest inn called Bolta Rece opened its doors in 1786 and offered business travelers a place to have a meal and quench their thirst. During the second half of the 19th century Bolta Rece was the meeting place for literary, artistic, and political figures of the city, and became a place where major decisions in the development of the country took place.

Bolta Rece (The Cold Vault) is still in its original house, and an excellent restaurant with lots of atmosphere. This recipe, a Moldavian specialty, was contributed by managers Mihai Valeriu and Bodoga Ioan Neculai.

Bolta Rece—Iaşi

2 cups water
1 cup rice
1 tsp. salt
2 tbsp. cooking oil
½ lbs. onion, finely chopped
3½ lbs. boneless pork loin, ground
2 tbsp. fresh parsley, chopped
1 tbsp. fresh dill sprigs, chopped
1 tsp. ground thyme
2 tsp. fresh ground black pepper
6 feet of hog casing
1 tbsp. salt
3 carrots, peeled and sliced

Serves 6-8
Preparation time: 45 min., Cooking time: 45 min.

❑ In a small kettle, heat 2 cups of water over medium-high heat. When water boils, add rice and 1 tsp. salt. Return to boil. Cover, lower heat to low, and simmer about 15 min. or until water is absorbed. Remove from heat and let cool.

❑ In a skillet, heat oil over medium-high heat. Add onion and sauté until it turns a nice light golden color, about 5 min.

❑ In a bowl, mix meat, rice, onion, parsley, dill, and thyme together. Add pepper. Mix well.

❑ Cut hog casing in 2ft. lengths, wash in warm water and rinse in cold water. Stuff meat mixture into casing using either a pastry bag or a stuffing horn. With string tie ends of casings and at intervals along each 2 ft. length.

❑ Cover sausages with water in a large kettle. Add 1 tbsp. salt and carrots. Boil sausages 30 min. After sausages have cooled, store in refrigerator.

Serve cold as appetizer with mustard or horseradish.

BREADED CAŞCAVAL CHEESE

Caşcaval Pane

¾ lbs. caşcaval cheese[*]
1 cup flour, sifted
1 egg, slightly beaten
1 cup bread crumbs, sifted
1 tbsp. cooking oil

Serves 4
Preparation time: 5 min., Cooking time: 6 min.

❑ Remove outer skin of cheese. Cut 2 slices per person, about ½ oz. each.
❑ Roll slices in flour, then in egg, and finally in bread crumbs.
❑ In a skillet heat oil over medium-low heat. Fry slices until nicely browned, about 3 min. on each side.

Serve as a hot appetizer, decorated with a few small cornichons pickles and buttered toast.

Special thanks to chefs Maria Pascu and Stefania Stoicescu of the Hanul Manuc in Bucharest who contributed this recipe for the book. See BREADED CALVES BRAINS, p. 44 for story.

---

* You can substitute caşcaval with such ewe milk cheeses as the Italian Pecorinos or Toscanellos, or the Greek Kaseri or Kefalotiri.

PAN-MELTED CAŞCAVAL CHEESE

Caşcaval la Capac

4 oz. caşcaval cheese*
1 tbsp. butter

Serves 4
Preparation time: 5 min., Cooking time: 6 min.

This starter dish is best cooked and served in individual French Le Creuset-type enamel egg dishes. However, any non-reactive, heavy skillet will do.

❑ Remove outer skin of cheese. Cut 2 slices per person, about ½ oz. each.
❑ In a skillet heat butter over medium-high heat. Fry slices about 2-3 min. on each side, watching them carefully. As soon as you notice some melting, quickly flip slices over, so that cheese is both melted and nicely browned.

Serve with pickled vegetables and bread.

---

* You can substitute caşcaval with such ewe milk cheeses as the Italian Pecorinos or Toscanellos, or the Greek Kaseri or Kefalotiri.

CHEESE SOUFFLÉ

Sufleu de Caşcaval

2 tbsp. butter
4 tbsp. flour
1 cup milk
4 eggs, separated
6 oz. caşcaval cheese[*]

Serves 4
Preparation time: 15 min., Cooking time: 35 min.

For this hot starter dish, use a non-reactive oven dish or mold, about 6 in. in diameter and 4 in. deep.

❑ Preheat oven to 400°F.

❑ In a saucepan, heat butter over medium heat. When butter has melted, slowly blend in flour with a wooden spoon. Cook until flour turns a golden yellow, about 2 min. Remove from heat and let cool a few minutes.

❑ In a small saucepan, heat milk until hot but not boiling. Add milk to warm sauce. Mix well. Return to medium heat and cook 1-2 min. more. You should have a nice thick sauce. Remove from heat.

❑ Fold egg yolks into sauce, one by one, whipping sauce with a wire whip.

❑ Whip egg whites with wire whip or electric mixer until they are stiff. Fold egg whites into sauce.

❑ Add grated cheese little by little while you fold in egg white.

❑ Pour batter into oven dish until dish is about ¾ full. Bake about 2 min. at 400° and then lower to 375°. Continue cooking for about 30 min. or until soufflé has risen and has turned a nice golden brown. Do not open oven the first 20 min., and do not overcook.

Serve immediately.

---

[*] You can substitute caşcaval with such ewe milk cheeses as the Italian Pecorinos or Toscanellos, or the Greek Kaseri or Kefalotiri.

ROMANIAN LAMB HAGGIS (Version I)

Drob de Miel (I)

This dish is a traditional component of the Romanian Easter meal. The lamb is usually slaughtered and all parts of it, including the head and the offal, will be used for a festive meal after the long fasting period. A typical Easter meal is composed of hand-painted hard-boiled Easter eggs, a lamb sour soup, lamb haggis, a lamb main course, and a festive Easter cake.

1½ lbs. lamb pluck (heart, liver, and lungs)
1 lamb paunch (stomach)
salt to taste
3 tbsp. cooking oil
3 oz. scallions, chopped
2 garlic cloves, peeled and chopped
2 tbsp. water
1 egg, slightly beaten
2 tbsp. fresh parsley, chopped
1 tbsp. fresh dill, chopped
2 tsp. salt
1 tsp. fresh ground black pepper

Serves 4
Preparation time: 15 min., Cooking time: 30 min.

You will need a meat grinder for this dish. If one is not available, ask your butcher to chop lamb very fine. Then mix your ingredients as well as you can.

❏ Wash lamb pluck and stomach well in cold water. Cover stomach with cold water until you are ready to wrap lamb mixture in it.
❏ Fill a kettle with water, add salt, and bring to boil. Lower heat to medium, add lamb pluck, and cook about 10 min. Skim surface scum during cooking.
❏ Remove meat from water, drain, and let cool.
❏ In a skillet, heat 2 tbsp. oil over medium-high heat. Add meat, scallion, garlic, and 2 tbsp. water. Stir, cover, and braise about 5-6 min. Drain and cool.
❏ Pass mixture through fine meat grinder. Put ground mixture in a bowl. Add egg, parsley, dill, salt, and pepper, and mix well.
❏ Cut the stomach into 4 pieces and fill each with a quarter of the mixture, or leave whole and fill with all the mixture. Work the filled skin into a rounded shape and seal well all around.
❏ Oil an oven dish. Place haggis in dish and bake in oven about 25-30 min. Let cool a few minutes.

Serve immediately sliced into serving portions as a warm starter, or cool in the refrigerator and serve them cold the next day.

ROMANIAN LAMB HAGGIS (Version II)

Drob de Miel (II)

This version does not use a lamb stomach. See preceding recipe for other ingredients.

You will need a meat grinder for this dish. If one is not available, ask your butcher to chop lamb very fine. Then mix your ingredients as well as you can.

❑ Wash lamb pluck well in cold water.

❑ Fill a kettle with water, add salt, and bring to boil. Lower heat to medium, add lamb pluck, and cook about 40 min. Skim surface of scum during cooking.

❑ Remove meat from water, drain, and let cool.

❑ In a skillet, heat 2 tbsp. oil over medium-high heat. Add meat, onion, garlic, and water. Stir, cover, and braise about 5-6 min. Drain and cool. Save skillet.

❑ Pass mixture through fine meat grinder. Put ground mixture in a bowl. Add egg, parsley, dill, salt, and pepper, and mix well.

❑ With a tablespoon, take portions of the mixture, and make into small balls.

❑ Add another tbsp. of oil to skillet. Place over medium-high heat. Add meatballs and fry, turning them with a wooden spoon for 10 min., or until they are well browned all around.

You can serve them immediately as a warm starter, or let them cool in the refrigerator, and serve them cold the next day.

CALVES BRAINS

Creier de Viţel

In Europe, where brains are considered a delicacy, there is a universal joke: the lady calls her butcher and asks if he has brains. "If I had any brains would I be in this job?" The reason people often call the butcher to check if there are any brains in stock is that the demand is high, and brains cannot be stocked for long as they are very perishable.

Unlike the French escargots and the Japanese sashimi, which are now accepted as delicacies in the United States, brains are still not well known. However, if you want to surprise your family and friends with some deliciously delicate dishes, give them a try. They are very popular in Romania and you will find them on almost every restaurant menu as a hot appetizer.

You will find them at better butchers mostly during the colder seasons because brains are so perishable. Buy them just before you are ready to cook them. Calves brains are the easiest to find, but pork and lamb brains are equally good. Calves brains are usually sold in pairs, and you will need one pair per person. Handle brains gently before they are cooked to avoid tearing them.

To prepare calves brains for cooking, follow the these steps:

1. Wash brains in cold water. Very delicately, pull away some of the thin membranes which cover any dark spots.

2. Place brains in a big bowl of cold water and let stand for about 20 min., changing water once.

3. Very delicately pull off as many more of the membranes as you can without tearing any of the flesh.

4. Soak them again in water adding a bit of vinegar and salt. Let them soak about 30 min., changing solution several times. Then peel off as many more of the membranes as possible.

BREADED CALVES BRAINS

Creier de Vițel Pane

The most beautiful and picturesque hotel in Bucharest is the Hanul Manuc (Manuc's Inn). The hotel includes two wooden buildings built in the 16th century that were used as a princely court through the 18th century. The Russian-Turkish peace treaty was signed here in 1812. The original owner, an Armenian named Manuc-bey, was poisoned by a fortune-teller who had predicted his death and could not risk his reputation. The hotel includes the Crama Restaurant. Its cozy architecture of timbered ceilings and heavy arches overlooks a garden giving it a pleasant dining atmosphere. The cuisine is well-known for its Romanian and international dishes, and the inn also boasts a wine cellar with an excellent list of Romanian vintage wines. This recipe was contributed to the book by chefs Maria Pascu and Stefania Stoicescu of the Hanul Manuc.

½ onion, peeled and sliced
2 oz. carrots, peeled and sliced
10 peppercorns
1 bay leaf
1½ lbs. calves brains, prepared for cooking*
2 tbsp. vinegar
1 tbsp. salt
1 cup flour
1 egg, slightly beaten
1 cup bread crumbs

Serves 4

Preparation time: 15 min. (not counting preparation of brains for cooking.)* Cooking Time: 50 min.

❑ In a non-reactive kettle, add onion, carrot, peppercorns, and bay leaf. Add 2 qt. water and heat over high heat. Cook vegetables about 20 min. Lower heat to low, add vinegar and salt.

❑ Gently place brains in the simmering water, and cook another 20 min. Remove from heat and let cool in the water.

❑ When brains are cool, remove gently from kettle, place on kitchen towels to absorb the water. Slice brain into serving portions.

---

* Brains have to be prepared for cooking in accordance with description under CALVES BRAINS, p. 43.

❑ Roll slices first in flour, then in egg, and finally in bread crumbs.
❑ In a skillet, heat oil over medium heat. Fry brain slices until nicely browned, about 4 min. on each side.

Serve hot, garnished with slices of lemon, and accompanied by a refreshing salad.

Hanul Manuc—Bucharest

CALVES BRAINS FRITTERS

Frigănele de Creier

3 eggs, slightly beaten
2 tbsp. bread crumbs
3 tbsp. cașcaval cheese,* grated
2 tsp. sgrated
2 tsp. salt
1 tsp. fresh ground black pepper
1½ lbs. calves brains, prepared for cooking*
3 tbsp. butter

> *Serves 4*
>
> *Preparation time: 10 min. (not counting preparation of brains for cooking)**, Cooking time: 10 min.*

❑ In a bowl, mix eggs, bread crumbs, and cheese. Add salt and pepper.

❑ Dice brains, and add to mixture. With a fork, beat mixture until it becomes a creamy batter. If the batter is too wet, add bread crumbs until it has a stiffer consistency.

❑ In a skillet, heat butter over medium-high heat.

❑ Fry teaspoonfuls of batter in butter, turning fritters with a spatula or wooden spoon. It should take about 4-5 min. on each side.

Serve hot, garnished with lemon slices, and accompanied by french fries and a salad.

---

* You can substitute cașcaval with such ewe milk cheeses as the Italian Pecorinos or Toscanellos, or the Greek Kaseri or Kefalotiri.

** Brains have to be prepared for cooking in accordance with description under CALVES BRAINS, p. 43.

SALATĂ ȚĂRĂNEASCĂ
AND OTHER SALADS

COUNTRY STYLE SALAD

Salată Țărănească

2 eggs, hard-boiled and cooled
2 large boiling potatoes, peeled and sliced
2 green peppers, cored and sliced
2 tomatoes, sliced
6 radishes, sliced
1 large onion, peeled and sliced
salt and pepper to taste
6 ripe black Greek olives
1 tbsp. fresh parsley, chopped
1 recipe vinaigrette*

Serves 4-6
Preparation time: 35 min., Cooking time: 15 min.

❏ Peel and slice eggs. Keep them cool.
❏ Boil the sliced potatoes just until slices become soft, about 15 min. Don't overcook them. Let cool in refrigerator.
❏ Place all vegetables in a large salad bowl. Season to taste, add eggs and olives, season again, and then sprinkle with parsley.

Keep cool in refrigerator. Just before serving, pour vinaigrette over salad, and then toss salad well with the help of two spoons or salad mixers.

---

* see chapter on SAUCES, p. 251.

EGGPLANT SALAD

Salată de Vinete

2 medium eggplants, about 1-1½ lbs. each[*]
1 tbsp. salt
½ cup olive oil
1 lemon, juice
½ onion, finely chopped
8 black ripe Greek olives

Serves 4
Preparation time: 30 min., Cooking time: 60 min.

❏ Pierce the eggplant skin in several places with a fork. Place on a rack over a broiler pan. Place the rack so that the surface of the eggplant is about 2½" to 3" from the source of heat. Set oven to broil. It is preferable to cook them over charcoal.

❏ Broil for 45 min. to one hour, turning eggplant each 15 min., first 90 degrees, and then 45 degrees on each side, until they are soft and the skin is partly blackened and charred. It is normal for the skin to break open during cooking and juices to drop into broiler pan.

❏ Remove cooked eggplant from broiler, place on a wooden cutting board or carving board. Let stand 2 min. While still hot, pull off skin (dip fingers in cold water to keep them from burning).

❏ After eggplants are peeled, and no charred skin is left, cut off the stem end. Press eggplant meat to squeeze out water. With the edge of a wooden spoon or wooden spatula chop the eggplant meat until very fine.

❏ Put chopped eggplant in a deep wooden, glass, or china dish, cover, and place in refrigerator to cool.

❏ When cold, add salt. Then, while beating with a fork, add olive oil very slowly, in a steady thin stream. Add lemon juice, also very slowly, continuing to beat another minute or two.

Serve as a refreshing appetizer or salad on small plates, decorated with a few olives. Place chopped onion in a dish, and let each person, according to taste, add some and mix into the salad.

You can also serve this salad accompanied with grilled peppers. (see GRILLED PEPPER SALAD, p. 52)

---

[*] Buy eggplant that are long and slim, not round. They should have a firm, smooth skin.

CARP CAVIAR SALAD, ANA

Salată de Icre de Crap, Ana

In Romania, this salad is usually made from pike roe, if available, or more commonly from carp roe. In Greece, it is called Tarama Salata, and is generally made from cod roe, but also from carp roe.Fresh roe is difficult to find most of the year at fish markets. Processed, pressed, and salted, carp roe can be found in supermarkets and ethnic Greek delis in jars. An easy to find brand is Kronos, imported from Greece. It is labeled Tarama Fish Roe, and comes in 10 oz. jars. Kronos also sells ready-made carp caviar salad in jars that look identical. They are labeled Tarama Fish Roe Salad. You have to be careful that you buy the roe, not the salad, if you want to prepare it yourself.

1 10 oz. jar tarama carp roe
1 qt. cooking oil
¾ cup club soda
1 lemon, juiced

Serves 8-10
Preparation time: 15 min.

❑ In a large electric mixer bowl, mix 6 oz. tarama carp roe at medium speed for about 1 min.

❑ As you continue to mix, add oil slowly in a thin stream, taking about 3 min. to pour a cup.

❑ Keep mixing, while you add ¼ cup club soda, little by little, taking about 1 min.

❑ Add another cup of oil slowly, while mixing, taking about 2 min.

❑ Add half the quantity of lemon juice, still mixing while you do this. Salad should begin to grow in size and become fluffy.

❑ Continue beating while you slowly add another 1 to 2 cups of oil alternately with rest of club soda and lemon juice. Taste a bit of salad to determine if it is too salty and if it is sufficiently fluffy and light for your taste.

If you use up all the ingredients and the salad is still too salty (fish caviar salad is normally salty), add more oil while mixing, but not so much as to make salad greasy.

Serve cold, 2-3 tbsp. portions per person, on small plates, decorated with Greek Calamata black olives. Many people like to add some chopped onion. This can be served separately, and each person can add it to his or her taste. Serve carp caviar salad as part of a Romanian Appetizer Table, see ROMA-

NIAN APPETIZER TABLE, p. 32, or accompanied by a grilled pepper (see GRILLED PEPPER SALAD, p. 52.)

GRILLED PEPPER SALAD

Salată de Ardei Copţi

In the old days, when kitchens were equipped with wood-burning stoves, peppers were simply put on top of the hot plate to gril. They can be prepared on the barbecue grill over charcoal, or under the oven broiler.

4 red (or green) peppers*
salt to taste
1 vinaigrette recipe

Serves 4
Preparation time: 15 min., Cooking time: 30 min.

Salad

Leave peppers whole, and don't cut off the stems as they make good handles during preparation. Place peppers on a barbecue grill or about 3 in. under broiler. Turn them often, about every 4- 6 min., so that they char evenly. They will become soft and the skin will blacken and begin to peel. They should be done in about 30 min.

Place cooked peppers in a bowl or container. Sprinkle with salt and stack on top of each other. Cover with lid, plate, or towel, let sit for at least 15 min.

Take peppers one by one out of the container, hold by stem, and with wet hand peel skin off by pinching the skin and pulling. Keep wetting your hand and rubbing the peppers to remove all trace of blackness.

Pour the vinaigrette into a bowl with peppers. Stir gently so that all are coated, and refrigerate for at least 2 hours before serving.

To serve, place one pepper on each plate. The grilled peppers can be served by themselves as a salad, or with an eggplant salad (see EGGPLANT SALAD, p. 49), and a few slices of tomato.

Vinaigrette

3 tbsp. olive oil
2 tsp. vinegar
2 tsp. salt
1 tsp. freshly ground black pepper

❏ In a small bowl, mix ingredients well together.

---

* Buy 1 pepper per person. This recipe is for 4 persons. Select peppers that have flat surfaces if possible because those with bumps do not grill evenly. Red peppers are sweeter and more aromatic.

MUSHROOM SALAD

Salată de Ciuperci

1 lb. mushrooms
1 qt. water
1 tbsp. vinegar
1 tbsp. mayonnaise
2 tsp. lemon juice
6 scallions, chopped
salt and pepper to taste
2 tbsp. dill, chopped

Serves 4
Preparation time: 15 min., Cooking time: 15 min.

❑ Wash mushrooms with a damp towel and remove stems. Cut into thin slices.

❑ In a large kettle heat water to boil. Add salt and 1 tbsp. of vinegar. Lower heat to medium-low.

❑ Drop mushrooms into water and simmer about 15 min.

❑ Remove mushrooms gently with the help of a skimmer. Drain well, and place in a bowl to cool.

❑ In a small bowl, mix mayonnaise with lemon juice and scallions. Spoon over mushrooms. Salt and pepper to taste. Mix well, sprinkle with dill, and serve.

This makes a good addition to a Romanian appetizer table (see ROMANIAN COLD AND HOT APPETIZER TABLE, p. 32), or just as a starter by itself.

TOMATO SALAD

Salată de Roşii

2 large tomatoes, red, ripe, and firm
salt to taste
1 tbsp. olive oil
1 tsp. apple cider vinegar
1 tsp. salt
1 tbsp. fresh parsley, chopped
½ onion, chopped
1 garlic clove, crushed

Serves 4
Preparation time: 10 min.

❑ Wash and slice tomatoes.

❑ On 4 flat salad plates, layer half slices of tomato so that they overlap slightly. Use about half a tomato per person. Sprinkle with salt to taste.

❑ In a small bowl, make a vinaigrette with oil, vinegar, salt, and parsley. Dribble over tomatoes just enough to moisten them.

❑ In a separate small bowl, mix onion with garlic. Sprinkle mixture over tomatoes. Let stand in refrigerator for 15-30 min. before serving.

CUCUMBER SALAD

Salată de Castraveţi

1½ lbs. fresh young cucumbers, peeled and thinly sliced
salt to taste
3 oz. scallions, cleaned, washed, and chopped
2 tsp. fresh ground black pepper
1 tsp. sweet paprika
1 recipe vinaigrette[*]
2 tbsp. fresh dill, chopped
Serves 4
Preparation time: 10 min. (not including standing time)

❏ Spread cucumber slices on kichen towels, and sprinkle with salt. Let stand about 30 min. to remove excess water from cucumbers.

❏ Place cucumbers in a salad bowl, add scallion, pepper, and paprika.

❏ Prepare the vinaigrette.

Just before serving, pour vinaigrette on salad, mix well, and sprinkle with dill.

---

[*] see chapter on SAUCES, p. 251.

APPLE , CHEESE, AND NUTS SALAD

Salată de Mere, Brânză, și Nuci

4 apples, peeled and cored
½ lbs. cașcaval cheese[*]
2 oz. chopped walnuts
1 tsp. granulated sugar
½ tsp. salt
2 tsp. mayonnaise
4 lettuce leaves

Serves 4
Preparation time: 15 min.

❏ Grate apples and cheese. Mix together in a bowl. Add walnuts, sugar, and salt. Mix. Add mayonnaise, and mix everything well together.
❏ In each individual salad bowl, place a lettuce leaf. Place a scoop of salad on the lettuce.

---

* If you cannot find cașcaval cheese, you can use any hard ewe milk cheese, or a sharp cheddar cheese will do well for this salad. p. 37.

BEET SALAD

Salată de Sfeclă

2 beets, cleaned, with stems cut off
1 small horseradish
2 tbsp. salad oil
2 tsp. vinegar
1 tsp. salt
1 tbsp. chives
salt and pepper to taste

Serves 4-6
Preparation time: 15 min.

❑ Wash beets, and cut most of the stem off. Do not peel.

❑ Option 1. In a kettle, heat enough water to cover the beets. Boil over medium-high heat about 40 min. or until a fork will pierce beets easily.

❑ Option 2. Preheat oven to 375°F and bake beets about 45 min. Beets will retain more of their flavor by baking.

❑ When beets are done, drain well, scrape skin off, and let cool.

❑ Wash, peel, and grate horseradish. Mix oil and salt together. Add chives, and grated horseradish to your taste.

❑ When beets have cooled, cut into thin slices, sprinkle with vinegar, and store in refrigerator until cold and ready to use.

Arrange slices on individual salad plates and sprinkle with the oil mixture. Season with salt and pepper to taste.

CALVES BRAINS SALAD

Salată de Creier

½ onion, peeled and sliced
2 oz. carrots, peeled and sliced
1 bay leaf
10 peppercorns
1½ lbs. calves brains, prepared for cooking*
2 tbsp. vinegar
1 tbsp. salt
1 head lettuce, washed, dried, and separated into leaves
1 recipe sauce vinaigrette**
2 tsp. ground tarragon
2 tsp. salt
2 eggs, hardboiled and sliced
4 tsp. mayonnaise

Serves 4

Preparation time: 15 min. (not counting preparation of brains for cooking, described under CALVES BRAINS, p. 43),   Cooking time: 50 min.

❑ In a non-reactive kettle, add onion, carrot, peppercorns, and bay leaf. Add 2 qts. water and heat over high heat. Cook vegetables about 20 min. Lower heat to low, add vinegar and salt.

❑ Gently place brains in the simmering water, and cook another 20 min. Remove from heat and let cool in the water.

❑ Cover bottom of each serving plate with lettuce leaves. Spoon some vinaigrette over the lettuce and sprinkle with tarragon and salt.

❑ Cut brains into slices, one or two slices per person. Arrange slices on top of lettuce. Pour the rest of the vinaigrette and tarragon over them. Decorate each plate with egg slices. Season with salt and pepper. Add one tsp. of mayonnaise on top of each serving.

---

* Brains have to be prepared for cooking in accordance with description under CALVES BRAINS, p. 43.
** See under SAUCE VINAIGRETTE, p. 258 .

SCROB CU SMÂNTÂNĂ AND OTHER EGG DISHES

POACHED EGGS, ROMANIAN STYLE

Ouă Fierte - Mod Românesc

2 eggs
1 tbsp. vinegar
few drops lemon juice
few drops olive oil
salt and pepper to taste

Serves 1
Preparation time: 5 min., Cooking time: 2 min.

❏ Fill a saucepan with enough water to cover the eggs, about 2 in. Add a pinch of salt and a tbsp. of vinegar. Bring to a boil.

❏ Warm a plate.

❏ When water boils, create a circular swirl by stirring the water with a spoon in a clockwise, circular motion. Then quickly break the eggs and drop them in the water. Continue to cook for about 2-3 minutes, or until egg yolk and egg white have coagulated and yolk is still soft.

❏ Remove eggs gently with a skimmer, and place them on the warm plate.

❏ Sprinkle with a few drops of olive oil and lemon juice. Add salt and pepper to taste and serve.

FRIED EGGS WITH SOUR CREAM

Ochiuri cu Smântână

2 tbsp. sour cream
1 pinch flour
1 tbsp. butter
2 eggs
salt and pepper to taste

Serves 1
Preparation time: 10 min., Cooking time: 3 min.

❑ Warm a plate
❑ In a cup or small bowl, thoroughly mix sour cream and flour.
❑ Heat butter in a small skillet over medium-high heat.
❑ As soon as the foam disappears from the melted butter, break eggs one by one into the hot butter. Add salt and pepper to taste.
❑ When eggs begin to solidify, gently spoon sour cream over them, cover, and let cook another half minute to a minute, depending on personal preference. With spatula, transfer eggs to warm serving plate.

SCRAMBLED EGGS WITH SOUR CREAM

Scrob (Jumări) cu Smântână

2 eggs
salt and pepper to taste
2 tbsp. sour cream
1 pinch flour
1 tbsp. butter
1 tsp. herbes de provence

Serves 1
Preparation time: 10 min., Cooking time: 3 min.

❑ In a small bowl, beat eggs lightly. Add salt and pepper.
❑ Warm a plate.
❑ In a cup or small bowl, thoroughly mix sour cream and flour.
❑ Add sour cream mixture to eggs and beat well until mixture is smooth.
❑ Heat butter in a small skillet over medium-hot heat.
❑ As soon as the foam disappears from the melted butter, pour egg mixture into skillet and stir with a wooden spoon until eggs are almost solid. Continue to stir while you slide the eggs onto warm plate. Sprinkle with herbs.

CHEESE OMELET
Omletă cu Brânză

2 eggs
1 tbsp. sour cream
1 tbsp. fresh parsley, chopped
2 tsp. fresh dill, chopped
salt and pepper to taste
1 tbsp. butter
2 oz. grated cheese[*]

Serves 1
Preparation time: 5 min., Cooking time: 6 min.

❑ Warm a plate.
❑ In a small bowl, beat the eggs slightly. Add sour cream, half of parsley, dill, salt and pepper. Stir well but don't beat.
❑ In a small skillet, heat butter over medium heat. When butter has melted, add egg mixture and let brown, shaking the skillet slightly, and lifting the edges of the egg with a spatula. When eggs are well browned on one side, flip and brown the other side, continuing to shake skillet sideways. The eggs should cook about 3 min. on each side.
❑ Place eggs on warm plate. Sprinkle half the grated cheese on surface. Fold omelet in two, sprinkle the rest of the cheese and parsley over it, and serve.

---

[*] It is more authentic to use a ewe cheese such as caşcaval, cacciocavallo, or a pecorino; but omelet will taste equally good with grated Swiss gruyère.

THE HERITAGE OF ROMANIA AND ITS PEOPLE

The Thinker (Neolithic)

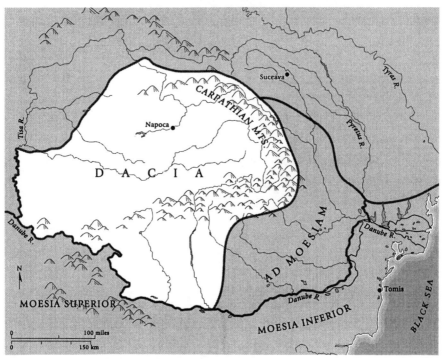

Map of Roman Dacia

Map of Romania, after World War II

*R*omanians can trace their ancestry as far back as the Bronze Age (roughly 2200 to 1200BC), although as a state, Romania has only been in existence since 1859. Because of their geographical location on the crossroads between the East and the West, the Romanians' history has been one of almost continual struggle to survive. For four thousand years they had to defend their land and their families through almost endless wars, invasions, occupation, oppression, and massacres.

The Romanians are descendants of the Getae and the Romans. The Getae, or Dacians, as the Romans called them, were an ancient Thracian tribe which inhabited the region where Romania now stands. Present day Romania's size is equivalent to the area of New York and Pennsylvania, and slightly smaller than the United Kingdom. It has a population of around 22 million. Romania is situated at the northern extremity of the Balkan Peninsula, with its southern frontiers along the wide, majestic, and, in places, spectacularly beautiful Danube.

67

The Getae were blessed with a fertile soil, rich in natural resources. The Carpathian Mountains soared to over 8000 feet, with dense forests, lakes, and mountain streams, a place to retreat from endless incursions by marauding foreign armies. The Black Sea and rivers provided an abundance of fish and navigation routes for trade with Greece. The Getae engaged in agriculture and stock raising, and mined the gold and iron ore, which they learned to process into tools and arms. They became the envy of empires and barbarian tribes alike. The Getae prospered for a while, became a kingdom, and built a powerful and well trained army to defend themselves against Cimcrians, Scythians, Illyrians, and the Celts. When the Getae themselves began to raid Roman lands south of the Danube, the Romans retaliated but were defeated and their armies massacred. However, when the Getic King Burebista began to scheme with the Roman General Pompey to overthrow Julius Caesar, Caesar decided to invade the Getic kingdom. He was assassinated before he could go through with his plans. It was Emperor Trajan who finally defeated the Getae, but only after two bloody wars lasting a total of four years.

The land of the Getae became a Roman province in 106AD, and was named Dacia. Rome sent merchants, craftsmen, and administrators from every part of the empire to settle there. They built roads, cities, and fortresses, and the province flourished. Romans referred to it as Dacia Felix (The Happy Dacia). Its population merged with the Roman colonists, and Latin became the official language. Romanian, as it is spoken today, is a Latin based language with elements of ancient Thracian, blended with elements from other languages of peoples with whom the Romanian ancestors fought and traded—and so traces of Greek, Slavic, Turkish, Bulgarian, and Hungarian are in the Romanian language. Some French and Italian words also crept into the language during the 19th century. Dacia, which had inclined towards the Hellenic Eastern culture, began to turn to the West. This had a profound influence on the Romanian cultural heritage.

Dacia remained a Roman province for over 150 years. While it flourished, the Roman Empire began to decline, and a new menace threatened the province—great barbarian invasions—that would eventually lead to the downfall of the Roman Empire and force the Romans to abandon Dacia in the year 271.

Without Rome's protection, Dacia became an open passage for invading tribes looking for new lands. For ten long centuries the valiant Daco-Roman population, by then known as Romanians, suffered as wave after wave of barbarians—the Visigoths, Ostrogoths, Huns, Gepids, Lombards, Avars, followed by the Bulgars, Magyars, and Mongols—massacred their families and plundered their settlements in passing. Dacian towns were abandoned, highway robbers menaced travelers along crumbling Roman roads, and rural life decayed. Fortunately the Romanians had the mountains and forests, which served as a retreat, where they could go in hiding and wait for quieter days. In those days, you could cross the entire country, from the Carpathians to the Black Sea, without ever having to leave the forest. The forest has been so much part of the Romanian's life and struggle to survive that references to the forest are common place in the Romanian folklore.

The Magyars, the last of the migrating tribes to establish a state in Europe, settled west of the Carpathian mountains and became the Hungarian Kingdom. More than a century later, they integrated Transylvania, then a principality ruled by a Voivode, and inhabited by Romanians. During the 13th and 14th century, many Romanians left Transylvania under increasing economic and religious persecution. They came over the Carpathian mountains, eastward and southward, where they founded two principalities, Wallachia and Moldavia, each ruled by a voivode. The two principalities steadily gained strength in the 14th century, a peaceful and prosperous time throughout southeastern Europe.

About that time, however, the Ottoman Turks began to expand their empire, and in so doing attacked both principalities. A series of wars between the Turks and the two principalities were fought during the next century. Two voivodes gained fame as a result of successful battles against the Turks. One was the Wallachian ruler, Vlad Draculă, who hated the Turks and defied the sultan by refusing to pay tribute. In 1461 Hamsa Pasha tried to lure Vlad into a trap, but the Wallachian prince discovered the deception, captured Hamsa and his men, impaled them on wooden stakes, and abandoned them. He became known as Vlad Țepeș (Vlad the Impaler), and was the inspiration for the well known fiction character Count Dracula. The other was a Moldavian voivode, Ștefan cel Mare (Stephen the Great). During his reign (1457-1504) Moldavia reached its height of splendor. He fought off the Turks in battle after battle, and at the time when the whole of Christendom was shaking with fear before the all-conquering Islam, Stephen the Great was named "the athlete of Christ" by the Pope. After each victorious campaign, he had a beautiful church built to honor the victory, forty in all. Some of them still adorn Romania's countryside. The oldest and one of the most important of them is the church—with monastery—of Putna, in southern Bucovina. Completed in 1469, it is the burial place of Stephen the Great. Putna is one of a number of 15th and 16th century monasteries known as the Painted Monasteries of Southern Bucovina, acclaimed as masterpieces of art and architecture, steeped in history and perfectly in harmony with their surroundings. Unique in the world in style as well as in their exterior wall painted frescoes, they won UNESCO's Prix D'Or for their artistic, spiritual, and cultural value.

Exhausted and discouraged after a century of battling the Turks with not much support from the West, both principalities signed honorable accords granting the Turks suzeranity over their states. Wallachia and Moldavia remained under the Turkish yoke for five centuries. The Ottoman Empire appointed the princes who ruled the principalities. These princes made land grants to a class of noblemen, the boieri, in return for their military service. As a result, the boieri became wealthy, and in search of more wealth established serfdom and exploited the peasants. Corruption ran rampant, and conditions deteriorated badly. However, one brief moment of glory in the history of Romania came near the end of the 16th century. One of the nobles from Wallachia, Michael, used his wealth to buy many villages. By the age of 30 he owned twenty villages, and was very influential. He became Prince of Wallachia in 1593 with the blessing of the Ottomans. Once in power, however, he turned against the Turks. He was an astute politician, and a ruthless fighter.

He hated the Turks, and through a long series of battles against the Turks, Transylvania, and Moldavia, he managed for a brief period to make every Romanian's dream come true. In Iaşi, in July 1600, Michael the Brave, as he was known, declared himself "by the grace of God, prince of Wallachia, Transylvania, and all of Moldavia." It was not to last long, but the brief union became the driving force behind later efforts for the unification of Romania.

From the turn of the 18th century through the middle of the 19th century, Moldavia and Wallachia were battle grounds in the wars between Russia and Turkey. The Russians were defeated in the Crimean War in 1853, and in 1856, under the Treaty of Paris, they were forced to withdraw from the two principalities. With the support of France, the two principalities united in 1859, and formed the modern Romanian state.

Four years later, Romania chose to nominate a foreign prince to the throne. Prince Charles of Southern Germany's Hohenzollern-Sigmarinen family was elected. At the outbreak of the Russian-Turkish War of 1877-78, during which Romanian troops backed Russia, and the Ottomans were defeated, Charles proclaimed Romania's independence, ending five centuries of vassalage. In 1881 the parliament proclaimed Romania a Kingdom, and Charles was crowned in Bucharest's cathedral as King Carol I.

Mainly foreign events thereafter shaped Romania' fate. The Balkan Wars began in 1912, and soon ignited the fire that was to become World War I. Romania joined the Allied Forces in 1916. Under the postwar treaties, Romania's size more than doubled, adding Transylvania, as well as the provinces of Dobrogea, Bessarabia, Bucovina, and part of the Banat to the Old Kingdom. These treaties also fulfilled the centuries-long Romanian dream of uniting all Romanians in a single country.

A period of peace, prosperity, and economic growth followed, but not for long. World War II and communism pushed Romanians once more into a long period of hardship and suffering. In 1939, France and Great Britain pledged to ensure the independence of Romania. Then, the Soviet Union and Nazi Germany signed a non-aggression pact, giving the Soviet Union the sphere of influence over the Balkans. Germany invaded Poland and ignited World War II. King Carol II of Romania tried to maintain neutrality, but France's surrender and the defeat of Britain's first attempt to invade Europe made this difficult. In September 1940, the King was forced to abdicate, Romania aligned itself with Germany, and joined the Axis Powers. In June 1941, the German armies with Romanian support attacked the Soviet Union. The troops were decimated by the Russians at Stalingrad. Some 700,000 Romanian lives were lost. At the same time, Romanian oilfields were destroyed by allied bombing, and finally Soviet troops entered Romania and occupied Bucharest. From 1945, rapid communist takeover followed. Romania also lost the province of Bessarabia the northern part of the province of Bucovina, the southern part of Dobrogea. Its industrial and petroleum industries were badly damaged, and excessive war reparations threw Romania into economic chaos. In 1948, Romania became a full fledged communist state, and remained part of the Eastern Block until the revolution of 1989, which opened a new page in Romania's contemporary history. After 45 years under communism and dictatorial regimes, conditions were created for restoration of democracy based on a multi-party system and a market economy. A new constitution was introduced on 21 November 1991 and free parliamentary and presidential elections took place.

CIORBĂ DE POTROACE
AND OTHER SOUPS

VEGETARIAN SOUP STOCK

Zeamă de Legume

4 tbsp. butter
4 oz. carrots, peeled and sliced
1 large onion, sliced
4 oz. celery stalks, cut into small pieces
1½ cups mushrooms, sliced (with stems)
1 tbsp. salt
2 bay leaves
12 black peppercorns
3 tbsp. fresh parsley, chopped
1 qt. water

Serves 6
Preparation time: 20 min., Cooking time: 70 min.

❑ In a large (2-3 qt.) kettle, heat butter over low heat.
❑ Add carrot, onion, celery, mushroom, and salt. Stir well. Cook, covered, stirring occasionally over low heat until vegetables are lightly browned (about 25-30 min.).
❑ When vegetables are cooked, add bay leaves, peppercorns, and parsley. Stir well.
❑ Add water. Stir. Bring to a boil over medium high heat. Reduce heat, and simmer, partially covered, about 40 min. Remove from heat and let cool.
❑ When cool, strain through a fine sieve, pressing solids to remove all the juice; discard solids.

Store in refrigerator until needed. To freeze, let first cool, skim any solid fat on surface, then freeze.

FISH STOCK

Zeamă de Peşte

4 tbsp. butter
1 large carrot, peeled and sliced
1 large onion, chopped
4 oz. celery, chopped
1½ cups mushrooms, sliced (with stems)
1 tbsp. salt
2-2½ lbs. fish carcasses*
1 bay leaf
12 white peppercorns
6 fresh parsley sprigs
2 tsp. dried thyme

Serves 6
Preparation time: 45 min., Cooking time: 70 min.

❏ In a large (2-3 qt.) kettle, heat butter over low heat.

❏ Add carrot, onion, celery, mushroom, and salt. Stir well. Cook, covered, over low heat until vegetables are lightly browned (about 25-30 min.), stirring occasionally.

❏ Break the fish carcasses into smaller pieces. Do not use entrails, scale, or gills. When vegetables are ready, add fish heads and carcasses, bay leaf, peppercorns, parsley, and thyme. Then add enough water to cover all solids. Stir well.

❏ Bring slowly to boil over medium heat. Reduce heat and simmer, partially covered, about 40 min. Remove from heat and let cool.

❏ Strain through a cheesecloth-lined strainer, and dispose of all solids.

For fish soups, add 1 cup dry white wine. For fish ciorbă, add 1 cup sauerkraut juice instead of wine. Don't mix wine with sauerkraut juice.

Fish stock can keep in refrigerator for about 3 days. If you make a larger quantity for future use, chill fish stock, skim any solid fat from surface, and freeze.

---

* Use heads and carcasses of any non-oily white fleshed fish. Flounder, sole, perch, monkfish are some good fish to use. Any fish market should be able to give you the quantity you need.

good !!

BEAN SOUP

Supă de Fasole

1 lb. dry white beans (lima, butter, or navy)
1 large onion, chopped
3 celery stalks, chopped
1 tomato, quartered
2 carrots, sliced
2 garlic cloves, peeled
6 fresh parsley sprigs

pork

¾ lb. smoked sausage, sliced

house

¾ lb. smoked pork, diced
1 tbsp. salt
2 tsp. fresh ground black pepper
1 tsp. sweet paprika
2 tsp. granulated sugar
1 handful spinach, chopped
2 tbsp. butter
2 egg yolks
3 tbsp. sour cream
1 tbsp. flour

Serves 6
Preparation time: 30 min., Cooking time: 2 hours

The night before (or at least 3-4 hours before preparing this soup), place beans in a bowl and cover with enough cold water to reach at least 2-3 in. above bean level. Soak beans.

❏ Drain beans, saving the water in which they soaked.

❏ Put beans in a large kettle. Top up the saved water with enough fresh cold water to make 2½ qts., and pour over the beans. Heat over high heat until water comes to a boil.

❏ Skim. Then lower heat to medium, and simmer for about 45 min. If beans absorb an excessive amount of water, add hot water.

❏ In a cheesecloth, prepare the onion, celery, tomato, carrots, garlic, and parsley, en bouquet.

❏ After 45 min., add bouquet of vegetables, and continue to simmer for another 30 min., stirring occasionally with a wooden spoon, and skimming the top if needed.

❏ Add the meat, stir, and simmer 15 min. more. Season with salt, pepper, and paprika.

❏ Taste. If beans are not quite tender, simmer another 10-15 min. Remove vegetables. Taste again and season with salt, pepper, and paprika, if needed. Add sugar and stir.

❏ Add spinach, cover, and simmer another 10-15 min. Add butter and stir.

❏ In a small bowl, mix egg yolks, sour cream, and flour until smooth. Stir the mixture into the simmering soup, and continue to simmer while stirring another 5 min.

This soup can be served as a main meal, with bread and a glass of wine. It is a very popular and nourishing Romanian dish.

POTATO SOUP WITH WHEY

Sârbuşcă

3½ cups buttermilk*
½ lemon, juice
2 tsp. cooking oil
2 oz. slab bacon, rind removed, cut into 1 in. cubes
4 oz. onion, chopped
1 garlic clove, crushed
1 tbsp. flour
1 tbsp. salt
2 tsp. fresh ground black pepper
1 tsp. hot Hungarian paprika
2 cups vegetarian soup stock**
1 lbs. potatoes, peeled and diced
1 parsnip, peeled and sliced
3 scallions, chopped
2 bay leaves
1 tbsp. parsley
1 tbsp. fresh dill sprigs, chopped
1 tbsp. chopped chives

Serves 6
Preparation time: 30 min., Cooking time: 55 min.

❑ Add lemon juice to the buttermilk, and leave at room temperature.
❑ In a skillet, heat oil over medium-high heat. Add bacon and sauté for about 5 min., tossing bacon to brown on all sides. Add onion, and garlic, and continue to cook until onion is soft and golden yellow, about 15 min. Add flour, and spices.
❑ In a kettle, bring the soup stock to a boil. Add potatoes, bay leaves, parsnips, scallions and vegetables; cook about 15 min. over medium heat. Add the onion and bacon mixture, and the buttermilk. Stir, and continue to cook until soup begins to bubble.
❑ Reduce the heat to medium-low, and simmer the soup for another 20 min., or until potatoes are done. Stir in herbs, taste, and season accordingly.

---

* Whey is the liquid part of the milk drained off the curd during cheese making. It is a low fat milk drink, but not readily available. Buttermilk, soured with lemon juice is a good substitute.
** Use VEGETARIAN SOUP STOCK, p. 74, or any other vegetarian stock.

CREAM OF CAULIFLOWER SOUP

Cremă de Conopidă

1½ lbs. cauliflower
3 tbsp. butter
3 tbsp. flour
5 cups water
1 cup chicken stock
2 tsp. salt
1 tsp. fresh ground black pepper
2 tbsp. sour cream
1 egg yolk
2 tbsp. fresh parsley, chopped
1 tsp. chervil

Serves 6
Preparation time: 40 min., Cooking time: 40 min.

❏ Cut all green leaves and most of the stem from cauliflower. Cover with cold water, and let soak for about 30 min.

❏ While cauliflower soaks, prepare a white sauce roux, as follows: heat 2 tbsps butter in a small heavy skillet over medium heat. When butter is melted, blend in flour with a wooden spoon or spatula. Let butter and flour foam together for about 2 min. or until sauce turns a light yellow. Remove from heat and let cool until bubbling stops.

❏ In a kettle, mix water with chicken stock. Add 1 tbsp. butter, and bring to a boil.

❏ Cut cauliflower into small pieces. Set aside ½lb., of the smaller florets. Add the rest to the boiling stock. Add salt and pepper. Reduce heat to medium-low, and cook covered until cauliflower is cooked, about 15-20 min.

❏ In a small bowl, mix sour cream and egg yolk.

❏ In a separate bowl mix roux with 3-4 tbsp. hot soup, and beat well with a wooden spoon or wire whip to avoid lumps. Add mixture to the roux sauce, and mix well to make a smooth sauce. Add to soup, and stir well. Sprinkle with parsley and chervil.

❏ Separately, boil remaining cauliflower florets about 10 min. in a small amount of water to which 1 tsp. of salt has been added. Add cooked florets to soup, and continue to simmer over medium-low heat for another 10 min.

Serve hot, with buttered toast.

CREAM OF POTATO SOUP

Cremă de Cartofi

3 tbsp. butter
3 onions, peeled and cut into small pieces
1 celery stalk, cut into small pieces
1 tbsp. salt
2 tsp. fresh ground black pepper
2 bay leaves
1½ qt. water
6 potatoes, peeled and quartered
12 slices French baguette
1 cup milk
2 tbsp. fresh parsley, chopped
½ cup caşcaval cheese, grated*
½ cup sour cream

Serves 6
Preparation time: 25 min., Cooking time: 1 hour 25 min.

❏ In a large kettle (2-3 qt.), heat butter over low heat.
❏ Add onion and celery. Stir well. Cover and cook until vegetables are soft and lightly golden, about 25 min.
❏ Add salt, pepper, and bay leaves. Stir. Add water. Stir. Bring to a boil over medium-high heat. Skim surface. Reduce heat to low.
❏ Add potatoes and simmer, partially covered, about 40 min. Remove from heat and let cool.

❏ In the meantime, preheat oven to 450°F. Heat slices of bread a few minutes.
❏ When cool, strain stock through colander and save soup stock. Press vegetables through a sieve, or pass through food processor, to make a purée.
❏ Return soup stock to the kettle. Add the vegetable purée and milk. Stir and heat over medium-high heat until hot but not boiling.
❏ Turn hot soup into a heated tureen.
❏ Place two slices bread in each soup plate. Pour soup over them, and sprinkle with parsley and cheese, then top with a dollop of sour cream.

---

* You can substitute a similar ewe cheese such as Kaseri, Pecorino, or Petit Basque.

TOMATO AND RICE SOUP

Supă de Roşii şi Orez

⅔ cup water
¼ cup rice
1 pinch salt
2 tbsp. butter
1 onion, peeled and chopped
3 oz. carrots, peeled and sliced
3 oz. celery stalks, chopped
1 green pepper, cored and cut into thin strips
1 qt. vegetable stock[*]
2 cups crushed tomatoes
6 oz. tomatoes, peeled and quartered
2 tsp. salt
1 tsp. fresh ground black pepper
2 tbsp. sour cream (optional)
1 tbsp. butter (optional)
2 tbsp. fresh parsley, chopped

Serves 4-6
Preparation time: 15 min., Cooking time: 60 min.

❑ In a kettle, combine 2/3 cup water, rice, and a pinch of salt. Heat to boiling, stir once, cover, reduce heat to medium-low, and steam rice 15 min. Remove from heat and let stand 5-10 min. Fluff rice with fork.

❑ In a large kettle (2-3 qt.), heat butter over low heat.

❑ Add onion, carrot, celery, and green pepper. Stir well, cover, and braise for 10 min., stirring occasionally.

❑ Add 1 cup vegetable stock, stir, cover, and continue to cook another 10 min.

❑ Add crushed tomatoes, peeled tomatoes, and the rest of the vegetable stock. Increase heat to high, and stir well. When soup begins to bubble again, lower heat to low, and simmer 30 min. uncovered.

❑ Strain soup through a fine sieve, extracting as much of the vegetable juices as you can through the sieve, with the help of a wooden spoon, then dispose of the remaining solids. Pour clear soup back into kettle. Add rice, salt, and pepper. Stir.

---

[*] Use recipe for VEGETABLE STOCK, p. 74, or any other stock.

❑ You may add sour cream and 1 tbsp. butter, stir and cook over low heat another 5 min., if you wish.

Serve hot and sprinkle with parsley.

CIORBĂ

The Romanian ciorbe are soups with a characteristically tangy tart aroma and taste due to the addition of a souring agent. Just a whiff of a ciorbă being prepared in the kitchen is sufficient to whet an appetite. It is equally delicious when tasted.

The word ciorbă derives from çorba, the Turkish word for soup, which in turn appears to be based on Persian word shurba, composed of shur, meaning "salty, brackish," and -ba, a suffix indicating food. However, shurba has long since disappeared from Persian usage.

Traditionally, a sour base called borş—not to be confused with the Russian borscht, which is a red beet soup—was used. Borş is made from fermented wheat bran, and can be prepared at home or bought at Romanian grocery stores. However, in recent years it is less frequently used because it requires too much time to prepare. Instead, the most common souring agents for the ciorbe are lemon juice and sauerkraut juice. Other souring agents are vinegar, sour grape leaves or green sorrel leaves.

In general, when the soup is soured with borş it is called borş. When other souring agents are used, it is called ciorbă.

In the recipes included in this book, sauerkraut juice is used. The easiest way to obtain it is to buy sauerkraut and press the juice out. Try to get fresh sauerkraut. Otherwise, buy it in plastic bags, glass jars, or cans. For other souring agents, you will have to experiment with quantities used to obtain a pleasing degree of acidity.

FISH CIORBĂ

Ciorbă de Peşte

1 qt. fish stock*
1 cup sauerkraut juice
1 cup peeled tomatoes
1 green pepper, cored and cut lengthwise into strips
3 tbsp. fresh parsley, chopped
3 tbsp. fresh dill, chopped
2 tbsp. fresh lovage, chopped (optional)
1-1½ lbs. fish**, cleaned, and cut
into boneless fillets or steaks
salt and pepper to taste
1 tsp. crushed hot red pepper

Serves 6
Preparation time: 20 min., Cooking time: 35 min.

❏ Mix fish stock with sauerkraut juice to make ciorbă stock.

❏ Pour into a 1½-2qt. kettle. Add tomatoes, green pepper, parsley, dill, and lovage.

❏ Bring to boil over high heat. Reduce heat, and simmer for 15 min.

❏ Cut fish into small chunks, and add to soup. Mix and simmer for another 15 min.

❏ Season with salt, pepper, and hot red pepper. Simmer another 2-3 min. and serve.

Ciorbă can be eaten with bread as a main dish, perhaps preceded by a shot of traditional Romanian ţuică, or as a starter.

See CIORBĂ, p. 83 for a description of this type of Romanian soup and suggestions for sources of sauerkraut juice.

***See footnote under ROMANIAN COLD AND HOT APPETIZER TABLE, p. 32.

---

* Use FISH STOCK recipe on page 75, or any other recipe, provided it contains no wine. Wine and sauerkraut juice don't mix well.

** You can use any one or a combination of sturgeon, carp, halibut, salmon, monkfish, tuna, prawns, or lobster tail.

LAMB CIORBĂ

Ciorbă de Miel

2 qts. cold water
2 lbs. lamb shoulder, cut into small pieces
1 lbs. lamb shank (bone and meat)
4 oz. carrot, peeled and sliced
½ lbs. parsnip, peeled and sliced
1 large onion, peeled and quartered
4 celery stalks, cut into small pieces
4 oz. fresh spinach, cut into small pieces
1 green pepper, cored, cleaned, and cut into small pieces
2 tbsp. salt
2 tomatoes, sliced
2 tbsp. rice
2 cups sauerkraut juice
2 tsp. crushed hot red pepper
1 tbsp. fresh ground black pepper
1 egg yolk
2 tbsp. sour cream
1 tbsp. fresh dill, chopped
1 tbsp. fresh fennel, chopped

Serves 6
Preparation time: 25 min., Cooking time: 45 min.

❑ Pour the water into a large kettle, add meat and bone, and bring to a boil over medium-high heat. As soon as it boils, skim the surface, then lower the heat to medium-low.
❑ Add carrots, parsnips, onion, celery, spinach, green pepper, and salt.
❑ Stir, and simmer for 15 min. Add tomatoes, and cook for another 5 min. Add rice, and cook another 10-15 min. or until meat and vegetables are cooked.
❑ Warm sauerkraut juice and add to soup. Add hot pepper, and black pepper. Cover kettle and remove from heat.
❑ Warm a soup-tureen.
❑ In a bowl, mix egg yolk and sour cream. Beat with a fork, and pour into tureen. Pour a ladle-full of soup liquid over it and stir well. Then add the rest of the soup, stirring while you pour.
❑ Sprinkle with dill and fennel, and serve.

You can serve this ciorbă as a main meal, either with the meat and vegetables in the soup, or you can pour the soup into the tureen through a sieve, and serve it on the side. It is a popular dish on Easter Day with red wine, painted Easter eggs, and cozonac, the festive Romanian cake(see ROMANIAN PANETONE, p. 263).

See CIORBĂ, p. 83 for a description of this type of Romanian soup and suggestions for sources of sauerkraut juice.

ZUCCHINI CIORBĂ

Ciorbă de Dovlecei

2 potatoes, peeled and diced
1 qt. vegetarian soup stock[*]
1 cup sauerkraut juice
3 zucchini, peeled and diced
3 tbsp. fresh parsley, chopped
3 tbsp. fresh fennel, chopped
3 tbsp. fresh chives, chopped
1 tbsp. salt
1 tsp. fresh ground black pepper
1 tsp. crushed hot red pepper
2 tbsp. sour cream
2 tsp. flour

Serves 6
Preparation time: 15 min., Cooking time: 55 min.

❑ Parboil potatoes.
❑ Mix soup stock with sauerkraut juice to make ciorbă stock.
❑ Pour into a 2-3 qt. kettle. Add all vegetables and herbs. Stir well.
❑ Bring to boil over high heat. Reduce heat, and simmer for 30 min. Stir well, then taste. Season with salt and pepper. Add hot pepper, stir, and simmer until vegetables are cooked, about 5-10 min.
❑ In a small bowl, mix sour cream with egg yolk and flour. Stir in a few tbsp. of ciorbă, mix thoroughly. Then blend mixture slowly into the ciorbă. Simmer another 5-10 min. and serve.

See CIORBĂ, p. 83 for description of this type of Romanian soup and suggestions for sources of sauerkraut juice.

---

[*] Use VEGETARIAN STOCK recipe on page 74, or any other recipe, provided it contains no wine. Wine and sauerkraut juice don't mix well.

Great!!!

MUSHROOM CIORBĂ

Ciorbă de Ciuperci

1 qt. vegetarian soup stock[*]
1 cup sauerkraut juice
3 tbsp. butter
½ lb. mushrooms, sliced
3 tbsp. fresh parsley, chopped
2 tbsp, fresh fennel sprigs, chopped
2 tbsp. fresh chives, chopped
1 tsp. ground thyme
1 tsp. black peppercorns
½ tsp. crushed hot red pepper
2 tsp. salt
3 tbsp. sour cream
1 egg yolk
2 tsp. all-purpose flour

Serves 6
Preparation time: 15 min., Cooking time: 35 min.

❑ Mix soup stock with sauerkraut juice to make ciorbă stock. Pour into a 2-3qt. kettle. Heat to boiling over medium-high heat.

❑ In a skillet, heat butter over medium-high heat. Sauté mushrooms about 5-6 min. while stirring and turning them with a wooden spoon.

❑ When stock begins to boil, reduce heat to low. Add mushrooms, herbs, spices, and seasoning. Stir well, and simmer, partially covered, about 20 min.

❑ In a small bowl, mix sour cream with egg yolk and flour. Stir in a few tbsp. of ciorbă, stir well. Then blend mixture slowly into the ciorbă. Simmer another 5-10 min. and serve.

see CIORBĂ, p. 83, for description of this type of Romanian soup and suggestions for sources of sauerkraut juice.

---

[*] Use VEGETARIAN STOCK recipe on page 74, or any other recipe, provided it contains no wine. Wine and sauerkraut juice don't mix well.

Excelent, cu carne de miel.!
Feb. 29' 2000

9 porții!

CIORBĂ WITH MEATBALLS

Ciorbă de Perişoare

Ingredients for the meatballs
  1 slice bread, crust removed
  1 lb. lamb meat (shoulder or leg)*
  ½ large onion, chopped
  1 egg, slightly beaten
  2 tsp. rice, boiled
  2 garlic cloves, crushed
  1 tbsp. fresh parsley, chopped
  2 tsp. salt
  1 tsp. fresh ground black pepper

Ingredients for the soup
  2 qts. cold water
  1½ lbs. lamb shank bones and meat*
  4 oz. carrots, peeled and sliced
  ½ lb. parsnips, peeled and sliced
  ½ large onion, cut into small pieces
  4 celery stalks, cut into small pieces
  4 oz. fresh spinach, cut into small pieces
  1 green pepper, cored, cleaned, and cut into small pieces
  1 tbsp. salt
  2 tomatoes, sliced
  2 tbsp. rice
  2 cups sauerkraut juice**
  1 tsp. crushed hot red pepper
  1 tbsp. fresh ground black pepper
  1 egg yolk
  2 tbsp. sour cream
  1 tbsp. fresh dill sprigs, chopped
  1 tbsp. fresh fennel sprigs, chopped

  Serves 6
  Preparation time: 25 min., Cooking time: 45 min.

---

* This soup can also be made with mixed pork and veal, in which case substitute the lamb bones with veal shank bones and fresh pork bones, and mix ground veal and ground pork meat for the meatballs.

Meatballs

❑ Soak bread in water and then squeeze out all excess.

❑ In a bowl, mix meat, bread, and onions. Pass through a fine or medium meat grinder. If a grinder is not available, ask the butcher to grind the meat mixture for you, or buy ground lamb and mix ingredients as well as you can.

❑ Return meat to the bowl. Add all the other ingredients, and mix well. With a teaspoon, take golf-ball pieces of the mixture and roll into balls. Coat each with flour, and let stand on work surface.

Soup

❑ Pour the water into a large kettle, add the meat bones, and bring to a boil over medium-high heat. Skim the surface, then lower the heat to medium-low.

❑ Add carrots, parsnips, onion, celery, spinach, green pepper, and salt. Stir, and simmer for 15 min. Add tomatoes, and cook for another 5 min. Add rice and meatballs, and cook for another 20 min or until meat and vegetables are cooked.

❑ Warm the sauerkraut juice and add to soup. Add hot pepper and black pepper. Cover kettle and remove from heat.

❑ Warm a soup tureen.

❑ In a small bowl, beat egg yolk and sour cream with a fork, and pour into tureen. Pour a ladleful of soup broth over it and stir well. Then add the rest of the soup, stirring while you pour. Sprinkle with dill and fennel, and serve.

This ciorbă can be served as a main meal, either with the meat and vegetables in the soup, or you can pour the soup into the tureen through a sieve, and serve it on the side. Left-over ciorbă usually tastes even better the next day.*

---

* See description of CIORBĂ (see p. 83) for suggestions on sources of sauerkraut juice.

GIBLET CIORBĂ

Ciorbă de Potroace

This is one of the best-known and most popular ciorbă in Romania. It comes from the province of Moldavia.

2 qts. cold water
3½ lbs. giblets[*]**, cut into small pieces**
4 oz. carrots, peeled and sliced
½ lbs. parsnips, peeled and grated
2 onions, chopped
4 celery stalks, cut into small pieces
2 tbsp. salt
4 tomatoes, slice and cut slices in half
4 tbsp. rice
2 tbsp. fresh parsley, chopped
2 tbsp. fresh dill or fennel sprigs, chopped
2 cups sauerkraut juice[**]
1 tsp. crushed hot red pepper
2 tsp. fresh ground black pepper
2 egg yolks

Serves 6
Preparation time: 25 min., Cooking time: 60 min.

❑ Pour the water into a large kettle. Add giblets, and bring to a boil over a medium-high heat. Skim the surface, then lower the heat to medium-low.

❑ Add carrots, parsnips, onion, celery, and salt.

❑ Stir, and simmer for 15 min. Add tomatoes, and cook for another 5 min. Add rice, parsley, and dill. Cook for another 20-25 min or until giblets and vegetables are cooked.

❑ Warm the sauerkraut juice and add to soup. Add hot pepper and black pepper. Cover kettle and remove from heat.

❑ Beat egg yolks slightly. Blend into soup slowly and gradually, stirring continually so that egg yolk does not coagulate.

Serve this ciorbă hot, preceded if you like with a glass of ţuică.

---

* Giblets can be from turkey, chicken, duck, or goose. They usually include the heart, liver, and gizzard; and can include also the neck, spine, and wings.

** see description of CIORBĂ (p. 83) for suggestions on sources of sauerkraut juice.

CABBAGE CIORBĂ

Ciorbă de Varză

1½ lbs. white cabbage
2 tsp. cooking oil
½ lb. smoked pork, off bone, diced (optional)
3 tbsp. butter
4 oz. carrots, peeled and sliced
4 oz. parsnips, peeled and sliced
6 oz. onion, coarsely chopped
1½ qt. cold water
1 cup sauerkraut juice*
1 tbsp. salt
2 tsp. fresh ground black pepper
½ tsp. crushed hot red pepper
2 tbsp. fresh dill, chopped
1 cup sour cream

Serves 6
Preparation time: 20 min., Cooking time: 50 min.

❑ Wash cabbage. Remove outer green leaves, cut cabbage into quarters.
❑ Fill a kettle with water and bring to a boil. Blanch cabbage in boiling water, about 10 min. Strain and let cool.
❑ In a skillet, heat oil over medium-high heat. Add smoked pork, and sauté about 5 min. stirring and turning with a wooden spoon.
❑ While cabbage is cooling, heat butter in a large, 2-3 qt. kettle, over medium-high heat. Add carrot, parsnips, and onion. Stir, lower heat to medium-low, cover, and braise about 20 min., mixing from time to time with wooden spoon.
❑ Add 1½ qt. cold water, sauerkraut juice, salt, pepper, and hot red pepper. Stir, increase heat to medium-high. Heat until water begins to boil. Reduce heat to medium-low, add cabbage, and dill, and simmer until vegetables are done, about 30 min. Add smoked pork. Stir.

Serve hot. Spoon some sour cream on soup.

---

* See description of CIORBĂ (p. 83) for suggestions on sources of sauerkraut juice.

BEET BORŞ BALADA

Borş cu Sfeclă

2 beets, whole, with a bit of stem, unpeeled
1 tbsp. butter
1 onion, chopped
2½ qts. cold water
2 beef marrow bones
1 parsnip, peeled and grated
2 carrots, peeled and grated
1 turnip, peeled and grated
1 tbsp. salt
2 tsp. fresh ground black pepper
2 beets, cleaned and peeled
1 cup sauerkraut juice*
4 potatoes, peeled and diced
1 tbsp. Delikat**
1 cup sour cream
3 tbsp. fresh parsley, chopped

Serves 6
Preparation time: 30 min., Cooking time: 1 Hour 15 min.

❏ Fill a kettle with enough water to cover 2 whole beets. Heat over high heat. Boil beets until tender, about 40 min. Strain, and let cool.

❏ In the meantime, in a skillet, heat butter over medium-high heat. Sauté onion until it turns a nice golden color, about 5 min.

❏ In a large, 4-5 qt., kettle, add 2½ qt. cold water and bones. Heat over high heat. When water begins to boil, skim surface and lower heat to medium-low. Add onion, parsnips, carrot, turnips, salt, pepper, and 2 peeled beets (for color). Simmer about 30 min.

❏ At this point you can either strain the soup stock and have a clear broth, or leave shredded vegetables in. If you strain it, then return the bones and go to the next step.

❏ Return soup to medium-low heat, add sauerkraut juice and potatoes, and

---

* see description of CIORBĂ (p. 83) for suggestions on sources of sauerkraut juice.

** Delikat is a brand of concentrated soup and stew flavor enhancer which seems to be in wide usage in Romania, both by restaurants and by homemakers. Several brands are available in the United States, such as Aromat by Knorr, and Vegeta, from Croatia, imported by Jana Foods.

continue to simmer another 30-40 min., until potatoes are cooked. About 5 min. before potatoes are tender, add Delikat and stir.

❑ Scrape the skin off the 2 cooked and cooled beets. Grate them.

❑ When potatoes are done, remove bones and whole beets. Add grated beets, and stir well.

Serve hot. Spoon some sour cream on soup, and sprinkle with parsley.

This recipe was contributed by the kitchen staff of the Balada Hotel in Suceava, a delightful small, privately owned hotel, run more like a pension that you would find in Switzerland or France, with a cozy dining room, and home-cooked meals.

Save the 2 beets used for color. Let them cool, and prepare a delicious beet salad. (see BEET SALAD, p. 57)

A ROMANIAN FOLKTALE

ION CREANGĂ (1837-1889)

Ion Creangă was one of the greatest Romanian writers and a true storyteller. He was born in 1837 in a village of white-washed houses, high in the Carpathian Mountains, surrounded by dense forests, and cool, pure mountain streams—forests inhabited by wild boar, bears, lynx, wild cats, fox, and wolves. He spent a happy childhood there, though from his recollections he appears to have often driven his parents out-of-their-mind with his never ending mischief and tricks.

Much later, having left his beloved village to complete his studies, he often reminisced about his childhood. He thought about the long, dark winter nights when the family was gathered around the wood-stove fire, when he listened to his mother telling stories—stories that were handed down by word of mouth from generation to generation. Ion Creangă decided to write down those stories, and they were published in 1875. These folktales give us an insight into life in the village, and often they have a universal moral. Five Loaves* is such a folktale, and you may find some present-day validity in it.

---

* From *Folk Tales from Romania* by Ion Creangă, translated by Mabel Nandriş. Edited and abridged by N. E. Klepper.

FIVE LOAVES

Cinci Pâini

A ROMANIAN FOLK TALE

Once upon a time, two men were traveling together along a road one summer day. One had three loaves of bread in his sack, the other, two. After some time they felt hungry and stopped in the shade of a weeping willow next to a water well. Each took the bread out of his sack, and so as to enjoy their meal more, they sat down to eat together.

Just as they were taking the bread from their sacks, a third traveler, unknown to them, overtook them and stopping beside them, bade them good day. He then asked to share their food, as he was very hungry, had no provisions, and there was no place to buy anything.

"Come, good man! Share our hospitality," said the first two travelers to the stranger, "for, thank God, where two can eat, there is always enough for a third."

The stranger, being very hungry, did not wait to be asked twice, but sat down by the other two and all three ate dry bread and drank water from the well, for there was nothing else to drink. And the three of them ate and ate and ate, until the five loaves were all eaten, as if they had never been there at all.

When they had finished, the stranger took five coins from his purse and gave them to the man who had had the three loaves, saying: "Good fellows! Please accept this small token of my gratitude, for you have indeed been friends. Further on, you can buy yourselves a glass of wine each, or do whatever else you please with the money. I am unable to thank you for the kindness you have shown to me, for I was nearly blind with hunger."

The two travelers hesitated before accepting the money, but after a good deal of insistence on the part of the third, they accepted. Then, a little later, the stranger said goodbye to the others, and continued on his way.

The two companions stayed a little longer in the shade of the willow to rest their bones. Then, having talked about one thing and another, the one who had had three loaves gave two coins to the one who had had two loaves, saying: "Here, brother! This is your share. Do what you like with it. You had two loaves, so you ought to have two coins. For myself, I am keeping three coins, for I had three loaves the same size as yours, as you know."

"How do you figure that?" said the other disparagingly. "Why only two coins and not two-and-a-half each? The man was not obliged to give us anything. Then what would have happened?"

"What would have happened?" replied his companion. "I would have been paid in the next world for my three loaves and you for your two—and that's all. But now, the bread has been paid for by the stranger, and we have money in our purses; I with my three coins and you with your two; each according to the number of loaves we had. I don't see how the money could possibly be more fairly divided."

"Oh no, my friend!" said the one with two loaves. "I don't agree with your judgment. Let us take the matter to court, and we'll stick to whatever the judge decides."

"All right, come along, then. To the court," said the other, "if you are not content. I am sure the judge will agree with me, although I've never been to a court of law in my life."

So off they went, decided to take their quarrel to the law. And when they came to a place where there was a courthouse, they went before the judge and told their story, each giving his own version. The judge, after hearing their case attentively, asked the owner of the two loaves: "So you are not content with your share of the money, my man?"

"No, Your Honor," said the discontented one. "We had no intention of taking the money from the stranger for the bread we gave him; but as it turned out that he gave us some, we should have divided it equally. That is my idea of what is just."

"If it's a question of justice," said the judge, "then be good enough to return a coin to your companion."

"Well, that astonishes me, your Honor," said the discontented one. "I came here to see justice done, and I find that your Honor, who knows the law, is making me even more puzzled. If the Last Judgment is to be like that, then Heaven help us!"

"So it seems to you," said the judge quietly, "but you will see that it is not the case. Did you have two loaves?"

"Yes, your Honor. I had two."

"Did your companion have three loaves?"

"Yes, your Honor, he had three."

"Just a moment ago you told me that you all ate the same amount; is that so?"

"That is so, your Honor."

"Good. Now, let us get it all clear, so that we may know how much bread each of you ate: let us say that each loaf was divided into three equal parts; how many pieces did you have, for you had two loaves to begin with?"

"I had six pieces, your Honor."

"And your companion, who had three loaves to begin with?"

"He had nine pieces, your Honor."

"Now, how many does that make? Nine and six?"

"Fifteen pieces, your Honor."

"How many men ate those fifteen pieces of bread?"

"Three men, your Honor."

"Now, try to remember how many pieces you had."

"Six, your honor."

"But did you eat six?"

"Five, your Honor."

"And how many were left over?"

"Only one piece, your Honor."

"Do you remember how many pieces your companion had?"

"Nine, your Honor."

"And how many did he eat?"

"Five, the same as I, your Honor."

"And how many had he left?"

"Four, your Honor."

"Good! Now let us get this straight. You mean that you had only one piece left over, while your companion had four pieces left; now one piece from yours and four pieces from your friend's make five pieces together?"

"Exactly five, your Honor."

"Is it true that the stranger ate those five pieces and gave you five pennies for them?"

"Yes, that is so, your Honor."

"So only one coin was due you for you had only one piece left over, and it was just the same as selling it for one coin. As for your friend, he ought to have four coins because he had four pieces left over. So now, be so good as to return one coin to your companion. And if you feel that that is unjust then go to God and see if He will make a different judgment."

The owner of the two loaves, seeing there was no other solution, gave back a penny to his companion, very reluctantly, thanked the judge and went off blushing.

The owner of the three loaves, however, astonished at the verdict, thanked the judge and went off saying: "If there were judges like that everywhere who do not stand nonsense, then those who are in the wrong would never appeal to the law. And the so-called lawyers, having no longer any means of making a living from their talking, would either do an honest job of work, or else die of hunger. And good people would live in peace!"

MĂMĂLIGĂ (POLENTA) AND SOME OF THE WAYS TO PREPARE IT

POLENTA
Mămăligă

In 1906, Theresa Strătilescu writes the following about mămăligă in *From Carpathian to Pindus. Pictures of Romanian Country Life.*:

Romanian cookery is very elaborate, and there is a number of dishes a Romanian peasant woman can cook if she only can afford it, but as a matter of fact, want will come to the rescue and make things ever so much easier. The plainest kind of food, the real national dish, is the mămăligă with brânză (cheese, sheep cheese). The mămăligă takes the place of bread, which is considered a luxury in a peasant's house; the mămăligă is always made fresh for each meal and eaten warm; cold mămăligă can be eaten too, but if a fire is at hand, it is cut into slices and fried on the embers. The table, of white wood, is milk-white with scrubbing; the mămăligă is turned out in the middle of it from the ceaun (iron round kettle for mămăligă) and stands like a golden cupola smoking there until everybody has set down round the table. In the meanwhile the wife is careful to take off the fire the pirostrii (iron tripod on which the ceaun has been boiling) otherwise she might also burn in hell's flames. If the mămăligă is furrowed with cracks, this means that an unexpected journey is at hand for some one of the household. Then the mămăligă is cut into slices, with a thread, carefully from upside down, and not the other way, as then the maize grows ear, and divided among the members of the family.

We can trace the ancestry of the mămăligă back to the Etruscan civilization, which predated the Roman Empire by almost a 1000 years and was the highest civilization on the Italian peninsula before the rise of Rome. It is the Etruscans who created and introduced a sort of mush made from grain which at times had the consistency of porridge and at others that of a crumbly cake. When the Romans took it over from the Etruscans, it became a basic, nutritious, and inexpensive meal for peasants as well as for the soldiers of the Roman armies. They called it puls, and later pulmentum.

In 105 AD, the Roman armies conquered lands that were inhabited by a Thracian tribe, the Getae, to whom the Romans referred as the Dacians. On this newly conquered territory, roughly the area which is now Romania, the Romans set up the Province of Dacia and colonized it with legionnaires, peasants, merchants, artists, and officials from all parts of the Roman Empire.

Dacia, as a Roman province, lasted 200 years. There is little doubt that the Romans brought with them the pulmentum.

Maize, sweet yellow corn, originated in Central America and was cultivated by the Maya Indians. It was not known in Europe until Venetian explorers brought the seeds back from their voyages during the 16th and 17th centuries. They apparently chose to trade these corn kernals with the Turks for other commodities, and it was the Turks that introduced corn to the northern regions of Valle d'Aosta, Veneto, and Piemonte, where it grows so well and is still referred to as Turkish wheat. The Turks also introduced corn throughout the Ottoman Empire, including Romania, where it grew successfully. Corn meal proved ideal for preparation of mush and the pulmentum made from corn became polenta in Italy and mămăligă in Romania.

Recipes for mămăligă are numerous and vary with the region, the ingredients available or afforded, and imagination. It is easy to prepare, inexpensive, and delicious. Usually eaten by itself as a main dish, it can also be served as a side dish with vegetables, meat, fish, or fowl. Sour cream is often spooned on the hot mămăligă, or on the cold left-overs. In general (I plowed through a seemingly endless variety of recipes for mămăligă taken from cookbooks and from friends and family) it is classified as soft or hard mush, boiled, fried, or baked. It is most commonly cooked with or served with cheese, usually cheeses made from ewe milk, such as Telemea or Brânză de Brăila (which can be substituted with any good quality imported Feta cheese), or Caşcaval (which can be substituted with similar Greek cheeses such as Kaseri and Kefalotiri, or the Italian Pecorino and Toscanello).

TRADITIONAL POLENTA

Mămăligă

The old method of making the mămăligă is very time consuming, taking hours to prepare. This recipe is one of several more modern ways of preparing it. Each cook seems to swear by one method, but this is simple, has a good success rate, and takes only half an hour. A ceaun is usually used, but if one is not available, use a kettle with rounded sides and a non-stick surface.

3 cups water
2 tsp. salt
2 tbsp. butter
1½ cups yellow corn meal, coarse or medium ground*
1 cup sour cream

Serves 6
Preparation time: 15 min., Cooking time: 15 min.

❑ Heat water in a ceaun or a kettle over high heat until it boils vigorously. Add salt, and butter**

❑ Sprinkle about a tbsp. of cornmeal into the boiling water. As soon as the water starts boiling again, pour in the rest of the cornmeal all at once, and stir vigorously with a melesteu (alternatively, use the tail end of a long wooden spoon) to prevent the formation of lumps. As soon as the cornmeal mixture begins to bubble, turn the heat down to low and be careful not to get splashed with boiling hot chunks of cornmeal which tend to shoot up when the mixture starts bubbling. Continue to stir, always in the same direction. As it continues to cook over the low heat you will begin to see the polenta thickening and becoming unglued from the sides of the kettle as you stir. The mămăligă should be done in about 10-15 min. To test if it is done, you can insert the tail end of a wooden spoon, which has been moistened with water, vertically into the polenta and spin it a couple of times. If it comes out clean, the polenta is done.

❑ Shake the kettle and immediately turn the kettle upside down over a wooden board. The mămăligă should come out clean, retaining the shape of the kettle. Cut portions with a thread, like cheese. You may also turn it into a serving

---

* Quantity may vary somewhat depending on quality of cornmeal, and if it is coarse, or medium ground.

** The pat of butter makes the water fatty, which helps prevent formation of cornmeal lumps during cooking.

dish and cut slices with a knife. Serve immediately while it is hot and before it hardens.

Serve the mămăligă as a side dish with meat, fish, or eggs. Put a pat of butter on it and some sour cream. Save the left-over polenta to use in other recipes later in this chapter.

FLUFFY POLENTA

Mămăligă Moale

3 cups water
2 tsp. salt
2 tsp. butter
1 cup yellow corn meal, coarse or medium ground[*]
½ cup sour cream

Serves 4
Preparation time: 15 min., Cooking time: 15 min.

❑ Heat water in a ceaun or kettle over high heat until it boils vigorously. Add salt, and a pat of butter.[**]

❑ With one hand slowly start pouring the cornmeal into the boiling water, while stirring continuously with a melesteu (or use the handle of a long wooden spoon) until all the corn meal has been addded, and until the liquid bubbles again.

❑ As soon as the liquid starts to boil, lower the heat to medium-low, and continue stirring until polenta starts to thicken and all the water has been absorbed. Be careful, as the polenta tends to "spit" as it thickens. Total cooking time should be about 10-15 min.

❑ Cover kettle with a lid and let stand for another 2 min. Then shake the covered kettle to loosen the edges, and turn the polenta into a bowl or deep serving dish.

❑ Spoon polenta onto each plate while polenta is still hot and somewhat fluid. Top each portion with a pat of butter, and serve with sour cream.

The mămăligă can be served by itself as an appetizer, or as a side dish to any main course. A attractive way to serve this dish the next day or later that day is to pour it into greased individual round dishes, and refrigerate. When cold, loosen edges with a knife, turn upside down and reheat, either in the oven or in a microwave oven. Serve with sour cream.

---

[*] Quantity may vary somewhat depending on quality of cornmeal, and if it is coarse, or medium ground.

[**] The pat of butter makes the water fatty, which helps prevent formation of cornmeal lumps during cooking.

CLASSY POLENTA
Mămăligă Boierească

3 cups milk
2 tsp. salt
2 tbsp. butter
1½ cups yellow corn meal, coarse or medium ground[*]
6 oz. telemea cheese (or a good quality feta cheese)
1 cup sour cream

Serves 6
Preparation time: 15 min., Cooking time: 15 min.

❏ In a ceaun or a kettle, heat the milk, salt, and 1 tsp. butter over medium heat until it begins to bubble.

❏ Sprinkle about a tbsp. of cornmeal into the milk. As soon as the milk begins to bubble again, pour in the rest of the cornmeal all at once, and stir vigorously with a melesteu (or the handle of a long wooden spoon) for about 1 min. Then add the cheese and the rest of the butter. Turn the heat down to low, and continue stirring vigorously, always in the same direction. You will begin to see the polenta thickening and releasing from the sides of the kettle. The mămăligă should be done in about 10-15 min.

❏ Shake the kettle and immediately turn it upside down into a hot serving dish. Cut into slices and serve hot.

Serve the mămăligă as a side dish with meat, fish, or eggs, or by itself, with sour cream.

---

[*] Quantity may vary somewhat depending on quality of cornmeal, and if it is coarse, or medium ground.

BAKED POLENTA CAKES

Alivenci

A very popular Moldavian dish, simple and quick to prepare as a snack, an appetizer, or main dish with salad. This recipe is based on one prepared by the well-known Romanian writer and storyteller, Ion Creangă.(see ION CRE-ANGĂ, p. 96)

1 lb. farmers cheese
4 eggs
2 tbsp. butter, soft
1 cup sour cream
3 tbsp. yellow corn meal
2 tbsp. flour
2 tsp. salt

Serves 6
Preparation time: 15 min., Cooking time: 30 min.

❑ In a bowl, stir cheese well with a wooden spoon until it becomes creamy.
❑ Separate eggs. Beat egg yolks slightly. Whip egg whites until stiff.
❑ Preheat oven to 350°F.
❑ Add yolks to cheese and mix well. Add 4 tbsps. sour cream and 1 tbsp. butter, and again mix well. Next, add corn meal, flour, and salt. Mix again. Then fold in egg whites. Mix batter by hand or with an electric mixer until smooth.
❑ Butter an oven dish and bake batter until the surface is nicely browned, about 30-40 min.

Cut into squares and serve immediately. The cakes get hard quickly as they cool. Top with sour cream.

BAKED POLENTA, COUNTRY STYLE
Mămăligă Ţărănească la Cuptor

1 recipe traditional or fluffy polenta[*]
1 garlic clove
2 tbsp. butter
4 oz. caşcaval cheese[**], grated
8 strips of grilled smoked bacon
1 cup sour cream
Serves 4
Preparation time: 15 min., Cooking time: 20 min

This tasty dish can be made either with cold left-over mămăligă, or by first preparing either a traditional or a fluffy polenta and letting it cool on a plate in the refrigerator until it is hard and cold.

❑ Cut cold polenta into thin slices by using a cutting thread or cheese wire.
❑ Rub the bottom of an oven dish with garlic, and then butter it well.

❑ Preheat oven to 350°F.
❑ Cover bottom of oven dish with slices of polenta. Put a few pats of butter over them, then sprinkle half of the grated cheese over them. Place another layer of polenta slices on top. Lay the bacon strips over them, and cover with a third layer of polenta. Again, place a few pats of butter and sprinkle the rest of the cheese.
❑ Bake in oven about 20 min.

Serve hot with sour cream, as a snack or as a main dish with a tomato salad and a good Romanian wine.

---

* see POLENTA chapter, p. 102.
** Grated Swiss cheese is also a delicious substitute

MOLDAVIAN POLENTA BALLS

Bulz (Boţ)

1½ cups water
1½ cups buttermilk
2 tsp. salt
1 tsp. butter
1¼ cups yellow corn meal, coarse or medium ground*
4 oz. caşcaval cheese, grated**

Serves 4
Preparation time: 45 min., Cooking time: 20 min.

❑ In a ceaun or a kettle, add water, buttermilk and salt. Heat over high heat until it boils vigorously. Add butter.

❑ With one hand slowly start pouring the cornmeal in the boiling liquid, while stirring continuously with a melesteu (or use the handle of a long wooden spoon) until all the cornmeal has been poured out, and until the liquid bubbles again.

❑ As soon as liquid starts to boil, lower heat and continuing to stir cook over low heat until polenta starts to thicken. Remove from heat and stir until all the water is completely absorbed.

❑ Cover kettle with a lid and let stand for another 2 min. Uncover and test thickness of polenta. It should be fairly thick, almost solid. If it is not, return to heat, sprinkle with another few tbsps. of corn meal and cook another few minutes. Cover again and let stand a few minutes. Shake the kettle, then turn polenta upside down onto a plate. Let cool.

❑ Preheat oven to 350°F.

❑ When polenta is cold and fairly solid, mold by handfuls into balls about the size of an egg. Make a fairly large indentation in each ball, take a bit of grated cheese, work with fingers and stuff into cavity, then smooth over the indentation.

❑ Place polenta balls on a buttered oven tray, and bake about 20 min.

Serve hot with with butter or sour cream, as a snack or lunch, or to accompany a ciorbă.

---

* Quantity may vary somewhat depending on quality of cornmeal, and if it is coarse or medium ground.

** Instead of caşcaval cheese, you can use any ewe milk cheese such as Kaseri. Kefalotiri, Pecorino or Toscanello.

FRIED POLENTA WITH CHEESE
Mămăligă Friptă cu Brânză

1 recipe fluffy polenta[*]
1 egg, slightly beaten
1 cup grated cheese[**]
2 tbsp. cooking oil
½ cup sour cream

Serves 4
Preparation time: 10 min.(not including preparation of fluffy polenta),
Cooking time: 6 min.

This is yet another tasty way to serve mămăligă. Use either cold left-over polenta, or prepare a new fluffy polenta recipe, pour into a rectangular mold, and cool in the refrigerator.

❏ Cut polenta into ¼ in. thick slices. Dip slices first in egg and then in grated cheese.

❏ In a skillet, heat oil over medium-high heat. Fry polenta slices until nicely browned on both sides, about 3 min. on each side.

Serve hot with sour cream.

---

[*] see FLUFFY POLENTA, p. 106.
[**] Use cașcaval cheese or other similar hard ewe cheese. Otherwise, gruyére or emmenthal cheese will do.

SARAMURĂ DE CRAP
AND OTHER FISH DISHES

FISH

Peşte

The Black Sea, important rivers such as the Danube (with its uniquely beautiful delta), the Prut, the Olt, and the Mureş, and the Carpathian Mountain streams and lakes provide a rich variety of fish for the Romanians and for export.

The Danube delta, where the Danube River divides into three branches and continues its journey for sixty more miles before emptying into the Black Sea, is a major source of fish. It is the biggest nature reserve park in Europe. More than 250 species of birds, native and migratory, inhabit this region. It is a paradise for those who enjoy photography, fishing, hunting, and bird watching.

It is there that fishermen catch sturgeon and process one of the best gray caviars. Romania has some of the best sturgeon fishing grounds in the world. In addition to sturgeon, fishermen catch carp, pike, pike-perch, bream, sword-fish, shad, mackerel, catfish, trout, and sardines.

Since some of the fish used in Romanian recipes may not always be readily available at the fish market, other suitable fish are listed for some of the recipes. Many typically Romanian fish recipes are eaten cold. Some recipes have been modified to bring them more in line with our present tastes.

CARP IN BRINE
Saramură de Crap

Bucharest, the capital of Romania, became the capital of the Province of Wallachia in 1659. Princes and nobles built their palaces and churches along its main streets, one of them being Podul Mogoşoaiei, which later was paved and widened and was named Calea Victoriei (Avenue of Victory). Bucharest's most prestigious hotels, restaurants and shops followed, and it became the city's most fashionable street. The prettiest square along Calea Victoriei was the Piaţa Teatrului. On that square stood a luxury hotel, the Grand Hotel Broft, which changed its name to the Grand Hotel Continental in 1900. For almost half a century it boasted a restaurant run by one of the most famous chefs, Andrei Cernea. Personalities from the theater, politics, and high society gathered here to taste its traditional Romanian and international cuisine.

Damaged by an earthquake in 1940, then hit by bombardments during the war, followed by a period of economic difficulties, the hotel closed and did not re-open until 1974 as Hotel Continental. It underwent extensive repairs, and has now become again one of the smartest hotels in Bucharest. Its restaurant, too, is re-establishing its reputation for an excellent cuisine. Continental's master chef, Grigore Todea, has contributed this recipe.

4 fillets (6 oz. each) of carp[*]
3 tbsp. olive oil
4 cups water
2 tbsp. crushed hot red pepper
2 tbsp. sweet paprika
1½ tbsp. salt
2 garlic cloves, diced

Serves 4
Preparation time: 10 min., Cooking time: 25 min.

❑ Brush fillets on both sides with olive oil. Place on hot grill of a barbecue, or under a broiler, and grill for 4-5 min. on each side. Remove from grill and set aside.
❑ In a large kettle, add water, hot pepper, paprika, and salt. Over a high heat, bring brine solution to a boil. Lower temperature to medium-low. Add fish fillets and cook uncovered for 5 min. Add garlic and cook another 3 min.

---

[*] Instead of carp, this recipe works very nicely with catfish, swordfish, or monkfish.

Serve hot, with polenta (see POLENTA recipes, p. 102) and pickled vegetables.

This dish is equally delicious cold. To serve cold, follow above recipe but instead of cooking the fish in the brine solution, place it on a deep serving plate, pour some of the boiling hot solution over the fish, and then let it cool. It can be refrigerated in the brine and then eaten cold with hot polenta.

STUFFED SMOKED SALMON

Papiot de somon

Predeal is a small winter resort town nestled in the mountains, at an altitude of 3500 ft., about 95 miles from the capital of Bucharest. It is a popular base from where vacationers can access some of the best skiing facilities in Romania.

The Hotel Orizont is an attractive, modern hotel. It has a pleasant restaurant serving excellent Romanian and international cuisine, as well as a comfortable cocktail lounge. A good band helps skiers relax in the evenings with dance music. This recipe is the specialty of Chef Gheorghe Cătană at the Orizont.

1 lb. fillet of perch[*]
3 egg yolks, slightly beaten
4 tbsp. sour cream
salt and pepper to taste
1 lb. sliced smoked salmon
3 tbsp. butter, melted

Serves 4
Preparation time: 15 min., Cooking time: 20 min.

❏ Pass the fillet of perch through a fine meat grinder several times. In a bowl, mix the perch with the eggs. Add sour cream, salt and pepper.

❏ Arrange salmon as 4 flat squares, using about ¼ lb. per square, on a work surface. With a spoon, place an equal amount of perch stuffing on each slice. Roll slices around stuffing to form cylinders.

❏ Preheat oven to 350°F.

❏ Place salmon rolls side by side in a buttered oven dish. Baste with melted butter, and bake in oven about 20 min.

Serve warm with sautéed vegetables.

---

[*] For perch you can substitute fillet of cod, halibut, or pike.

TROUT WITH ALMONDS AND SOUR CREAM
Păstrăvi cu Migdale şi Smântână

4 trout (8-10 oz. each), cleaned
salt to taste
4 tbsp. mixed green herbs, chopped (parsley, dill, chervil)
1 cup milk
2 cups fine dry bread crumbs
3 tbsp. butter
3 oz. almonds, sliced
1 cup sour cream
juice of ½ lemon

Serves 4
Preparation time: 15 min., Cooking time: 20 min.

❏ Clean, gut, and rinse the trout well. Pat dry.
❏ Rub fish with salt, and then coat each cavity with 1 tbsp. chopped herbs.
❏ Dip the trout in milk, and roll in bread crumbs.
❏ In a skillet large enough to hold the 4 trout, heat 2 tbsps. butter over medium-high heat. When butter is melted and spread evenly on the bottom of the skillet, add the trout and fry about 4 to 5 min. on each side.
❏ While fish is frying, in a separate small skillet, heat the remaining butter over medium heat. Add the almonds. Toss and stir continuously about 2 min. or until almonds are nicely roasted but not burned. Take off heat. Add sour cream and lemon juice, and stir. Cover and let simmer over low heat another 3-4 min.
❏ Serve with parsleyed boiled potatoes. Either spoon the sour cream sauce on the fish or bone the trout and place in the sauce.

FISH WITH ONIONS

Peşte cu Ceapă

This is one of the many delicious but simple fish recipes from the Danube River area. Similar dishes can be found in all the neighboring countries.

5 tbsp. olive oil
1 large onion, peeled and sliced
1 tbsp. salt
2 tsp. fresh ground black pepper
1½ tsp. Hungarian hot paprika
1½ lbs. sturgeon steaks*
¾ cup water
1 tbsp. fresh dill, chopped
1 cup sour cream

Serves 4
Preparation time: 10 min., Cooking time: 25 min.

❏ Heat 3 tbsps. olive oil in a skillet over medium heat. When oil is hot, add onions, salt, pepper, and paprika. Sauté onions just until they are soft and yellow, about 2-3 min., stirring and turning them with a wooden spoon.

❏ Cut fish steaks into small cubes, about 1 in. x 1 in. Add to the onions. Add another 2 tbsps. olive oil, and sauté for another 5 min., stirring and turning fish and onions.

❏ Add the water and dill, stir, and cover skillet. Lower heat to medium-low, and let simmer for 15 min.

❏ Remove lid, stir in 2 tbsps. sour cream, and continue simmering, uncovered, for another 5 min.

Serve hot with polenta (mămăligă), and spoon some sour cream on the polenta.

---

* Swordfish is a good fish to substitute for sturgeon.

FISH CAKES

Chiftele de Peşte

This is a nice recipe to use when you have some left-over cooked fish. The use of a meat grinder is recommended. If one is not available, just mix ingredients together thoroughly.

3 tbsp. olive oil
1 small onion, chopped
4 slices white bread, crust removed
1 lb. left-over cooked fish*
2 eggs, slightly beaten
1 tbsp. salt
2 oz. parmesan cheese, grated
1 tsp. Hungarian hot paprika
1 tsp. fennel seeds
2 tbsp. lemon juice
2 tbsp. fresh dill sprigs, chopped
1 cup flour

Serves 4
Preparation time: 35 min., Cooking time: 15 min.

❑ Heat 1 tbsp. oil in a skillet over medium heat. Add onion, and sauté until soft and yellow, about 5 min. Set onion aside and let cool a few minutes. Save skillet.

❑ Soak the bread in milk, then squeeze out excess.

❑ In a bowl, mix bread, fish, and onion. Pass the mixture through a grinder using a fine or medium screen. Return mixture to the bowl.

❑ Add eggs, salt, cheese, paprika, fennel seeds, lemon juice, and dill. Mix well with a wooden spoon. Pick up tablespoonfuls with your hands, moistened with water, and roll mixture into balls about 2-2½ in. diameter. You should get about 8-10 balls. Flatten the balls into patties.

❑ Dip patties in flour.

❑ Heat the remaining oil in the skillet over medium-high heat. Fry patties until nicely browned on both sides, about 3-4 min. on each side.

Serve alone or with a sauce, with mămăligă and salad or pickled vegetables (murături).

---

* Use any fish without many bones.

BAKED TROUT

Păstrăvi la Cuptor

3 lbs. rainbow trout, gutted and washed[*]
salt to taste
1 tsp. Hungarian hot paprika
1 tsp. sweet paprika
3 tbsp. butter, melted
4 sprigs fresh parsley
2 sprigs fresh fennel
2 sprigs fresh coriander (cilantro)
2 tbsp. dry white wine
2 tbsp. white wine tarragon vinegar
1 tbsp. olive oil

> *Serves 4*
> *Preparation time: 15 min., Cooking time: 40 min.*

❏ Preheat oven to 350°.
❏ Rub salt and paprika on the inside and outside of the fish.
❏ Butter the bottom of an oven dish. Arrange fish in it, and spread the herb
sprigs on top.
❏ In a small bowl, mix vinegar, wine, and oil. Pour mixture over fish.
❏ Pour remaining melted butter over the fish, Bake for 30-40 min., basting fish
from time to time with the butter sauce.

Serve with braised leeks and boiled parsleyed potatoes.

---

[*] Any moderately lean, mild flavored white meat fish can be used for this recipe.
They include several varieties of sea bream such as porgy, scup, and sheepshead,
catfish, salmon, and seatrout. Large fish can be baked as steaks or fillets.

FISH PAPRIKA

Papricaş de Peşte

1½ lb. fish steaks*
salt to taste
juice of ½ lemon
2 tbsp. olive oil
½ onion, peeled and sliced
3 tbsp. sour cream
1 tsp. Hungarian hot paprika
1 tsp. fresh ground black pepper
2 tbsp. fresh dill, chopped
½ cup water or fish stock
1 bay leaf
1 egg yolk
2 tbsp. fresh parsley, chopped

Serves 4
Preparation time: 10 min., Cooking time: 25 min.

❑ Rub fish steaks with salt. Cut into cubes the size of stewing meat. Coat with half the lemon juice, and let sit.

❑ In a skillet, heat olive oil over medium-high heat. Sauté onion until it turns a nice golden color, about 5 min. Be sure that onion doesn't burn.

❑ Add sour cream, paprika, pepper, and dill. Stir well.

❑ Lower heat to medium-low. Add fish, water or stock, and bay leaf. Let fish simmer in sauce about 15 min., without stirring.

❑ When fish tests done, pass sauce through a sieve into a small bowl. Return fish and onion to the skillet. Remove bay leaf. Cover, and keep warm.

❑ To the sauce, add egg yolk slowly while you stir. Add salt to taste, and the rest of lemon juice.

❑ Place fish and onion in a heated serving dish. Sprinkle with parsley. Either pour sauce directly over fish, or serve separately.

Serve with hot mămăligă, or parsleyed boiled potatoes.

---

* For this dish use carp, salmon, sturgeon, or swordfish.

RAGOUT OF CARP

Plachie de Crap

Following are two methods of preparing this dish. In one version, the fish is first fried quickly in oil and then braised with the vegetables. In the other, the vegetables and the fish are braised together. Some prefer the additional flavor of the fish in the first recipe, but for the calorie-conscious, there is not that much difference. Both methods result in a tasty, light, and nutritious meal.

1½ lbs. carp* fillets or steaks
juice of ½ lemon
salt to taste
2 tbsp. olive oil
2 onions, peeled and sliced
½ cup dry white wine
6 tomatoes, peeled, seeded, and sliced**
1 lemon, peeled and sliced
6 peppercorns
2 bay leaves
3 tbsp. fresh parsley, chopped
½ cup cooking oil
2 cups flour

Serves 4
Preparation time: 35 min., Cooking time: 35 min.

Version 1
❏ Cut fish fillets or steaks into small pieces, as for stewing meat. Place pieces in a bowl. Add lemon juice, stir well, and sprinkle salt on top. Let stand at least 30 min.
❏ While fish is absorbing the lemon juice and salt, heat olive oil in a saucepan over medium-high heat. Sauté onion until it turns a nice golden color, but does not burn, about 5-6 min. Lower heat to low, add wine, tomatoes, lemon slices, peppercorns, bay leaves, and parsley. Stir well, cover, and braise about 15 min.
❏ In a skillet, heat a good quantity of cooking oil over high heat. Roll fish in flour, and fry in hot oil about 3-4 min. Remove fish and drain well.
❏ Place fish over the vegetables in the saucepan, pour a little of the oil in which

---

* Good substitutes for the carp are striped or sea bass, whiting, or swordfish.

** Instead of the fresh tomatoes, you can use about 8 oz. of canned peeled tomatoes.

it fried on top of the fish, cover, increase heat to medium, and braise with the vegetables another 10 min. Remove bay leaves, sprinkle with paprika, and serve.

The fish is excellent served hot. More commonly, in Romania, the fish is left to cool with the vegetables and sauce, and is served cold, decorated with quartered lemons.

Version 2

❑ Let fish stand in lemon juice and salt as in Version 1.

❑ Sauté onion as in Version 1. Add the rest of the ingredients as in Version 1, and also add fish, without rolling it in flour or frying it. Place a few pats of butter or some melted butter on top of the fish, cover, and braise over low heat about 25 min.

BAKED SOLE WITH MUSHROOMS

Calcan cu Ciuperci

1½ lb. sole fillets* (about 6-8 fillets)
salt and pepper to taste
2 tbsp. butter
1 tbsp. olive oil
1 onion, chopped
2 cups mushrooms, sliced
2 tbsp. fresh parsley, chopped
1 tbsp. fresh dill sprigs, chopped
½ cup dry white wine
2 tbsp. butter, melted
½ cup sour cream**
2 tsp. flour
1 tbsp. sweet paprika

Serves 4
Preparation time: 10 min., Cooking time: 30 min.

❏ Rub fish fillet with salt and pepper. Let stand for 45 min.
❏ During this time, prepare the rest of the ingredients.
❏ In a skillet, heat 2 tbsps. butter and 1 tbsp. olive oil over medium-high heat. Sauté onion, mushrooms, half the parsley, and dill until onion turns yellow gold but does not burn, about 5- 6 min.
❏ Preheat oven to 350°F.
❏ Grease a baking dish. Arrange half the fish fillets in a layer on the bottom. Spread mushroom mixture on top. Salt and pepper lightly. Place second half of fillets on top. Pour wine over the fish. Sprinkle with melted butter.
❏ Bake uncovered for 15 min. Spoon out sauce and save.
❏ Stir sour cream gradually into flour. Blend in fish sauce. Cook mixture in a small saucepan over medium heat, stirring continually, until sauce begins to thicken. Spoon over fish.
❏ Sprinkle with paprika, and bake 10 more min. Sprinkle with chopped parsley and serve hot, with boiled, parsleyed potatoes and a vegetable.

---

* You can substitute cod, halibut, or catfish for sole.

** In the United States, where the sour cream tends to be thick, it is best to dilute it with either créme fraiche or light cream.

BREADED CARP

Crap Pane

1½ lbs. carp[*] fillets (skinless), or steaks
salt and pepper to taste
1 cup flour
1 egg, slightly beaten
1 cup bread crumbs
3 tbsp. olive oil
juice of ½ lemon
½ lemon, sliced
2 tsp. sweet paprika
2 tbsp. fresh parsley, chopped

Serves 4
Preparation time: 10 min., Cooking time: 10 min.

❑ Rub fish fillets with salt and pepper.
❑ Roll fillets in flour, dip in egg, and then dip in bread crumbs.
❑ In a skillet, heat olive oil over medium-high heat. When hot, reduce heat to medium. Fry fish until nicely browned and crisp, about 3-4 min. on each side.
❑ Remove fish and place on kitchen towels to absorb excess oil. Then place on a heated serving plate. Sprinkle with lemon juice. Place a thin slice of lemon on each fillet. Sprinkle with paprika and parsley.

Serve hot with parsleyed boiled new potatoes and broccoli, cauliflower, carrots, or Brussels sprouts.

---

* Good substitutes are catfish and striped bass.

VEGETABLE CASSEROLE WITH FISH

Ghiveci cu Peşte

2 lbs. fish steaks or fillets[*]
1 tbsp. salt
6 tbsp. cooking oil
2 onions, peeled and sliced
3 garlic cloves, peeled and chopped
2 small eggplants, ends trimmed, blanched about 3 min.,
    squeezed, and sliced (unpeeled)
2 carrots, peeled and sliced
1 parsnip, peeled and sliced
¼ lbs. okra, ends cut and blanched about 2 min.
8 oz. peas, canned
8 oz. green beans, canned
1½ lb. potatoes, peeled and diced
1½ lb. tomatoes, quartered
½ cup tomato sauce
2 tsp. salt
1 tsp. black peppercorns
1 tbsp. sweet paprika

Serves 6
Preparation time: 40 min., Cooking time: 1 hour 10 min.

❏ Remove skin from fish fillets or steaks. Cut fish into small stew-size pieces, sprinkle with salt, and let stand about 20 min.

❏ Heat 3 tbsps. oil in a large skillet over medium-high heat. Add onion and garlic. Sauté until onion turns a nice golden brown, about 5 min. Lower heat to medium-low, add eggplant, carrot, parsnips, okra, peas, green beans, potatoes, tomatoes, and tomato sauce[**]. Stir well, cover, and braise about 30 min.

❏ Preheat oven to 350°F.

❏ Oil a 4-5 qt. earthenware or Pyrex casserole. Pour the mixed vegetables into casserole. Add peppercorns. Spread fish pieces on top of vegetables. Sprinkle with salt and paprika. Dribble 2 tbsps. oil over fish and vegetables.

---

* The best fish to use for this recipe are carp, swordfish, tuna, or halibut.

** The vegetables used in this recipe are the common ones for a Romanian ghiveci. However, others such as corn, broccoli, cauliflower, zucchini, turnips, and mushrooms can be used.

❏ Cover casserole tightly, and cook in oven for 30 min., shaking casserole from time to time to ensure that there is some liquid at the bottom to prevent vegetables from burning. Don't stir contents as the vegetables and potatoes will break up.

Serve hot from the casserole. This dish is also delicious eaten cold the next day.*

---

* For general information about ghiveci, see GHIVECI, p. 127.

FISH ZACUSCĂ (ZAKOOSKER)
Zacuscă de Pește

The Romanian zacuscă is very popular. It is tasty, easy to prepare, and can be cooked with fresh vegetables to be preserved for winter. The zacuscă is prepared either with vegetables, or with vegetables and fish, or vegetables and mushrooms. Although a fish zacuscă can be eaten warm, it is usually eaten cold.

The name comes from the Russian zakooska, but in Russia it means something quite different. It designates their appetizer table, similar to the Romanian mezeluri (see chapter on APPETIZERS, p. 31). The usage of the word probably comes from the center of the fish industry in Romania, the Danube delta region. It borders Russia, and many of the fishermen are of Russian origin.

1½ lb. fish steaks or fillets*
6 oz. whole dill pickles
4 tbsp. tomato paste
½ cup dry white wine
3 tbsp. olive oil
salt to taste
2 tbsp. cooking oil
1 onion, peeled and chopped
6 oz. carrots, peeled and sliced
2 tsp. salt
1 tsp. fresh ground black pepper
1 tsp. ground thyme
2 tbsp. chives, chopped
1 bay leaf
3 oz. Greek Calamate black olives

Serves 4
Preparation time: 30 min., Cooking time: 55 min.

❏ Remove skin of fish fillets or steaks. Cut fish into small stew-size pieces, and let stand 15-20 min.

❏ In the meantime, blanch pickles in boiling water for about 2 min. Remove, drain, and squeeze out excess water. Cut pickles into slices and let cool.

In a small bowl, prepare a tomato sauce by dissolving tomato paste in wine.

---

* For this recipe the best fish to use are carp, swordfish, salmon, halibut, or perch.

❏ In a skillet, heat olive oil over high heat. Fry fish in very hot oil, turning pieces with wooden spoons, for a total of about 8 min. Remove fish and drain. Save skillet with the oil. Place fish on a plate, sprinkle with salt, and let cool.

❏ To the skillet, add cooking oil, and heat over medium-high heat. Sauté onion about 3 min. Add carrot, pickles, salt, pepper, thyme, chives, and bay leaf. Stir well.

❏ Deglaze vegetables with the tomato sauce. Stir, and add enough water to cover the vegetables. Lower heat to medium-low, and simmer about 30 min.

❏ Cut olives in half, remove pits, and place olives in a sieve. Run cold water over them to remove salt.

❏ Add olives and fish to vegetables, stir well, and continue to simmer another 10 min. Add water if sauce becomes dry to keep the zacuscă moist.

Let cool and refrigerate, then eat cold. Serve with mămăligă (polenta). You may process the zacuscă in sterilized jars and store in cool place. See a resource on preserving fish for method.

This dish is from Ion Negrea's personal portfolio of recipes. Mr. Negrea is at the time of this writing the executive manager of the Inter-Continental Hotel in Bucharest, as well as vice-president of the Romanian Cooks and Pastry-Cooks Association.

A ROMANIAN FABLE

Illustration of King and Queen-to-be by Eve Wilder.

*T*his Romanian fable has been told to children over and over again, from one generation to another. Just as it happened over and over again throughout the history of the Romanians, here, too, a town in the mountains is invaded by barbarians who plunder, and kill, and leave the town burned to the ground. It is a moving story of pure young love, of a father's devotion to his children, of courage and bravery, of a harvest celebration; and it has a happy ending as all fables should have.

THE TOWN IN THE MOUNTAINS

Oraşul Dintre Munţi

Translated and abridged by N. E. Klepper

A very long time ago, in a Moldavian town high in the mountains, two little girls lived with their mother and grandmother. Their father, heartbroken, had had to leave because his wife's relatives did not want him around. Although he now lived far away, his heart and his thoughts were constantly there, where his daughters had been born, and he missed terribly not seeing them grow up. He worked very hard, and from what he earned, he always made sure to send them enough so that they would not be in need.

Time passed, and before long the two girls were old enough to go to school, and were learning to read, which they loved. The older daughter's name was Daniela. She was very beautiful and resembled her father, both in looks and in character. The younger one was called Doina, after the hauntingly beautiful and romantic Romanian folk music. Her parents had chosen her name well for, as it turned out, she not only loved to listen to the playing of the doina, but she had a lovely voice and she sang doinas with such tenderness that it brought peace of mind and tranquillity to all those that heard her.

Daniela had other qualities. She loved to read and to learn about everything. At school she was ahead of everyone in her class. She soon ran out of books, and begged her teachers to lend her more. The teacher who understood her best was a young professor whose name was Victor. He understood Daniela so well because he, too, was not very rich and he, too, loved to read. Daniela did what she could to finish each book as quickly as possible and return it to the young teacher, for whom she felt so much respect and admiration. When Victor taught a class, the pupils would be all eyes and ears, and would not stir until the end of the lecture because he taught them so beautifully. It seemed, however, as if Daniela concentrated and absorbed his every word even more than the others—and though Victor talked for all his pupils, he, too, sometimes felt that he was only addressing Daniela, and that she alone was listening.

One night, a band of barbarians stormed through the little town in the mountains and destroyed it, setting houses on fire. They burned the school down, too. They pillaged everything—the animals, the grain, all the people's possessions. The frightened townspeople ran to hide wherever they could. Some perished in the flames that engulfed the town, others in the dense forests surrounding the town, as they took unfamiliar paths.

That night, Daniela was awake, reading as usual by the yellow, flickering light of the kerosene lamp. Suddenly she heard pounding hoofs of galloping horses, terrifying screams, dogs barking, and farm beasts wailing as they trampled down the narrow alleys of the town. Instantly she got up and ran to awake her mother, her grandmother, and her sister Doina. They all slipped out of the house as quickly and as quietly as they could, leaving their beloved little house and everything in it, hidden behind the tall fir trees.

The two little sisters, their mother, and grandmother ran through the forest to another village, where they took refuge at the house of an uncle. Daniela was not as frightened as she was dejected. She thought about her school, and about Victor, the teacher who taught them so well.

In place of the little town with houses made of pine, with walls decorated with the bark of trees, with curtains as white as the mountain snow, hand painted with national motifs—only dust and ashes remained. Next to the green chain of firs, only silence and grief remained. A thick coat of soot covered everything.

Soon, however, the heavy stench of burning faded away, and was replaced by fresh scents of the forest, and the rains washed away all trace of the barbarians.

Much time passed, but the people who survived never forgot the barbarian attack which disturbed their tranquillity and shattered their lives. They met and swore to fight against their enemy and to destroy him. And then, on their old, ancestral land, they rebuilt their town. They gathered and worked side by side, hand in hand, and a new town rose from its ashes, a larger and more beautiful one. They built a new school, much better than the old one, with large windows and stairs made of cut stone from the mountains.

Daniela, who had no news from Victor, the young teacher, was overtaken with grief, but she never gave up hope that he was safe, and that some day she would see him again.

The girls' father eventually learned about the tragedy, and came as quickly as he could. He searched for his children, and after locating them, he got busy and built them a new house, more beautiful than the one that had burned down. He loved both his daughters equally, but he understood Daniela's free nature better. Daniela had a sort of wisdom of her own. She was very balanced in her thoughts and words, and especially in her deeds. Whenever she had any problem or concern, she consulted with her father because she felt closest to him. One day, when she was with her father, in the big city where he worked, her face suddenly saddened. Her father, noticing the change, and afraid that she might be ill, said:

"My dear daughter, what thoughts torture your mind and your heart? Has something happened? Can I be of help?"

Surprised, Daniela blushed, making her even prettier. Not wanting to worry him, she put on a smile and said:

"No, it's nothing, Father."

"My dear daughter, you do have something troubling your heart," said her father with kindness. "Maybe the reason for your sadness comes from there. Let's see, you are about 19," continued her father. "Have you by any chance fallen in love with a young man and you didn't tell me?"

Noting that she didn't answer, her father helpfully continued:

"If it's so, make sure that you know him well and that he is worthy of you. It's time that I tell you that we come from an honest and worthy family, Daniela." The love that her father showed in his eyes touched Daniela so that she could no longer keep her feelings hidden. She came close to him, put her arms around his neck, and kissed both his cheeks, just as she used to do so often when she was little. Daniela then pulled a chair close to her father, sat down, and told him her story:

"You see, Dad, I never ever told this to anybody else, not even to Mother, or to Grandmother, or to Doina, but I will tell you because I feel closer to you. You think like me and I see the world with your eyes." She told him about the time when she was 17 years old, just before the quiet little town had been destroyed, when she experienced, for the first time in her life, that sentiment, pure as a flower—the feeling of being in love, in love with the young teacher, Victor. She told him how much she still loved Victor, and about the grief she felt whenever she thought of him.

And so, her father learned Daniela's secret. It was later, when he went back with Daniela to their native town, that he was to learn the rest of the story. Two years had passed, and Daniela had no news about the fate of Victor. She continued her studies at another school, and her ambition was that she, too, should become a teacher, to teach the children as beautifully as Victor used to do.

After the barbarians left the burning town behind them, when the young workers and scholars alike set out to destroy their enemy, Victor was among them. That night he had managed to escape the flames, and he had walked for days, until he arrived at the emperor's palace. He was a kind emperor, who wanted only peace and tranquillity among his people. Victor presented himself and asked the emperor to give him men and arms to take with him to battle the plunderers. The emperor listened carefully, and then granted Victor's wish, but not before Victor agreed to spend two years at the emperor's palace to be taught the use of the arms and the art of fighting. Then, the emperpr wished him well and sent him on his way, back to his native lands, with many soldiers, arms, and all other things that he might need.

"Here," said the emperor, "you served me faithfully for two years. You proved yourself to be clever, agile, and cunning.

Therefore, I pronounce you King, to reign in peace and tranquillity over your native lands, with the assurance that it will be well defended."

After Victor crushed the enemies, people from all over welcomed him with much love. He united all the villages and towns into one kingdom, and he lived and ruled in peace thereafter.

Busy with affairs of state, Victor had had no time to visit the town where he had been a teacher, where he had taught Daniela, the one with the golden braids and with eyes the color of the sky; the one he fell in love with and never forgot, not for a second. He walked alone around his palace, for alone he remained. In the palace of the kind emperor, he had seen many beautiful daughters of noblemen, but not a single one attracted him. He only thought of Daniela, and seemed to see her face everywhere.

One day, when Victor was returning to his palace, tired from a long journey, two men from the faraway town in the mountains were waiting to see him. They told him that they were messengers from the town that had burned to the ground, and they were there to invite him to a harvest celebration. He accepted the invitation with pleasure. A few days later, with a heavy heart for fear that he may not find Daniela there, King Victor arrived at the edge of the town, the town that he had left just a few years before.

At the great harvest celebration, all the town's people were gathered. Beautiful young girls dressed in their colorful native costumes, carried flowers and golden ears of wheat in their arms. When the king arrived, everyone, young and old, lined the road. Victor dismounted his white horse, and walked into the town. On his shoulder he wore a cape embroidered with wreaths and bordered with gold thread. He was not so young anymore. He now had a small mustache, black as a crow's feather, and his hair was equally black and shiny.

And then, out of the multitude of young and beautiful girls, emerged one even prettier than all the rest. In one hand she carried a silk scarf, on which lay a loaf of bread as white as her skin and as ruddy as her cheeks, and in the other, a bowl of salt.. A town's elder spoke: "Welcome, your Majesty! We beg of you to taste this bread of good fortune."

The king approached, followed by the crowd that began to cheer with happiness. Then, suddenly, as he came closer to the girl who held the bread and the salt, he froze. The girl with the rosy cheeks, wearing a dress the color of a red rose, embroidered with gold edges, was none other than Daniela, the girl he loved even as he taught at that school, and she was even more beautiful now. When she realized who the king was, she nearly dropped the bread she was holding. Fortunately, Victor rushed forward and grabbed her just in time to steady her. Then he took a piece of the warm bread, dipped it in salt, and tasted it with great pleasure. The crowds cheered. He then dipped his piece of bread in the salt again, and smiling, in front of everyone, offered it to Daniela to taste, saying, "Just as you are sharing with me this bread, so shall you share with me this kingdom. Bless you, my love, for coming back into my life."

To Daniela, what was happening was like a dream, but she had no time for dreaming. The king was taking her by the hand and saying, "Dear Daniela, how I suffered! I thought you perished. I never stopped thinking about you. I felt that I should have run to your house to save you that terrible night. I reproached myself, I was dejected, but I never stopped thinking of you—and all along, these mountains of ours were hiding the person I longed for so much!"

Daniela found Victor even more handsome than she had remembered. "And so," the king went on, "I ask you here, in front of the good people of our little town which suffered so much, would you be my wife, and queen forever?"

Daniela, full of emotion, turned her head in the direction where she knew that her father was standing, and looked to see his expression. He gave her a big smile, and nodded his head just enough for her to understand that she had his blessing. Then she turned in the other direction, where her mother was standing. She did not forget her mother, and she received her blessing too. Daniela then turned to King Victor, and holding his hand, said, "With my parents' blessing, I am your queen and will be your wife forever."

A big wedding followed, as part of the celebration of the rich plentiful harvest. Her parents kissed her, and Doina, who knew how to sing so beautifully, sang a special song for the king and her sister, a song so lovely that it warmed the hearts of everyone who heard it. Then, the beautiful queen left with the king, and they traveled to a far away place, over the mountains and the two lived together many happy years.

Daniela did not forget her parents or her sister, and especially her father, whom she loved so much. And whenever life brought her difficulties, she always called on him to ask his advice. She became a teacher, and also helped the king with his duties. All their children were taught by Daniela. And they built a proud and beautiful kingdom, in which everyone lived happily for many years. And the people would have lived happily even to this day, had their King Victor and Queen Daniela still been alive.

MITITEI AND OTHER MEAT DISHES

CHARCOAL GRILLED STEAK
Fleică la Grătar

The Romanian tradition of eating charcoal grilled meats seems to have evolved from both the ancient shepherds who lived at the foot of the Carpathian Mountains, and from the nomadic gypsies. Charcoaled steak is served at Romanian restaurants sizzling hot on a wood platter.

1½ lbs. beef steak*
1 recipe cold garlic sauce**
salt and fresh ground black pepper to taste
3 tbsp. butter, melted
3 tbsp. fresh parsley, chopped

Serves 4
Preparation time: 5 min., Cooking time: 10-16min.

❏ Meat must be at room temperature.
❏ Brush steaks on both sides with garlic sauce. Sprinkle them with fresh ground black pepper, and let stand for about an hour before grilling.
❏ Brush steak with melted butter. Weather permitting, grill outside on a barbecue grill. Otherwise, broil them under the broiler. Continue to baste with melted butter, while cooking. For medium steaks, grill about 6 min. on each side.

Serve steaks on wooden platters or heated plates. Season with salt and pepper to taste, and sprinkle with parsley. You can also pour a little of the garlic sauce on top if you like garlic and your family and friends don't mind.

Serve with baked potato or french fries and murături(see PICKLED VEGE-TABLES, p. 34)

---

* For this recipe, try to use that part of the beef flank (fleică) which is called flank steak fillets in the U.S., and goose skirt in Britain. This is not easy to find as many butchers save this cut for themselves. Or use tenderloin (fillet steak).
** See COLD GARLIC SAUCE,p. 252.

TENDERLOIN WITH ONION

Muşchi cu Ceapă

2 tbsp. cooking oil
¼ lb. shallots, chopped
1 tbsp. black peppercorns, whole
~~2 tsp. salt~~
½ cup beef stock
4 tbsp. sour cream
1 tbsp. all purpose flour
2 tbsp. butter
1½ lbs. tenderloin, rib-eye, or other lean beef cut
2 tbsp. fresh parsley, chopped
1 tbsp. chives, chopped

Serves 4
Preparation time: 20 min., Cooking time: 35 min.

❏ Heat the oil in a skillet over medium heat. Add shallots, peppercorns, and salt. Sauté until shallots are golden brown, about 5 min. Add beef stock, stir, and cook another 5 min. Lower heat to medium-low.

❏ In a small bowl, mix sour cream with flour. Add mixture slowly to the simmering beef stock and shallots, and stir well. Cover and keep warm on low heat.

❏ Separately, heat the butter in a skillet over medium-high heat. Pound meat lightly, then cook it in hot butter, about 3 min. on each side, then lower heat to medium-low.

❏ Pour sauce from the other skillet over meat, sprinkle with parsley and chives, cover, and cook for another 10 min.

Serve with french fries and salad.

ROMANIAN BOILED BEEF
Rasol de Vacă

Rasol is the Romanian version of boiled meat. The term "boiling" is not really correct. The meat is actually cooked over low heat so it is actually simmered. This method of cooking is probably the oldest form of preparing food, and it is found universally in almost all ethnic foods. It is a simple and economical method, and results in a very tender, tasty, and nutritious meal. Furthermore, in addition to a great meat dish, all the vegetables to garnish it and the stock in which the meat is cooked provides a ready, wholesome soup.

The tastiest cuts for this dish are from the foreshank with the marrow-bone, the brisket, and the oxtail meat.

4 qts. water
2 lbs. beef, foreshank with marrow bone.
4 oz. carrots, peeled and sliced
4 oz. celery stalks, sliced
3 oz. parsnips, peeled and sliced
3 oz. leeks, sliced
8 oz. onions, sliced
4 parsley sprigs
4 dill sprigs
8 oz. white cabbage, cut in pieces
4 potatoes, peeled, and quartered
1 tbsp. salt
2 tsp. fresh ground black pepper

Serves 4
Preparation time: 25 min., Cooking time: 2H30 min.

❑ Fill a large kettle with water, and place over high heat. Add meat. Bring water to boil. When water begins to boil, skim surface several times to remove any scum, lower heat to medium-low, add all vegetables except cabbage and potatoes, and greens. Simmer for 2 hours.

❑ In a separate kettle, parboil cabbage for about 20 min.

❑ After simmering meat and vegetables for 2 hours, add cabbage, potatoes, salt, and pepper. Continue to cook another 30 min. or until meat is tender.

Place drained meat on a serving platter, surrounded by the drained vegetables and potatoes. Serve with a mustard or horseradish sauce*.

---

* See chapter on SAUCES.

PAN-FRIED LAMB CHOPS

Cotlete de Miel la Tigaie

8 loin lamb chops
2 tsp. salt
2 tbsp. butter
3 tbsp. cooking oil
2 tsp. crushed hot red pepper
2 eggs, well beaten
1 cup bread crumbs

Serves 4
Preparation time: 20 min., Cooking time: 30 min.

❏ Bone the chops. Pound them slightly. Then, with a sharp knife, score several times to speed up cooking.
❏ Rub chops with salt.
❏ Heat butter in a skillet large enough to hold the 8 chops. Sauté chops over medium-low heat just enough to whiten the meat—about 2-3 min. on each side.
❏ Remove chops from skillet to a plate. Let cool until chops are at room temperature. Leave skillet on the side.
❏ Heat oil in the skillet in which you sautéed the chops, over medium-high heat. Add red pepper. Roll chops in egg, then in bread crumbs. Fry about 3 min. on each side in the hot oil.

Serve hot with mashed potatoes and a vegetable.

BREADED LAMB SCALLOPS

Şniţel de Miel

2 lbs. lamb, center-cut from the leg
salt and pepper to taste
1 tbsp. butter
3 tbsp. olive-oil
3 garlic cloves, peeled and cut in half
1 tbsp. fresh thyme, chopped
1 tsp. cumin
1 cup all-purpose flour
2 eggs, slightly beaten
1 cup bread crumbs
¼ cup dry white wine
6 slices lemon

Serves 6
Preparation time: 30 min., Cooking time: 20 min.

❑ Cut slices of lamb about ¾" thick. Remove any bones and pound slices into thin scallops. Then, with a sharp knife, score several times to speed up cooking time. Rub scallops with salt and pepper, and let stand about 15 min.

❑ In the meantime, heat the butter and oil in a skillet large enough to hold the 6 scallops. Add the garlic, thyme, and cumin. Sauté over medium-high heat, shaking the skillet, for about 3-4 min. Remove garlic and thyme and let stand in a covered warm dish. Keep skillet hot.

❑ Coat the scallops on both sides, first in flour, then in eggs, and finally in bread crumbs.

❑ Place the meat in the hot skillet, and brown quickly on both sides over medium-high heat about 3-5 min. on each side. Remove scallops to warm serving plates.

❑ Deglaze skillet with the wine, scraping up any browned bits from the bottom. Return the garlic and thyme to the skillet. Stir and spoon the sauce over the lamb, and decorate with lemon slices.

PORK ROAST BALADA

Friptură de Porc

The recipe for this roast is simple, but you must follow the instructions carefully to ensure succulent meat, full of flavor, which melts in your mouth.

The tastiest cut for this dish is the shoulder butt. Ask your butcher to bone it for you.

> 2½ lbs. pork butt roast, boneless
> 2 onions, peeled and sliced
> 2 carrots, peeled and sliced
> 1 bay leaf
> 4 tsp. Delikat[*]
> ½ cup dry white wine
> 3 garlic cloves, peeled and chopped
> 2 tsp. salt
> 1 tsp. fresh ground black pepper
> 2 tsp. ground thyme
> 3 tbsp. sour cream (optional)

> *Serves 6*
> *Preparation time: 15 min., Cooking time: 1H45 min.*

❏ Fill a large kettle with water. Place over high heat. Add meat. Bring water to boil. When water begins to boil, skim surface several times to remove scum; add onion, carrots, bay leaf, and Delikat. Boil for 20 minutes. Meat should be about half cooked. Remove from water and place on a work surface. Let cool several minutes, then cut meat into slices.

❏ Preheat oven to 325°.

❏ Grease a roasting pan. Place meat slices in one layer, slightly overlapping each other, to cover bottom of the pan. Sprinkle chopped garlic around meat. Add salt, pepper, and thyme. Pour wine over it.

❏ Place roasting pan on a middle rack in the oven, and let roast about 1¼ hours. It is very important to keep meat moist. Therefore, about every 10 min., baste slices well with the wine sauce from the pan. During the last 10 min. increase temperature to 400° to brown the roast nicely.

---

* Delikat is a brand of concentrated soup and stew flavor enhancer used in Romania, both by restaurants and homemakers. Several brands are available here, in the United States, such as Aromat by Knorr, and Vegeta, from Croatia, imported by Jane Foods.

Serve with baked or roasted potatoes. Use the pan sauce as gravy, or add sour cream to it.

This recipe was contributed by the kitchen staff of Hotel Balada in Suceava. (see BEET BORŞ BALADA, p. 93 for the story)

PORK ROAST WITH PICKLED CUCUMBER SAUCE

Friptură de Porc cu Sos de Castraveţi

3 tbsp. butter
3 shallots, chopped
2 garlic cloves, crushed
1 tbsp. salt
2 tsp. fresh ground black pepper
1 sage leaf
1 tbsp. fresh thyme, chopped
1½ lbs. center cut loin pork, cut in 1 in. thick slices
2 medium dill pickles, sliced julienne style
1 tbsp. French Dijon mustard
¾ cup tomato sauce
¾ cup dry white wine
4 tbsp. sour cream
1 tbsp. all-purpose flour

Serves 4
Preparation time: 25 min., Cooking time: 50 min.

❑ Heat the butter in a large heavy skillet over medium heat. Add shallot, garlic, salt, pepper, sage, and thyme. Sauté until shallots are soft and translucent, about 3-4 min.

❑ Increase temperature to medium-high. Add slices of pork, and sauté, turning over so that both sides brown, about 2 min. on each side.

❑ Preheat oven to 350°F.

❑ Transfer meat and sauce to an oven casserole. Add cucumber, mustard, tomato sauce, and wine. Cook covered for about 30 min.

❑ In a small bowl, mix sour cream with flour, then add 3-4 tbsps. of sauce from the casserole. Mix well, and add to sauce around the meat. Cook uncovered for another 5 min.

PORK LOIN AU GRATIN SIBIU STYLE

Muşchi de Porc "Sibian"

This is a specialty of Chef Nicolae Turean who oversees the restaurant of the Hotel Împaratul Romanilor (The Roman Emperor Hotel) in the town of Sibiu. Sibiu was originally called Hermannstadt in 1241 by the German Saxons who colonized Transylvania. It still retains the medieval German character.

In 1555, the corner building in which this beautiful hotel is located was an inn called The Turkish Sultan. In 1772 the inn was re-named The Blue Star. In 1773 Emperor Joseph II stayed here, at which time the name of the inn was changed to The Roman Emperor. Other famous guests at this hotel include Brahms, Liszt, and Johann Strauss. The restaurant has a reputation for its fine Romanian and international cuisine.

> 1½ lbs. boneless pork loin, cut into ½ in. slices
> salt and pepper to taste
> ½ lb. caşcaval cheese[*], cut into 8 slices
> 4 medium thick slices boiled ham
> 3 tbsp. cooking oil
> 2½ cups mushrooms, sliced
> ½ cup tartare sauce

Serves 4
Preparation time: 20 min., Cooking time: 17min.

Meat:

❑ Pound the pork slices with a mallet to form two thin scallops per serving. Sprinkle slices with salt and pepper.

❑ Place a slice of cheese and a slice of ham on each of half of the slices, and cover with the other half of the slices.

❑ In a skillet, heat oil over medium-high heat. When oil is hot, sauté meat about 6 min. on each side. Then remove from skillet and let stand.

❑ In the same skillet, sauté mushrooms in the remaining oil for about 5 min., turning mushrooms over several times.

❑ Pre-heat oven to 350°F.

❑ In an oven dish, place meat. Cover each portion with mushrooms, and another slice of cheese. Bake in oven about 10 min.

---

* In place of caşcaval, you can use other similar ewe milk cheeses such as the Greek Kaseri and Kefalotiri, or the Italian Pecorino and Toscanello.

Serve hot, with french-fried potatoes and sautéed petit-pois peas. Spoon tartare sauce over meat.

Tartare Sauce:
   1/3 cup mayonnaise
   1 egg, slightly beaten
   4 scallion tips, chopped
   1 tsp. salt
   1 tsp. fresh ground black pepper
   1 tsp. French Dijon mustard

❏ In a small bowl, mix mayonnaise well with each of the above ingredients, one at a time, until mixture is homogeneous. Refrigerate until ready to serve.

PORK ROLL WITH SPINACH

Rulou de Porc cu Spanac

1¼ lbs. boneless pork cutlet, sliced in 4 pieces and pounded thin
2 oz. onion, chopped
1 tbsp. fresh parsley, chopped
1 tbsp. fresh dill, chopped
2 oz. pork sausage
2 oz. mushrooms, diced
2 eggs, slightly beaten, each egg separately
2 tsp. salt
2 oz. green pepper, thin sliced and chopped
2 tbsp. cooking oil
3 oz. spinach, chopped, either canned or frozen
1 egg white

Serves 4
Preparation time: 40 min., Cooking time: 30 min.

❑ Place pounded slices of pork on squares of aluminum foil. Trim each cutlet into a rectangle. The scraps you cut off should equal about ¼ lb.
❑ In a bowl, mix the scraps with onion, parsley, dill, and sausage. Pass through fine meat grinder. Put ground mixture back in the bowl. Add mushroom, 1 beaten egg, salt, and pepper. Mix well. Then spread mixture evenly on the 4 slices of pork.
❑ Preheat oven to 350°.
❑ In a skillet, heat 1 tbsp. oil over medium-high heat. Add 1 beaten egg and tilt skillet to spread egg around. Turn quickly over, and remove from heat. Let thin omelet cool.
❑ Cut omelet in four and place one on top of each slice of meat.
❑ In a bowl, mix spinach and egg white. Spread evenly over the four slices of meat. Sprinkle green pepper on each slice.
❑ Carefully roll meat around the stuffing. Baste rolls with oil, sprinkle a few drops of water on each, and wrap them in the foil, closing sides tightly.
❑ Place rolls in an oven dish. Bake about 30 min.

Unwrap, and serve hot with a mushroom sauce, accompanied with french fried potatoes and a salad.

This is a specialty of Chef Nicolae Turean at the Hotel Împăratul Romanilor in Sibiu.
(See PORK LOIN AU GRATIN SIBIU STYLE, p. 148, for the story)

VEAL ROLL WITH SPINACH

Rulou de Viţel cu Spanac

1 lb. veal cutlet, sliced in 4 pieces and pounded thin
1 tsp. thyme
1 tsp. salt
½ tsp. fresh ground black pepper
1 tbsp. butter
8 egg yolks, slightly beaten
2 cups cooked chopped or creamed spinach*
3 tbsp. olive oil

Serves 4
Preparation time: 20 min. (not including preparation of spinach),
Cooking time: 45 min.

❑ Place slices of veal on a work surface. Sprinkle with thyme, salt, and pepper.
❑ In a large skillet, heat butter over medium heat until melted. Add egg yolks and tilt skillet to spread egg around. Cook just until egg begins to solidify into omelet, about 1 min. Remove from heat and let cool.
❑ Preheat oven to 350°.
❑ Cut omelet into 4 pieces. Place one piece on each slice of veal. Spread a thin layer of creamed spinach on top of egg.
❑ Roll each slice of veal around the spinach and egg. Fasten rolls with thread or a few toothpicks. Baste with oil.
❑ Place rolls in a well greased oven dish. Roast uncovered about 45 min., basting occasionally with oil.

Slice each roll, and serve with a selection of potatoes and vegetables.
* Buy frozen or canned creamed spinach, or prepare as follows:

1 lb. spinach
1 tsp. salt
½ tsp. pepper
1 tbsp. butter
2 tsp. flour
¾ cup milk or light cream

❑ Discard wilted spinach leaves. Wash spinach quickly in warm water (not hot), then several times in cold water. Place in saucepan. Do not add water. Cover tightly and steam over low heat for about 10 min. and drain.
❑ Finely chop spinach and sprinkle with salt and pepper.

❑ In a skillet, heat butter, stir in flour, and cook over medium-low heat, stirring until smooth. Add spinach and simmer over low heat about 5 min. Add milk and cook 3 min., stirring constantly.

This is a specialty of Chef Cheorghe Cătană at the Orizont Hotel in Predeal (see p. 117, STUFFED SMOKED SALMON)

ROMANIAN VEGETABLE CASSEROLES
Ghiveci

These very popular dishes in Romania are both nutritious and delicious. They are reminiscent of the well-known French Provençal vegetable casserole ratatouille. In the ghiveci, however, many more vegetables go into the casserole. Also, whereas for the ratatouille various vegetables are braised separately, for the ghiveci, all the vegetables steam together so that their different flavors and aromas blend.

Other Balkan countries claim this dish as their own. In Bulgaria it is called Gjuvec, in Serbia, Djuvec. However, the ghiveci appears to originate in Turkey, where it is called Güveç, a word which means both "a dish of vegetables baked together with meat or poultry," and "an earthenware pot" in which this dish is prepared.

In Romania, ghiveci is usually made with either fish, beef, or a combination of beef and pork. It is also popular as a vegetable casserole without meat, particularly during Lent.

VEGETABLE CASSEROLE WITH MEAT

Ghiveci cu Carne

6 tbsp. cooking oil
1 lb. beef shoulder, cut in 1 in. cubes
1 lb. pork shoulder, cut in 1 in. cubes
2 large onions, chopped
2 tbsp. salt
2 tsp. fresh ground black pepper
1 tsp. hot Hungarian paprika
2 garlic cloves, crushed
¼ lb. carrots, peeled and sliced
½ lb. green peppers, cored and sliced julienne style
¼ lb. white cabbage, cut into small pieces
¼ lb. fresh green beans, ends cut and cut into small pieces
1½ lbs. potatoes, peeled and diced
¼ lb. okra, ends cut and blanched about 2 min.
¾ lb. zucchini, sliced
2 small eggplants trimmmed, blanched about 3 min., squeezed,
    and sliced unpeeled
¼ lb. green peas, canned or frozen
½ lb. cauliflower, cut in small florets
4 tomatoes, peeled, cut in half, and seeded[*]
2 tsp. fresh parsley, chopped

Serves 6

Preparation Time: 20 min[**], Cooking Time: 3 hours

❑ Heat skillet over medium-high heat. Brown meat with the onion, stirring
and turning from time to time for about 10 min., until onion turns a nice
golden yellow.

❑ Lower heat to low, add 2 tsps. salt, 1 tsp. pepper, ½ tsp. hot paprika, and
garlic. Mix, cover, and simmer for 60 min. While the meat is simmering,
prepare the vegetables, except the tomatoes, and mix them in a large bowl.

❑ Preheat oven to 350°F.

❑ Butter a 4-5 qt. earthenware or Pyrex casserole. Pour half of the mixed

---

* You can substitute canned peeled, stewed, tomatoes

** In addition to the 20 min. preparation time, the vegetables can be prepared for
cooking while the meat and onion are browning. This will take almost 60 min.

vegetables into casserole. Sprinkle with salt, pepper, and hot paprika. Pour 2 tbsps. oil over vegetables. Then layer meat and onions over the vegetables with half of the meat sauce over it.

❑ Pour the rest of the mixed vegetables over the meat. Sprinkle the rest of the salt, pepper, and hot paprika over them. Then cover with tomatoes, and add the rest of the oil. Sprinkle with parsley.

❑ Cover casserole tightly, and cook in oven for 1½ hours, shaking casserole from time to time to ensure that there is some liquid at the bottom to prevent vegetables from burning. Don't stir contents as the vegetables and potatoes will break up.

❑ Remove lid, and cook another 30 min.

Serve hot in the casserole.

The vegetables used in this recipe are traditional for a Romanian ghiveci. However, others, such as corn, broccoli, turnips, parsnips, and mushrooms can be added.

CIULAMA

Ciulama are Romanian meat dishes prepared and served with a roux sauce called ciulama in Romanian. The roux is made from butter and flour, and is usually deglazed with milk, meat stock, or a combination of the two. The meat is usually boiled with soup vegetables.

A ciulama can be prepared with veal, lamb, chicken, or turkey, as well as veal kidney. On the next page you will find the recipe for a Veal Ciulama. For lamb, use cuts from the neck or shoulder, and add some basil. Don't add mushrooms to the roux. For the lamb kidney ciulama, cut kidney in 3-4 pieces lengthwise. When cooked and tender, slice thinly.

You will find a recipe for Chicken Ciulama on p. 204. Use the same recipe using turkey.

VEAL CIULAMA

Ciulama de Viţel

1¼ lbs. veal*, cubed
2 tsp. salt
1 bay leaf
1 carrot, peeled and sliced
1 onion, peeled and sliced
1 turnip, peeled and sliced
1 parsnip, peeled and sliced
1 parsley root, peeled and sliced
½ lb. mushrooms, sliced
1 tbsp. butter
1 garlic clove, crushed
¾ cup milk, hot
¾ cup veal stock, hot, strained
4 tbsp. butter
4 tbsp. all purpose flour
½ tsp. crushed red hot pepper
salt and pepper to taste
1 tsp. sweet paprika

Serves 4
Preparation time: 30 min., Cooking time: 1 Hr. 30 min.

❑ Put meat in a large kettle. Add enough cold water to cover meat well. Add salt. Heat over high heat until water starts to boil.
❑ When meat starts to boil, lower temperature to medium-low, and skim well, 2-3 times. Then add bay leaf and vegetables. Simmer, partially covered, until meat is tender, about 1¼ hour.
❑ While veal is cooking, prepare mushrooms. In a skillet, sauté in 1 tbsp. butter over medium-high heat with garlic, about 8-10 min.
❑ In a small bowl, mix the hot milk with the hot, strained veal stock.
❑ When veal is almost ready to serve, prepare a ciulama roux as follows:
❑ In a heavy saucepan or skillet, heat the rest of the butter over medium heat. When butter is melted, blend in flour, stirring continually for about 2-3 minutes, or until roux is a buttery yellow color.

---

* The best cut of veal for this dish is the meat around the marrow bone of the leg, the Osso Buco cut. Otherwise, use cuts from the neck or shoulder.

❑ Remove from heat and let stand about 1 minute, or until roux stops bubbling.

❑ Return roux to heat over medium-low heat. Add milk/stock liquid little by little, stirring continually to avoid lumps. Continue until roux becomes the consistency of creamy sour cream. Add salt, pepper to taste, hot pepper, and mushrooms.

❑ Strain stock, remove vegetables, place meat on a serving dish, and spoon ciulama over it. Sprinkle with paprika.

Serve with warm mămăligă and carrots or salad.

ROMANIAN RAGOUT

Tocană

Romanian tocană recipes are so varied that it is difficult to define a specific method of preparation, except that every recipe I have researched includes lots of onion. Traditional tocană, as prepared by shepherds, was braised in its own juice, but other recipes add water or soup stock, which results in a moister meat; some cover the meat with water or stock, as in a stew. Other variants use wine, most use soured cream, and paprika is used extensively in Transylvania.

RAGOUT OF VEAL

Tocană de Vițel

1 garlic clove, peeled
2 tbsp. butter
2 onions, chopped
1½ lbs. veal shoulder, cut into pieces about 1½ x 1½ x ½ in.
2 tsp. salt
2 tsp. fresh ground black pepper
1 bay leaf
5 tbsp. sour cream
1 tbsp. flour
1 cup beef stock
1 tsp. crushed hot red pepper

Serves 4
Preparation time: 15 min., Cooking time: 60 min.

❑ Rub the bottom of a large skillet with the garlic clove.
❑ Heat butter in the skillet over medium heat. Add onion and garlic, and sauté until light brown, about 10 min.
❑ Add meat, salt, pepper, and bay leaf. Stir once and cover tightly. Cook about 5 min.
❑ In a small bowl, stir flour in 4 tbsps. sour cream, and mix well.
❑ Add sour cream mixture to the meat, and cook another 5 min. while stirring.
❑ Lower heat to low, add beef stock, stir well, and simmer for about 45 min., or until meat is tender.
❑ About 10 min. before meat is ready to serve, add another tbsp. of sour cream and the hot pepper. Stir well.

March 25
Just great!!!

RAGOUT OF VEAL WITH MUSHROOMS

Tocană de Viţel cu Ciuperci

1 garlic clove, peeled
5 tbsp. butter   *½ x ½ x ½*
1½ lbs. veal shoulder, cut into pieces about 1½ x 1½ x ½ in.
2½ cups mushrooms*, sliced *— Shitaake*
1 onion, chopped   *vegeta*
2 tsp. salt *—*
2 tsp. fresh ground black pepper
¾ cup beef stock
4 tbsp. sour cream
1 tbsp. flour
1 tsp. crushed hot red pepper
½ cup dry white wine
1 tsp. sweet paprika
1 tbsp. fresh fennel, chopped *had none*
1 tbsp. fresh parsley, chopped *(dry just as good.)*

Serves 4
Preparation time: 20 min., Cooking time: 1 H 10 min.

❑ Rub the bottom of a large skillet with the garlic clove.
❑ Heat 3 tbsps. butter in the skillet over medium-high heat. Add meat and sear, about 2 min. on each side. Add mushrooms, and cook another 5 min., while stirring.
❑ Remove meat and set aside. Lower heat to medium. Add 2 tbsps. more butter and onions. Crush the rest of the garlic clove and add to onions. Continue to cook 5 min. Add meat and cook another 10 min. while stirring.
❑ Add salt and pepper. Stir well. Add beef stock. Cover, reduce heat to medium low, and simmer for 25 min. Remove cover. Continue to simmer.
❑ In a small bowl, stir flour in sour cream and mix well, add sour cream mixture to the meat, increase heat to medium, and cook another 10 min. while stirring.
❑ Lower heat to low, add beef stock, stir well, and simmer for about 45 min., or until meat is tender. *4-5-!!*
❑ About 10 min. before meat is ready to serve, add another tbsp. of sour cream and the hot pepper. Stir well.
❑ Add wine, paprika, fennel, and parsley. Stir well, and serve.

---

* If available, use Crimini, Shitaake, Oyster, or a combination of these mushrooms.

RAGOUT OF LAMB WITH MUSHROOMS

Tocană de Miel cu Ciuperci

2 tbsp. butter
1 tbsp. olive oil
1½ lbs. lamb cut from leg into small stewing size cubes
½ lbs. onion, chopped
2 garlic cloves, peeled and sliced
3 cups mushrooms*, sliced
1 tbsp. salt
2 tsp. fresh ground black pepper
½ cup beef stock
3 tbsp. sour cream
1 tbsp. flour
1 tbsp. fresh parsley, chopper
1 tbsp. fresh dill, chopped

Serves 4
Preparation time: 30 min., Cooking time: 50 min.

❑ Heat butter and oil in a skillet over medium-high heat. Add meat and sear on all sides, about 4 min. Remove meat and keep warm.

❑ In the same skillet, add onion, garlic, and mushrooms. Sauté over medium-high heat until onion turns a golden yellow, about 8-10 min.

❑ Add salt, and pepper, and stir well. Then add the meat and beef stock. Stir well, lower heat to medium-low, cover and simmer for 25 min. Remove lid, stir, and continue to simmer.

❑ In a small bowl, stir flour in sour cream and mix well. Add about 1 tbsp. of the sauce from the meat to the sour cream mixture and mix well. Then add mixture to the meat ragout, stir, increase heat to medium, sprinkle with parsley and dill, and cook another 10 min.

---

* If available, use Crimini, Shitaake, Oyster, or a combination of these mushrooms.

BRAISED LAMB

Stufat de Miel

A very tasty Romanian dish, often served as part of the traditional Easter dinner.

20 scallions
8 shallots
2 tbsp. olive oil
1½ lb. boneless lamb for braising (from shoulder or neck), cut
    into small pieces
1 tbsp. flour
½ cup tomato sauce
5 tbsp. sauerkraut juice*
2 tsp. salt
1 tsp. fresh ground black pepper
1 tbsp. fresh parsley, chopped
1 tbsp. fresh dill sprigs, chopped
fresh mint leaves

Serves 4
Preparation time: 20 min., Cooking time: 1 hour 10 min.

❑ Cut roots off scallions, trim greens. Wash. Peel shallots and leave whole. Blanch onions and shallots about 3 min.

❑ In a skillet, heat 1 tablespoon olive oil over medium-high heat. Sauté onions and shallots until they turn a nice yellow gold, about 5 min. Remove and put in a casserole.

❑ Preheat oven to 350°F.

❑ In the same skillet, add 2 more tbsps. olive oil. Sauté meat pieces until nicely browned all around, turning them often with wooden spoons, about 5-6 min. Transfer meat and any meat sauce from the skillet into casserole with the vegetables.

❑ In a small bowl, mix flour, tomato sauce, sauerkraut juice, salt, pepper, parsley, and dill. Mix well, and pour over meat and vegetables. Place mint

---

* The best source for sauerkraut juice is fresh sauerkraut found in supermarkets in clear plastic bags. If not available, use canned sauerkraut, preferably imported from Germany or Poland. Squeeze out the juice through a sieve. Alternately, use the juice of a half lemon.

leaves on top. Cover, and braise in the oven for about 50-60 min., or until meat is tender.

Serve with hot mămăligă or boiled, parsleyed potatoes.

RAGOUT OF PORK WITH SAUERKRAUT

Tocană de Porc cu Varză Acră

½ lb. sauerkraut
4 strips smoked bacon, cut into small pieces
1½ lbs. onions, chopped
5 tbsp. cooking oil
1½ lbs. boneless pork for braising(from the loin), cubed
3 garlic cloves, peeled and sliced
2 tbsp. fresh parsley, chopped
1 tbsp. fresh dill sprigs, chopped
1 tsp. caraway seeds
½ tsp. thyme
2 tsp. salt
2 tsp. fresh ground black pepper
1 tsp. sweet paprika
1 cup beef stock
4 tbsp. sour cream
1 tbsp. flour

Serves 4
Preparation time: 25 min., Cooking time: 1 hour 20 min.

❑ Wash sauerkraut, and drain through a sieve, squeezing all juice and water out. Set aside.

❑ In a large heavy skillet or casserole, fry bacon in its own fat over medium-high heat. Add onion and 2 tbsps. cooking oil, and sauté until it softens and turns golden yellow, about 8 min.

❑ In a separate skillet, heat 2 tbsps. cooking oil over high heat. Sear meat, turning pieces constantly with wooden spoons, until browned on all sides, about 5-6 min. After the first 2 min., add garlic.

❑ Add the meat to onion. Add sauerkraut, mix well, and cook another 5 min. over medium-high heat.

❑ Add parsley, dill, caraway seeds, thyme, salt and pepper, and paprika. Mix well. Add enough beef stock until it just covers the meat. Cover tightly, and cook over low heat about 45 min.

❑ Ladle 3-4 tbsps. of sauce from the ragout, and mix in a small bowl with sour cream and flour. Pour back over meat, mix well, cover, and cook another 15 min., or until meat is tender.

Serve meat in its sauce, with hot mămăligă, and spoon sour cream over it.

PAN-FRIED PORK WITH POLENTA
Tochitură Moldovenească

In the center of Iaşi, a beautiful city and the cultural center of the Province of Moldavia, stands the Moldova Hotel. A modern, high-rise, luxury hotel, it is a striking contrast to the wealth of priceless old buildings, villas, and churches which surround it and still dominate Iaşi. The hotel has a very nice restaurant, and this delicious Moldavian specialty was contributed by its chef, Dumitru Moisă.

¾ lb. center-cut pork loin, cut into stew-size pieces
3 tbsp. cooking oil
¾ lbs. pork liver, cut into stew-size pieces
2 garlic cloves, sliced
2 tsp. salt
1 tsp. pepper
1 tsp. Hungarian hot paprika
1 recipe fluffy polenta[*]
1 tbsp. butter
4 eggs
6 oz. telemea cheese[**], grated

Serves 4
Preparation time: 15 min., Cooking time: 45 min.

❏ In a skillet, heat oil over medium-high heat. Add pork, sauté meat, turning with spatula or wooden spoons, about 5-6 min.
❏ Add liver, garlic, salt, pepper, and paprika. Sauté another 5-6 min.
❏ Add water, stir, lower heat to medium, and continue to cook another 15 min.
❏ While meat is cooking, prepare polenta.
❏ In a skillet, heat butter over medium-high heat. Fry eggs.

Arrange plates as follows: Place large scoop of polenta on upper half of plate. Put mixed pork and liver on lower half. Place a scoop of grated cheese on right and left of polenta, and one fried egg on top of polenta. Serve hot.

---

[*] see FLUFFY POLENTA, p. 106.
[**] You can use a good quality imported Feta cheese.

BRAISED PORK WITH SAUERKRAUT

Stufat de Porc cu Varză Acră

½ lb. sauerkraut
½ cup water
4 tbsp. rice
2 tbsp. cooking oil
1 tsp. black peppercorns, slightly crushed
1 cup beef stock
2 tsp. salt
1 tsp. sweet paprika
2 tsp. caraway seeds
½ cup dry white wine
1½ lbs. boneless pork for braising (from shoulder or neck),
  cubed
½ lbs. onions, coarsely chopped
½ tsp. crushed hot red pepper
2 garlic cloves, peeled and sliced
1 cup sour cream

Serves 4
Preparation time: 20 min., Cooking time: 1 hour 20 min.

❑ Rinse sauerkraut and let sit in cold water for 30 min. Drain through a sieve, squeezing all juice and water out.

❑ In a small kettle, bring ½ cup water to boil. Add rice, lower heat to low, cover, and steam for about 20 min. Remove from heat and let stand until all water is absorbed.

❑ In a saucepan, heat 1 tbsp. cooking oil over medium high heat. Add sauerkraut, peppercorns, and ¼ cup beef stock. Stir, lower heat to low, and cover. Simmer for about 50 min., stirring occasionally; add beef stock if needed to keep sauerkraut moist. Add rice, salt, paprika, and caraway seeds. Stir well. Add wine, cover, and continue to simmer another 10 min.

❑ Preheat oven to 350°F.

❑ While sauerkraut is cooking, heat 1 tbsp. cooking oil in another large saucepan over medium-high heat. Add meat, onions, red pepper, and garlic. Brown, turning often with wooden spatula or spoon, until meat is browned and onion softened, about 5-6 min.; add rest of the beef stock, little by little, and stir occasionally.

❏ Cover the bottom of an oven dish with cooked sauerkraut, add meat mixture, cover well, and cook in oven for 20 min.

Serve hot with hot mămăligă or boiled, parsleyed potatoes. Spoon some sour cream over the meat and mămăligă.

STUFFED EGGPLANT

Vinete Umplute

4 small round eggplants
2 tbsp. cooking oil
1 lb. medium-lean beef, ground
1 large onion, chopped
4 tsp. mixed herbs (basil, chervil, parsley)
1 tbsp. salt
2 tsp. fresh ground black pepper
2 cups beef stock
2 tsp. flour
4 tbsp. sour cream (optional)

Serves 4
Preparation time: 20 min., Cooking time: 40 min.

❑ Trim eggplants.
❑ Bring large pot of water to boiling. Boil eggplants for about 5-6 minutes. Remove from boiling water and let stand in cold water to cool.
❑ In a skillet, heat oil over medium heat. Sauté ground beef, half the quantity of onion, and 2 tsps. mixed herbs (basil, chervil, parsley), salt and pepper, about 15 min., breaking up the meat and stirring with wooden spoon occasionally.
❑ Remove eggplants from cold water and press excess water out gently, being careful not to split skins. Cut in half either lengthwise or crosswise, and gently scoop out center of each half. Chop leftover eggplant and put aside.
❑ Stuff eggplant halves with the cooked ground beef.
❑ Prepare a sauce as follows:
❑ Heat beef stock gently in a medium size kettle, add the rest of the onion, another 2 tsps. of mixed herbs, and blend in 2 tsps. flour. Add the chopped eggplant and stir well.
❑ Set the stuffed eggplant in the sauce. Cover, and simmer for about 20 min.

Serve with sour cream. Accompany with a small mixed salad.

STUFFED ZUCCHINI

Dovlecei Umpluţi

4 zucchini, about 8 in. long
1 lb. medium-lean beef, ground
4 tbsp. onion, chopped
2 eggs, slightly beaten
1 tbsp. fresh parsley, chopped
1 tbsp. bread crumbs
¼ lb. Swiss gruyère cheese, grated
2 tsp. salt
1 tsp. black pepper
2 tbsp. olive oil
2 tbsp. butter
2 cloves garlic, crushed
1 tbsp. flour
2 cups tomato sauce
1 tbsp. fresh basil, chopped
1 tsp. salt
1 tsp. black pepper
3 tbsp. sour cream

Serves 4
Preparation time: 45 min., Cooking time: 35 min.

❑ Trim zucchini.
❑ Bring large kettle of water with 1 tsp. salt to boiling point. Boil zucchini for about 6-7 minutes. Remove from water and drain. Cut in half lengthwise, and scrape the seeds out with a spoon.
❑ Put the ground beef in a large bowl. Add 2 tbsps. chopped onions, eggs, parsley, bread crumbs, cheese, salt and pepper. Mix all ingredients. Fill zucchini with the beef mixture.
❑ In large skillet heat olive oil and butter. Sauté stuffed zucchini, the rest of the onion, and the garlic for about 10 min.
❑ Place zucchini in a lightly buttered oven dish. Preheat oven to 350°F. Cook uncovered for 35 min.
❑ Stir flour in the tomato sauce. Add basil, salt and pepper, and simmer.

When zucchini are tender, add sour cream to tomato sauce, stir, and spoon over each zucchini. Serve with french fries and a salad.

LITTLE GRILLED SAUSAGES

Mititei (The Wee Ones)

Mititei have been associated with Romanian cuisine since 1865-1866. In Bucharest on Covaci street, a popular inn named La Iordachi (At Iordachi's) was well known for its delicious sausages. One night, so the story goes, the kitchen ran out of one kind of beef sausage, so they mixed the ingredients left over, rolled them into small sausage-shaped patties, and grilled them on charcoal without the usual casing. Regular customers loved them so much that they asked for more of "the wee ones without skin," and with time they became known as mititei, or "the wee ones."

2 lbs. medium-lean ground beef*
2 tbsp. olive oil
2 tbsp. water
3 garlic cloves, crushed
2 tsp. bicarbonate of soda
½ tsp. dried thyme
½ tsp. crushed hot red pepper
½ tsp. hot Hungarian paprika
1 tsp. caraway seeds
2 tsp. salt
1 tsp. fresh ground black pepper

Serves 4
Preparation time: 45 min., Cooking time: 15 min.

❏ Place ground beef in a bowl, and add all the ingredients in the order listed. Mix well and then knead mixture with your hands for not less than 5 minutes, wetting your hands frequently. This is important because the water from your wet hands mixes with the meat and helps keep the mititei moist. Place mixture in a bowl, cover with a plate or foil, and refrigerate at least 5 hours or overnight.

❏ By tablespoonfuls, with damp hands, make small meatballs. Then roll between your hands into sausages about 3" long and 1" thick.

❏ Grill or barbecue, turning mititei frequently to cook evenly**.

---

* Mititei can also be made from ground lamb, mutton, pork, or a combination of meats.

** Use tongs, not a fork, to turn the mititei, so as not to pierce them. This will keep the juices in the meat.

Serve with baked potatoes or french fries and salad as a main course, or serve them as part of a Romanian appetizer table (see ROMANIAN COLD AND HOT APPETIZER TABLE, p. 32). They are also very good with French mustard.

MOLDAVIAN BREADED MEAT PATTIES
Pârjoale Moldoveneşti

Ground meat patties, meatballs, meat croquettes, or hamburgers, are a favorite worldwide in ethnic cuisines. These days, the American hamburger is eaten in almost every country in the world, courtesy McDonalds, Burger King, Burger Haven, and the like. However, the Middle East has its kefta, kufta, and kefteda, and most European countries, from Finland to Italy to Poland, have their own favorites. In Romania, it is the pârjoale and chiftele.

Pârjoale can be made from beef, pork, lamb, or from a mixture of meats; many regional variations are found in Romania. This recipe is from the Moldavian province, and uses all beef.

Romanians often prepare extra patties, and eat them cold the next day or for picnics. Many think the pârjoale taste even better cold, with mustard and bread.

1 tsp. olive oil
1 onion, finely chopped
2 garlic cloves, crushed
½ raw potato, peeled and grated
1½ lbs. medium-lean beef, cubed
1 tbsp. salt
1 tbsp. fresh ground black pepper
½ tsp. crushed hot red pepper
2 slices multi-grain bread, without crust
2 tbsp. fresh parsley, chopped
2 tbsp. fresh dill, chopped
1 egg, slightly beaten
1½ cups bread crumbs
2 tbsp. olive oil
4 tbsp. water

Serves 4
Preparation time: 45 min., Cooking time: 45 min.

❑ Heat 1 tbsp. olive oil in a large skillet over medium heat. Add onion, garlic, and potato. Sauté lightly—about 5 min. Let cool in skillet.

❑ Place the meat in a bowl. Add salt, pepper, and hot pepper. Add cooled onion, garlic, and potato mixture, including any oil from the skillet, and set skillet aside. Mix ingredients well with a wooden spoon.

❑ Wet bread with warm water, then squeeze out excess. Add bread to the meat mixture. Stir well.

173

❏ Pass meat mixture through a meat grinder*

❏ Shape meat with moist hands into 2-inch balls, about 9 or 10.

❏ Place each ball in bread crumbs, flatten with your palm, and shape into an oval patty. Turn twice to cover well with crumbs.

❏ In the skillet used to sauté onion, garlic and potato, add 2 tbsps. olive oil and cook over medium heat. When hot, add meat patties. Then add about 2 tbsps. water. Cover and cook for 1-2 min. Turn patties, add a little more water, cover, and cook another 1-2 min.

❏ Remove cover. When water has evaporated, brown patties well, about 6-7 min. on each side, while you savor the delicious aroma. Serve hot.

---

* If a meat grinder is not available, choose a nice cut of medium-lean beef and ask the butcher to grind it fine for you. Chop ingredients as fine as possible, and mix well.

MEATBALLS WITH TOMATO SAUCE

Chifteluţe de Carne cu Sos de Roşii

2 tbsp. cooking oil
1 small onion, chopped
2 garlic cloves, crushed
1 lb. medium-lean beef[*]
2 slices bread, crusts removed
1 large potato, peeled and grated
1 egg, slightly beaten
1 tbsp. fresh parsley, chopped
1 tbsp. fresh dill, chopped
½ tsp. crushed hot red pepper
2 tsp. salt
1 tsp. fresh ground black pepper
1 cup all purpose flour
1 tbsp. cooking oil
2 cups tomato sauce

Serves 4
Preparation time: 30 min., Cooking time: 25 min.

❑ In a skillet, heat 2 tbsps. oil over medium-high heat. Sauté onion and garlic until they turn a nice golden color, about 3-4 min. Remove from heat and let cool in skillet.

❑ Cut meat into small cubes. Place in a bowl.

❑ Soak bread in warm water, then squeeze out excess water. Add bread to meat. Add potatoes and onions. Mix well and then pass through fine or medium meat grinder.

❑ Return ground meat to bowl. Add egg, parsley, dill, red pepper, salt, and pepper. Mix well, first with a wooden spoon, then with your hands.

❑ Roll small portions of meat between your palms to form 1 inch balls, about 24 balls. Roll each ball in flour.

❑ In skillet in which you browned the onion, add 1 tbsp. oil and cook the meatballs over medium-high heat, turning often to cook evenly, about 8-10 min., or until they are browned well on all sides.

❑ Add tomato sauce, lower heat to medium-low, and simmer for another 10 min.

---

* If a meat grinder is not available, buy ground meat, chop ingredients as fine as possible, and mix well.

Serve with warm mămăligă, potatoes, or pasta, and salad. These meatballs will taste even better re-heated next day.

EGGPLANT MOUSSAKA

Musaca (pronounced Musacá) de Vinete

2 large eggplants, about 1½ lbs.
2 tsp. salt
1½ lbs. medium-lean beef, cubed[*]
2 onions, peeled and chopped
1 tbsp. butter
2 tsp. olive oil
1 cup all purpose flour
2 garlic cloves, crushed
1 egg, slightly beaten
2 tbsp. sour cream
2 tbsp. fresh parsley, chopped
1 tsp. fresh ground black pepper
1 tbsp. butter
¼ cup bread crumbs
1 green pepper, washed, cored, and chopped
2 tomatoes, sliced
2 cups tomato sauce (or canned peeled crushed tomatoes)
salt and pepper to taste

Serves 6
Preparation time: 60 min., Cooking time: 50 min.

❏ Trim eggplants and peel alternate strips lengthwise to create stripes. Slice into medium thick slices. Sprinkle with salt. Stack slices and cover with a weighted plate to drain off bitter juice, about 30 min.

❏ Meanwhile, place meat in a bowl. Add onion, and mix well. Pass mixture through fine meat grinder.

❏ In a skillet, heat butter and olive oil over medium-high heat. Cook ground meat until it begins to brown, stirring well, about 5 min. Remove from heat and let cool.

❏ While meat is cooling, rinse eggplant slices in warm water, dry on kitchen towels, then dip in flour to coat both sides.

❏ Either pan-fry or deep-fry eggplant slices over medium-high heat, about 3-4 min. on each side.

---

[*] If a meat grinder is not available, buy a good quality ground beef, chop ingredients as fine as possible, and mix well.

❑ Preheat oven to 400°F.

❑ When meat has cooled off, place in a bowl. Add garlic, egg, sour cream, salt, pepper, and parsley. Mix well.

❑ Butter the bottom and sides of a deep oven dish. Sprinkle with bread crumbs.

❑ Place a layer of eggplant slices on the bottom of the dish as well as against the sides. Next, spread a layer of half the meat mixture. Cover meat with half of the green peppers, and then half the tomato sauce. Repeat with eggplant, meat and peppers, then add half of the tomato slices, another layer of eggplant slices, then another layer of tomato slices, and finally the rest of the tomato sauce. Sprinkle with salt and pepper, and bake for about 45 min.

❑ When moussaka is done, take out of the oven, let stand about 5 min., then turn it over onto a serving dish.

Serve with a refreshing salad.

CABBAGE MOUSSAKA

Musaca (pronounced musacá) de Varză

1 cabbage, about 2 lbs.
2 tsp. salt
2 tbsp. olive oil
1 tbsp. butter
1 onion, peeled and chopped
2 garlic cloves, peeled and chopped
1½ lbs. lean ground beef
1 tbsp. salt
2 tsp. fresh ground black pepper
2 tsp. crushed hot red pepper
½ cup sour cream
1 tbsp. flour
2 tbsp. tomato paste
1 cup beef stock

Serves 4-6
Preparation time: 25 min., Cooking time: 50 min.

❑ Wash cabbage, cut off loose green leaves. Save 3-4 nice big leaves. Shred the rest of the cabbage. Blanch leaves and shredded cabbage in boiling water about 5 min. Drain, place in a bowl, sprinkle salt on top, and let cool.

❑ Preheat oven to 350°F.

❑ In a skillet, heat oil and butter over medium heat. Add onion, garlic, and meat. Mix and sauté until meat is brown all around, about 10 min.

❑ In a bowl, mix sour cream, flour, tomato paste, and beef stock together into a sauce.

❑ Grease an oven dish. Cover the bottom and sides with cabbage leaves. Add a layer of shredded cabbage, then a layer of meat. Season with salt, pepper, and hot pepper, and pour ½ cup of sour cream sauce over it. Repeat the layering process beginning with shredded cabbage and ending with the sour cream sauce until all ingredients have been used up.

❑ Cook in oven, uncovered, 40 min. Baste the moussaka with its own juices from time to time while cooking.

Serve with mashed potatoes or mămăligă.

STUFFED GRAPE LEAVES

Sarmale în Foi de Viţă

5 oz. grape leaves[*]
4 tbsp. olive oil
¼ lbs. onion, chopped
2 tbsp. rice
½ cup hot water
1 lb. boneless lamb meat[**]
1 slice bread, without crust
½ tbsp. fresh parsley, chopped
1 tbsp. fresh coriander, chopped
1 tbsp. fresh dill, chopped
1 tbsp. salt
2 tsp. fresh ground black pepper
1 lb. tomatoes, sliced
1 tbsp. rosemary
¾ lbs. tomato sauce
3 tbsp. sour cream
1 tbsp. all purpose flour
½ lemon, juice

The size of the sarmale is a matter of choice, and also depends on the size of the grape leaves. In general, natives of Transylvania make them big; in the Walachian region, somewhat smaller; and in Moldavia where they usually make them minuscule, they refer to them as sărmăluţe, which is a diminutive of sarmale. In Moldavia, which has a reputation for providing the best and most authentic Romanian food, natives insist that their way is the tastiest because the flavor of the sauce gets into the meat mixture.

Serves 4
Preparation time: 1 hour 30 min., Cooking time: 1 hour 15 min.

❏ Rinse grape leaves individually, and cut off stems. To make about 24 stuffed leaves, you will also need an additional 6-8 leaves, or a total of 32.

---

[*] You can usually find grape leaves in jars, imported from Greece, in better supermarkets. If not, you will find them in Greek or Middle Eastern ethnic groceries. Be sure they have been refrigerated, and check the freshness date.

[**] Buy boneless meat from the leg or shoulder. If a meat grinder is not available, buy ground meat, chop ingredients as fine as possible, and mix well.

❏ Blanch leaves in boiling water for about 2 min. Then lay them flat on a work surface.

❏ In a skillet, heat 1 tbsp. olive oil over medium-high heat. Sauté onion and raw rice, stirring with a wooden spoon, until onion and rice turn a nice golden color, about 5-6 min.

❏ Add hot water. Lower heat to medium-low, stir, and continue to simmer for about 10 min. Remove from heat, cover, and let stand for about 5 min. or until rice has absorbed all water. Let stand to cool.

❏ Cut meat into small pieces. Place in a bowl. Dip bread in water, and then squeeze out excess. Add bread, onion, and rice to meat. Stir well. Pass twice through a fine or medium meat grinder. Return mixture to bowl. Add parsley, dill, coriander, salt, and pepper. Mix well with your hands or a wooden spoon.

❏ Take one leaf at a time in the palm of your hand. Center a small amount of meat (walnut-size chunk) near base. Roll leaf around meat, folding in sides of the leaf, then roll to seal sides well. Form into small sausages, about 3½ in. long. Continue until all meat is used up.

❏ Oil a large saucepan with 2 tbsps of olive oil. Cover the bottom with a layer of tomato slices, then a layer of flat grape leaves, and another layer of tomato slices. Sprinkle with rosemary. Place stuffed grape leaves on top of tomato slices, making sure that you place them with the open end down.

❏ Pour tomato sauce over the stuffed grape leaves. Sprinkle another tbsp. of olive oil on top. Cover, and simmer over low heat about 45 min.

❏ In a small bowl, mix sour cream with flour. When the stuffed leaves are cooked, ladle up about ½ cup of sauce, let cool, and then mix with the sour cream and flour. Stir well. Heat mixture in a small saucepan over low heat, about 5 min. Add lemon juice, and then slowly pour mixture over stuffed grape leaves. Simmer, uncovered, another 10-15 min.

Serve hot, alone or with warm mămăligă, potatoes, or pasta, and salad. These sarmale will taste even better next day, hot or cold. Serve with sour cream.

STUFFED PEPPERS

Ardei Umpluţi

1½ cups water
½ cup rice
4 big green peppers
5 tbsp. olive oil
1 onion, chopped
2 garlic cloves, chopped
2 lbs. tomatoes, peeled*
1 lb. medium-lean beef, finely ground
4 tbsp. fresh parsley, chopped
2 tbsp. fresh dill sprigs, chopped
2 tsp. salt
1 tsp. fresh ground black pepper
4 large tomato slices
4 tbsp. sour cream

Serves 4
Preparation time: 30 min., Cooking time: 1 hour 45 min.

❑ Heat water, add salt, and bring to boil. Add rice, lower heat to medium-low, cover, and parboil rice about 5 min. Remove from heat and leave covered.

❑ Wash peppers. With a sharp knife, remove top, stem, and core with seeds, keeping peppers whole. Rinse and drain.

❑ In a skillet, heat 3 tbsps. olive oil over medium-high heat. Place peppers on their sides, sauté, and turn gently with two forks so that they brown slightly all over. It's a tricky operation, as peppers tend to move around as the skin breaks and sizzles, but it should only take 5 min. Remove peppers, and place right side up on a working surface.

❑ In the same skillet, add another 2 tbsps. olive oil. Sauté onion and garlic over medium-high heat until onion is soft and a light yellow-gold, about 5 min. Let cool.

❑ In a covered saucepan, heat the peeled tomatoes over medium heat until juice begins to boil. Lower heat and steam another 5-10 min. Remove from heat, and leave covered.

❑ Preheat oven to 350°F.

❑ Place meat in a bowl. Add rice, onion, parsley, dill, salt, and pepper. Mix

* You can use the equivalent weight of canned peeled tomatoes.

well with wooden spoon, and then with your hands, until all ingredients are combined.

❏ Fill peppers with the meat mixture. Place a slice of tomato on top of each pepper to prevent meat from falling out during cooking. Place peppers in a casserole on their sides.

❏ Pour cooked tomatoes into skillet in which you cooked peppers and onion. Stir to crush tomatoes and mix with the remaining oil in the skillet. Pour the sauce over the peppers. Bake peppers, covered, in oven for 1 hour 15 min.

❏ Remove lid, ladle 2-3 tbsps. sauce into a small bowl. Let cool, then mix well with sour cream until smooth, then pour back into casserole.

❏ Cook another 5-10 min. uncovered.

Serve hot, or cold. Stuffed peppers taste even better reheated.

STUFFED CABBAGE

Sarmale în Foi de Varză

Stuffed cabbage is not at all difficult to prepare but it does take a lot of time. However, the time spent is well worth it. Everyone loves these sarmale. In fact, prepare them in large quantities, as they taste even better reheated the next day, and they can be frozen. In Romania, they are a special treat for Christmas dinner.

> 1 head of cabbage, 3-4 lbs.
> 6 tbsp. olive oil
> 1 onion, peeled and chopped
> 2 garlic cloves, peeled and chopped
> 2½ tbsp. rice
> ¼ cup hot water
> 1½ lbs. pork*
> 1 slice bread, without crust
> 2 tbsp. fresh dill, chopped
> 1 tsp. ground thyme
> 2 tsp. salt
> 1 tsp. fresh ground black pepper
> 1 tsp. crushed hot red pepper
> 2 tbsp. water
> 3 cups water
> 1 cup sauerkraut juice**
> 1 tbsp. Vegeta***
> 10 black peppercorns
> 4 bay leaves

---

* Buy boneless meat from the shoulder butt. If a meat grinder is not available, ask your butcher to grind a piece of pork butt, chop ingredients as fine as possible, and mix well.

** The best source for sauerkraut and sauerkraut juice is fresh sauerkraut found in supermarkets in clear plastic bags. If they are not available, buy a can of sauerkraut, preferably imported from Germany or Poland. Squeeze out the juice through a sieve. Use the quantity required in this recipe and save the rest to make a Romanian ciorbă with.

*** Vegeta is a brand of concentrated soup and stew flavor enhancer. It is imported from Croatia by Jane Foods. Several other brands are available here, in the United States, such as Aromat by Knorr.

3 cups sauerkraut
6 strips smoked bacon
6 fresh dill sprigs
2 lbs. tomatoes, sliced

Serves 4-6
Preparation time: 2 hours, Cooking time: 3 hours

❏ Place cabbage on a work surface. Remove loose outer green leaves, and save. With a sharp knife, cut out the hard core of the cabbage. Wash cabbage well. Blanch outer green leaves about 2 min., and save.

❏ Blanch cabbage in boiling water, with the hole down, for about 1 min. Remove, drain, and place on work surface with hole up. Gently, with the aid of two forks, try to peel off whole leaves, as many as will come off easily. Place leaves in a large bowl. Return cabbage to boiling water and blanch another minute or two, and repeat operation, until all leaves at least 3 x 3 in. have been removed.

❏ Chop up the remaining cabbage, and save to add to sauerkraut.

❏ Take each leaf from the bowl, and with a sharp knife, shave off some of the thick center vein so that it is the same thickness as the rest of the leaf.

❏ In a skillet, add 1 tbsp. olive oil, and heat over medium-high heat. Sauté onion, garlic, and raw rice, stirring with a wooden spoon, until onion and rice turn a nice golden color, about 5-6 min.

❏ Add hot water. Lower heat to medium-low, stir, and simmer for about 10 min. Remove from heat, cover, and let stand for about 5 min. or until rice has absorbed all water. Let stand to cool.

❏ Cut meat into small pieces. Place in a bowl. Dip bread in water, and then squeeze to remove excess. Add bread, onion, and rice to meat. Stir well. Pass twice through a fine or medium screen meat grinder. Return mixture to bowl. Add dill, thyme, salt, pepper, hot pepper, and 2 tbsps. water. Mix well with your hands or a wooden spoon.

❏ In a bowl, mix 3 cups water with sauerkraut juice, add Vegeta, peppercorns, and bay leaves.

❏ Place sauerkraut in a sieve, rinse well with cold water, strain, and press well with spoon against sieve to squeeze out excess juice and water. Add chopped cabbage.

❏ Take one cabbage leaf in the palm of your hand with the base at your wrist. With your other hand, center a small amount of meat mixture, the size of a walnut or larger, depending on the size of the leaf. Shape meat in the form of a little sausage near the base of the leaf, cover with one side of the leaf, roll leaf around meat, and end up by tucking the other side in so as to seal it. Continue until all meat is used up.

❏ Oil a large casserole with lid, using 2 tbsps of olive oil. Cover the bottom with a thin layer of sauerkraut. Place 3 strips of bacon across sauerkraut. Cover with a layer of stuffed cabbage placed side by side. Add another layer of sauerkraut, strips of bacon, and stuffed cabbage. Then add the rest of the sauerkraut. Spread the dill sprigs over the sauerkraut. Sprinkle the rest of the olive oil over the top. Then pour the water and sauerkraut juice mixture over all. Cover with the large outer leaves to keep moisture in.

❏ Preheat oven to 375°F.

❏ Place casserole over high heat, and heat until sauce begins to bubble. Lower heat to medium-low, cover, and simmer about 20 min.

❏ Cook, covered, in oven 1½ hours. Add sliced tomatoes, cover, and braise another 45 min. Remove lid and continue cooking about another 15 min. Don't worry about overcooking. Romanians say that the longer the stuffed cabbage cooks the better it tastes.

Serve hot, by itself or with warm mămăligă (polenta), potatoes, or pasta, and salad. If you like a sour taste, ladle some of the juice over the polenta as well as over the stuffed cabbage. Sarmale taste even better reheated.

Recipe makes about 20 rolls of stuffed cabbage.

MITITEI AND OTHER MEAT DISHES

STUFFED SOUR CABBAGE
Sarmale în Foi de Varză Acră

If you want to prepare stuffed cabbage the traditional Romanian way, use sour cabbage. Sour heads of cabbage are not commercially available; it takes at least 3 weeks to prepare your own. For method of preparation, see SOUR CABBAGE IN A BARREL, p. 286. Otherwise, go to STUFFED CABBAGE, p. 184, and you will achieve equally delicious sarmale.

Stuffed cabbage is not at all difficult to prepare, but it does take a lot of time. However, the time spent is well worth it. Everyone loves sarmale. Prepare them in large quantities, as they taste even better reheated, and they can be frozen. In Romania, they are a special treat for Christmas dinner.

1 head of cabbage, 3-4 lbs.
6 tbsp. olive oil
1 onion, peeled and chopped
2 garlic cloves, peeled and chopped
2½ tbsp. rice
¼ cup hot water
1½ lbs. pork [*]
1 slice bread, without crust
2 tbsp. fresh dill sprigs, chopped
1 tsp. ground thyme
2 tsp. salt
1 tsp. fresh ground black pepper
1 tsp. crushed hot red pepper
2 tbsp. water
1 qt. water
1 tbsp. Vegeta[**]
10 black peppercorns
4 bay leaves

---

* Buy boneless meat from the shoulder butt. If a meat grinder is not available, ask your butcher to grind a piece of pork butt, chop ingredients as fine as possible, and mix well.

** Vegeta is a brand of concentrated soup and stew flavor enhancer. It is imported from Croatia by Jane Foods. Several other brands are available in the United States, such as Aromat by Knorr.

3 cups sauerkraut[*]
6 strips smoked bacon
6 fresh dill sprigs
2 lbs. tomatoes, sliced

Serves 4-6

Preparation time: 1 hour, Cooking time: 3 hours

❑ Wash sour cabbage. Place on a work surface, and gently, with the aid of two forks, peel off all full leaves that are at least 3 x 3 in. in size. Reserve 3 or 4 of the very largest that may not be perfect.

❑ Chop up the rest of the cabbage, and save to add to sauerkraut.

❑ Take each leaf and with a sharp knife, shave off some of the thick center vein to make it the same thickness as the rest of the leaf.

❑ In a skillet, add 1 tbsp. olive oil, and heat over medium-high heat. Sauté onion, garlic, and raw rice, stirring with a wooden spoon, until onion and rice turn a nice golden color, about 5-6 min.

❑ Add hot water. Lower heat to medium-low, stir, and simmer for about 10 min. Remove from heat, cover, and let stand for about 5 min. or until rice has absorbed all water. Cool.

❑ Cut meat into small pieces. Place in a bowl. Dip bread in water, and then squeeze out excess. Add bread, onion, and rice to meat. Stir well. Pass twice through a fine or medium screen meat grinder. Return mixture to bowl. Add dill, thyme, salt, pepper, hot pepper, and 2 tbsps. water. Mix well with your hands or a wooden spoon.

❑ In a bowl, mix 1 qt. water with Vegeta, peppercorns, and bay leaves.

❑ Place sauerkraut in a sieve, rinse well with cold water, strain, and press with spoon to squeeze out excess juice and water. Add chopped cabbage.

❑ Take one leaf at a time in the palm of your hand with the base of the leaf at your wrist. With the other hand, center a walnut-size ball of meat mixture on the leaf. Shape meat into a little sausage, cover with one side of the leaf, roll leaf around meat, and tuck the other side in to seal it. Continue until all meat is used up.

❑ Oil a large covered casserole, using 2 tbsps. of olive oil. Cover the bottom with a thin layer of sauerkraut. Place 3 strips of bacon across sauerkraut. Cover with a layer of cabbage rolls placed side by side. Add another layer of sauerkraut, strips of bacon, and more stuffed cabbage, then the rest of the

---

[*] The best source for sauerkraut is fresh sauerkraut found in supermarkets in clear plastic bags. If they are not available, buy a can of sauerkraut, preferably imported from Germany or Poland. Squeeze out the juice through a sieve. Save the juice to make a Romanian ciorbă with.

sauerkraut. Arrange the dill sprigs over the sauerkraut. Dribble olive oil over the top, then pour the water and sauerkraut juice mixture over all. Cover the whole surface with the 3 or 4 large outer green leaves to keep more moisture in.

❑ Preheat oven to 375°F.

❑ Place casserole over high heat, until sauce begins to bubble. Lower heat to medium-low, cover, and simmer about 20 min.

❑ Cook, covered, in oven 1½ hours. Add sliced tomatoes, cover, and braise another 45 min. Remove lid and continue cooking about another 15 min. Don't worry about overcooking. Romanians say that the longer the stuffed cabbage cooks the better it tastes.

Serve hot, by itself or with warm mămăligă (polenta), potatoes, or pasta, and salad. If you like a sour taste, ladle some of the juice over the polenta as well as over the stuffed cabbage. Sarmale taste even better next day, heated up.

Recipe makes about 20 rolls of stuffed cabbage.

POEMS

Mihai Eminescu (1850-1889)

MIHAI EMINESCU (1850-1889)

Mihai Eminescu, born January 15, 1850, in Botoşani in the Province of Moldavia, is considered the national poet of Romania. He was highly intelligent, an avid reader, and had a wide range of interests. At the age of 14 he ran away with a theater company and traveled throughout Romania and Transylvania. At the age of 16 he was already interested in the Romanian language and culture, and published his first poem.

In 1859, Eminescu went to Vienna to study at the University, where he enthusiastically absorbed the works of the great philosophers. Briefly back in Romania in 1872, he published much of his literary work before he left his country again to obtain his doctorate at the University of Berlin. There he became interested in mythology, the history of religion, law and history, and even the Sanskrit language. He also translated Kant's *Critique of Pure Reason* into Romanian, but lost interest in his doctorate.

Later in Romania he held a number of positions, including editor of the newspaper *Timpul*, where he gained fame and a reputation as an insightful journalist. In the meantime he continued to write and publish poetry.

Aside from his work and poetry, Eminescu was totally indifferent to the material world, to events occurring around him, and social conventions! He was equally indifferent to wealth or lack of it, and class distinctions. His life also became somewhat unstable—he often lived only on narcotics and stimulants, excesses of tobacco and coffee. Titu Maiorescu, who had published Eminescu's first collection of poems, wrote in 1889:

not only was he indifferent to life's outward events but he was also unusually so in love affairs.... No one single woman ever managed to win and keep him completely to herself. Like Leopardi in Aspasia, the woman he loved was only an imperfect copy of an unattainable prototype. Whether the copy of the moment loved him or left him, she remained merely a copy, while he ensconced himself melancholically into a world which was closer to his own spirit, that of reflection and poetry...

At the age of 33, Eminescu's health deteriorated, and he began to suffer from periodic fits of madness. He spent the last six years of his life in and out of sanitariums, both in Romania and abroad. He died in Bucharest on 15 June 1889.

*From Selected Works of Ion Creangă and Mihai Eminescu.

DOINA

Doina, 1883

Doina, written in 1883, is one of Eminescu's most explicit nationalistic poems. In it he bemoans foreign oppression of the Romanian people, referring especially to the Russians and the Hungarians. Because of its anti-Russian, nationalist character, the poem was not allowed to be published for many years under the communist regime in Romania. In it, Eminescu calls on Ştefan cel Mare, the famous prince of Moldavia, who defended his country against the Turks, Hungarians, Poles, and Tartars in the 15th century, to rise again from his grave in the Putna Monastery in northern Moldavia, and defend his people against foreign oppression. Eminescu intended this poem for the inauguration of a statue dedicated to the renowned prince in Iaşi in 1883.

From Tisa to Dniester's tide
All Romanians to me cried,
That they could no longer dwell
Amidst the foreign swell.
From Hotin until the sea
Rides Muscovite cavalry,
On their way they're always seen
From the seashore to Hotin,
And from Dorna to Boian
Plague is spreading on and on.
The foreigner is everywhere
Like you were no longer there;
Up to mountains, down to valley
Enemies on horses rally,
From the seashore to Hotin,
They as flooding waters are.
Oh, the poor Romanians all
Like the crab they backwards crawl;
A cruel fate to them begotten

TASTE OF ROMANIA

Autumn is no longer autumn,
No more summer in their hand,
Now all strangers in their land.
From Dorohoi to Turnu
Enemies in steady strew
All, together overcome you,
As they arrive by railway
All our songs they drive away,
All the birds fly out of sight
From wretched foreign plight.
Over shadows of a thorn
Are the poor Christians born,
Ravaged is the country's face
Forests - our refuge place
Bending, their axe bide,
Even pure springs are dried,
Poor in poor countryside.
He who loves the foes about
May his heart the dogs rip out,
May desert his home efface,
May his sons live in disgrace!
Rise, O' Stephen, mighty Prince,
From sacred Putna come hence,
Let the holy Prelacy
Guard alone the monastery,
Let the saints and their deeds
In the trust of pious priests,
Let them ring the bell with might
All the day and all the night,
And may mercy grant thee Lord
Redeem thy people from the horde.
Rise, O' Stephen, from the ground
So I may hear your horn sound
And gather all Moldavia 'round.
If you blow your horn one blare

All Moldavia will be there,
If you sound a second time
All the woods will fall in line,
If your horn is blown again
All the enemies will be slain
And our borders we regain,
That the crows may hear their cry
Above gallow trees so high.

*From Selected Works of Ion Creangă and Mihai Eminescu

Commentary is by the Editor, Kurt W. Treptow, and the translation is by Kurt W. Treptow and Irina Andone

LUCIAN BLAGA(1895-1961)

Lucian Blaga was a poet, philosopher, essayist and diplomat. His poems have been translated into several major languages. He is also the author of an original philosophical system. His autobiographical novel *Luntrea lui Caron* (Caron's Boat), published for the first time in 1990, is a chronicle of the tragic destiny of an intellectual, and the Romanian people in general, after World War II. Blaga became a member of the Romanian Academy in 1936.

Following is one of his poems, "Sufletul Satului" (The Soul of the Village). The translation is by Laura Treptow.

THE SOUL OF THE VILLAGE

Sufletul satului

Historically, Romania has been an agricultural state, where the village, the peasant, and the shepherd have remained important parts of the culture much longer than in Western European countries. Despite collectivization of farms during communism, and industrialization, the village remains close to the heart of the Romanian.

This poem describes so well the Romanian's attachment to the village. The village is eternal. "Eternity was born in the village.... Here every thought is more profound." In the village, it feels as if your own heart beat comes from somewhere deep within the earth. Here, nature has healing powers: "...and if you bloodied your feet/you stand upon a mound of clay."

Come child, put your hand on my knee.
I believe that eternity was born in the village.
Here every thought is more profound,
and your heart pounds more slowly,
as if it were not beating in your chest,
but somewhere deep within the earth.
Here the thirst for salvation is cured
and if you bloodied your feet
you stand upon a mound of clay.
Look, it's evening.
The soul of the village flutters all around us,

like a soft smell of fresh-cut grass,
like smoke settling on thatched roofs,
like young goats playing upon graves.

RAŢĂ CU VARZĂ ACRĂ
AND OTHER POULTRY
DISHES

CHICKEN WITH SOUR CREAM SAUCE

Pui cu Smântână

3 tbsp. butter
3 lbs. chicken, cut into 8 serving pieces
salt and pepper to taste
1 bunch scallions, cleaned and chopped
3 large garlic cloves, chopped
2 tbsp. fresh dill sprigs, chopped
4 tbsp. sour cream
1 tbsp. flour
1 tsp. lemon juice
2 potatoes, peeled, boiled, and cut into small pieces
2 tbsp. fresh parsley, chopped

Serves 4
Preparation time: 15 min., Cooking time: 30 min.

❏ In a large skillet, melt 2 tbsps. butter and brown chicken pieces on medium-high heat. When nicely browned (about 10 min. on each side), sprinkle with salt and pepper, cover, and simmer on low heat for 20 min.

❏ In a separate skillet, melt the rest of the butter, and lightly sauté scallions, garlic, and dill on low heat.

❏ In a small bowl, mix sour cream and flour well, and add lemon juice.

❏ When chicken is cooked, add sautéed ingredients, potatoes, and sour cream mixture, then stir well. Let simmer uncovered for 10 min.

❏ Sprinkle with fresh chopped parsley and serve with a light salad with lemon or balsamic vinegar dressing.

CHICKEN FRICASSEE WITH OLIVES
Pui cu Măsline

6 lbs. chicken, cut into 16 serving pieces
2 garlic cloves, peeled, whole
4 tbsp. olive oil
1 tbsp. flour
1 tbsp. fresh fennel sprigs, chopped
1 tbsp. fresh chives, chopped
1 tbsp. fresh parsley, chopped
1 cup dry white wine
2 oz. black Greek calamate olives, pitted and cut in half
1 tsp. sweet paprika

Serves 6
Preparation time: 20 min., Cooking time: 50 min.

❏ Rub chicken pieces well with salt.
❏ Rub the bottom of a large skillet with garlic. Add 3 tbsps olive oil. Heat over medium heat.
❏ Add the chicken pieces (if the skillet is not large enough, use two skillets). Brown chicken pieces on all sides (about 4 min. on each side).
❏ Remove chicken pieces.
❏ In the same skillet, slowly blend flour into drippings, while stirring, and cook for about 2 min.
❏ Add fennel, chives, and parsley, mix well, and continue to stir until sauce is brown (about 3-4 min.)
❏ Lower heat to medium low. Thin sauce with wine, and continue to cook for 5 min.
❏ Add olives, garlic, chicken pieces, paprika, salt and pepper to taste, and 1 tbsp. olive oil. Stir well. Cover and cook over low heat 25 min. or until chicken is tender. Baste chicken occasionally with sauce.

BRAISED CHICKEN WITH GARLIC

Pui cu Usturoi

5 tbsp. butter
6 lbs. chicken, cut into 16 serving pieces
4 oz. onion, chopped
1 tbsp. tarragon, chopped
6 garlic cloves, crushed
1 tbsp. salt
1 tbsp. fresh ground black pepper
1 large potato, boiled and mashed
2 tbsp. chives, chopped
1 tbsp. chervil
juice of ½ lemon
1 cup chicken stock
2 tbsp. sour cream
1 tbsp. flour
2 tbsp. fresh parsley, chopped

Serves 6
Preparation time: 25 min., Cooking time: 1 hour

❑ Heat 3 tbsps. butter in a skillet over high heat. Sear chicken pieces, about 1 min. each side. (If skillet is not large enough, use two skillets.) Remove from heat and cover. Let stand.

❑ In a saucepan, heat 2 tbsps. butter over medium heat. Add onion and sauté until golden yellow, about 5 min.

❑ Add tarragon, garlic, pepper, and salt. Stir well.

❑ Add potato, chives, chevril, and lemon juice. Stir well, and then stir in chicken stock.

❑ Re-heat the chicken. When warm, add sauce slowly to the chicken. If sauce is too thick, add a small amount of water. Cover, and simmer over low heat until chicken is tender (about 30 min.).

❑ In a small bowl, mix flour and sour cream together.

❑ Remove the skillet from heat, slowly stir in sour cream mixture, then return to heat and continue to simmer, uncovered, for another 5 min.

Spoon sauce over chicken and sprinkle with parsley. Serve with mămăligă.

CHICKEN PILAF

Pilaf de Pui

3 lbs. chicken, cut into 8 serving pieces
2 large tomatoes, quartered
1 tbsp. salt
1 tbsp. fresh ground black pepper
2 tbsp. fresh dill, chopped
2 tbsp. fresh parsley, chopped
4 tbsp. butter
4 oz. onion, chopped
2 garlic cloves, crushed
¾ cup rice
1 tbsp. flour
¼ cup grated parmesan

Serves 4
Preparation time: 35 min., Cooking time: 1 hour 30 min.

❑ Place the chicken pieces in a large kettle and add enough water to cover. Bring to boil over medium-high heat, and cook about 10 min.

❑ Skim well, and reduce heat to medium. Add tomatoes, salt, pepper, dill and parsley. Cover and continue to cook for another 20 min.

❑ In a saucepan, heat 1 tbsp. butter over medium-high heat. Add onion and garlic, and sauté until golden yellow, about 5 min. Add another 2 tbsps. butter and rice, and continue cooking, stirring rice with a wooden spoon, until rice turns brown, about 10-15 min. Turn the rice and onion mixture into a large greased casserole.

❑ Pre-heat oven to 400°F.

❑ Lift chicken pieces from the kettle, remove skin, and keep chicken warm.

❑ Strain chicken stock into a bowl through a sieve, pushing tomatoes through. In a saucepan, heat 1 tbsp. butter over medium heat. Blend in flour and cook, stirring with wooden spoon, until flour begins to brown, about 2 min. Add 2 cups chicken stock slowly, and stir continually until gravy is creamy.

❑ Pour 3 cups of the chicken stock over the rice, cover, and cook in oven about 20 min., or until the stock is completely absorbed by the rice. Remove lid, stir the rice with a fork to fluff, and arrange the chicken on top. Pour gravy over the chicken, and return to oven for another 15 min.

❑ Remove from oven, dot chicken and rice with butter and chopped parsley.

Serve with grated Parmesan on the side.

CHICKEN CIULAMA[*]

Ciulama de Pui

3½ lbs. chicken, cut into serving portions
2 tbsp. salt
½ lb. carrots, sliced
1 onion, peeled and quartered
4 oz. parsnip, peeled and sliced
4 oz. celery, cut into small pieces
2 bay leaves
4-5 dill sprigs
2-3 thyme sprigs or 2 tsp. ground thyme
3 tbsp. butter
3 tbsp. flour
1 tsp. salt
2 tsp. sweet paprika
¼ cup dry white wine

Serves 4
Preparation time: 25 min., Cooking time: 55 min.

❑ Place chicken pieces in a large kettle, add cold water to about 2 in. above meat, and salt. Heat over high heat until water begins to boil. Skim scum several times. Lower heat to medium-low. Add carrot, onion, parsnip, celery, bay leaves, dill, and thyme. Simmer, partly covered, until chicken is tender, about 35-40 min.

❑ When chicken is done, remove from broth and place on a warmed plate.

❑ Strain broth. Place vegetables in a bowl and save. Set 2 cupfuls of broth aside to cool. Place chicken back in the rest of the broth and keep warm.

❑ Prepare a roux (ciulama) as follows:

❑ In a saucepan, heat butter over medium heat. When butter has melted, blend in flour, little by little, stirring continually, for about 2-3 min. or until roux is a buttery yellow color. Remove from heat and let stand about 1 min. or until it stops bubbling.

❑ Return roux to heat over medium-low heat and slowly add the cooled chicken stock, stirring continually, until roux has a creamy consistency. Add 1 tsp. paprika, 1 tsp. salt, and wine. Cook another minute or two, stirring constantly.

---

* For a description of Ciulama, see CIULAMA, p. 156.

Set chicken on a warm serving plate and spoon the ciulama over it. Sprinkle with paprika.

In addition to a delicious chicken dish, you now also have a tasty and nutritious homemade soup. You can either drink it clear, purée the cooked vegetables and add them, or add noodles or other ingredients.

PAN-ROASTED CHICKEN

Ostropel de Pui

Ostropel (or Ostropat) is a poultry dish prepared similar to what the French call poêlé, or pot-roasting, and is smothered with onion and garlic.

3 lbs. chicken, cut into 8 serving pieces
salt and pepper to taste
2 cups flour
2 tbsp. cooking oil
1 medium-sized onion, finely sliced
2 garlic cloves, peeled and sliced
2 tsp. salt
2 tsp. fresh ground black pepper
1 tsp. tarragon
1 fresh thyme sprigs
¾ cup tomato sauce
2 tsp. flour
½ cup dry white wine
1 bay leaf

Serves 4
Preparation time: 20 min., Cooking time: 65 min.

❑ Completely coat chicken pieces in flour and sprinkle with salt and pepper.

❑ Heat 1 tbsp. cooking oil in a large skillet over medium heat. Place chicken pieces skin side down, and brown about 4-5 min., then turn them over and brown another 4-5 min. Remove from heat.

❑ In a separate skillet, heat 1 tbsp. cooking oil over medium-high heat. Add onions and sauté, turning them over frequently with wooden spoons, until they begin to soften and turn a yellow gold, about 3-4 min. Add garlic, and continue cooking another 2 min.

❑ Add onions to chicken, then salt, pepper, tarragon, and thyme. Mix well. Cook over medium-high heat for about 4 min. Turn pieces over, and continue cooking another 4 min.

❑ In a small bowl, mix tomato sauce with flour. Pour into juices around the chicken, mix well, cover skillet and reduce heat to medium-low. Cook slowly for about 15 min., turning chicken pieces over once or twice.

❑ Add wine and bay leaf, cover, and continue to cook until meat is done and sauce has thickened sufficiently, about 10-15 min.

Serve with mămăligă or sautéed potatoes and vegetables.

CHICKEN, COUNTRY STYLE

Pui Ţărănesc

3 lbs. chicken, cut into 8 serving pieces
2 cups flour
2 eggs, slightly beaten
1 cup yellow corn meal
1 onion, peeled and chopped
3 garlic cloves, peeled and chopped
2 green peppers, cored and sliced
¼ cup cooking oil
1 tbsp. salt
2 tsp. fresh ground black pepper
¼ cup chicken stock
½ lb. tomatoes, peeled and sliced
½ cup tomato sauce
2 tbsp. fresh dill, chopped

Serves 4
Preparation time: 20 min., Cooking time: 55 min.

❏ Dip chicken pieces first in flour, then in egg, and finally in corn meal. Let stand.
❏ Heat 2 tbsps. cooking oil in a large skillet over medium-high heat. Add onion, garlic, and green pepper. Sauté together about 5 min. Remove ingredients from skillet and reserve on a plate. Save skillet with remaining oil.
❏ In the same skillet, add the rest of the oil, and over medium-high heat fry chicken until nicely browned all around, about 10 min.
❏ Preheat oven to 350°F.
❏ In a greased oven dish, place chicken pieces. Cover with the onions, garlic, and green peppers. Add salt and pepper. Pour chicken stock over chicken. Cover with tomato slices, and pour tomato sauce over everything and sprinkle with dill.
❏ Cover and braise in oven 30 min. Remove lid, baste well with pan juices, and continue cooking, uncovered, for another 10 min.

Serve hot with sour cream and hot mămăligă.

ROAST DUCK WITH SAUERKRAUT

Raţă cu Varză Acră

4-5 lb. duck (or two 2-3 lb. ducklings)
salt and pepper to taste
3 cups flour
4 tbsp. butter
juice of 2 oranges
1 garlic clove
1 sage leaf
1 lb. sauerkraut, soaked in water and drained
1 tbsp. herbes de provence (or mixed dry thyme, basil,
    rosemary)
½ cup dry white wine
1 cup chicken stock
1 tbsp. granulated sugar
12 peppercorns
½ cup medium dry sherry
¼ cup cointreau
¼ lb. bacon, cut into small pieces
3 tbsp. shallot, chopped
1 tbsp. fresh fennel sprigs, chopped
1 tbsp. flour
½ cup sauerkraut juice

Serves 6

Preparation time: 1 hour 45 min., Cooking time: 2-2½ hours

❑ Puncture duck in several places to allow excess fat to drain. Salt and pepper inside and out.

❑ Place in preheated 400°F oven, breast down over a drip pan, for about 10 min. to release some of the fat.

❑ Remove from oven and let cool for a few minutes. Then roll duck in flour.

❑ Melt 3 tbsps. butter in a large skillet over medium heat, and brown duck slowly on all sides (about 10 min.). Pour orange juice over it. Remove duck and set aside.

❑ Prepare a brown sauce (see below).

❑ Rub the bottom of an oven casserole with garlic.

❑ In the skillet used for browning the duck, add sage, sauerkraut, herbes de provence, 1 tbsp. butter, wine, ¼ cup chicken stock, sugar, and peppercorns.

Brown sauerkraut over medium heat, stirring constantly (about 20 min.). Place sauerkraut in casserole.

❏ Cut duck into pieces, and add to sauerkraut in casserole. Pour brown sauce over it.

❏ Bake, covered, in preheated 375°F oven for 15 min. Reduce heat to 325°F and continue to cook for 1 hour 45 min. Uncover, and cook for another 30 min. or until duck is well browned.

❏ Before serving, pour sherry and cointreau over duck.

Serve with baked potatoes or sweet potatoes.

BROWN SAUCE

❏ In a skillet, fry bacon for about 3 min. over medium heat. Add shallots and fennel. Fry another 2 min. Stir in 1 tbsp. flour. Brown well, stirring constantly. Thin with remaining chicken stock and sauerkraut juice.

❏ Cook for another 10 min. while continuing to stir. Strain sauce through fine sieve.

PAN-ROASTED DUCK

Ostropel de Rață

Ostropel (or Ostropat) is a poultry dish prepared similarly to what the French call poêlé, or pot-roasting, and is smothered with onion and garlic.

4-5 lb. duck (or two 2-3 lb. ducklings), cleaned, washed,
 and patted dry
salt and pepper to taste
3 cups flour
4 tbsp. cooking oil
2 medium onions, finely sliced
4 garlic cloves, peeled and sliced
2 tsp. salt
2 tsp. fresh ground black pepper
1 tsp. tarragon
2 fresh thyme sprigs
1 cup tomato sauce
1 tbsp. flour
½ cup dry white wine
1 bay leaf

> *Serves 6*
> *Preparation time: 45 min., Cooking time: 65 min.*

❏ Puncture duck in several places to allow excess fat to drain. Salt and pepper inside and out.

❏ Place in preheated 400°F oven, breast down over a drip pan, for about 10 min. to release some of the fat.

❏ Remove from oven and let cool for a few minutes. Cut into serving portions, and dip pieces in flour to coat them completely.

❏ Heat 2 tbsps. cooking oil in a large skillet over medium heat. Place duck pieces skin side down, and brown about 4-5 min., then turn them over and brown another 4-5 min. Remove from heat and pour out excess fat.

❏ In a separate skillet, heat 2 tbsps. cooking oil over medium-high heat. Add onions and sauté, turning frequently with wooden spoons, until they begin to soften and turn yellow gold, about 3-4 min. Add garlic, and continue cooking another 2 min.

❏ Add onion mixture to duck, then salt, pepper, tarragon, and thyme. Mix well. Cook over medium-high heat for about 4 min. Turn pieces over, and continue cooking another 4 min.

❑ In a small bowl, mix tomato sauce with 1 tbsp. flour. Pour into sauce around the duck, mix well, cover skillet, and reduce heat to medium-low. Cook slowly, turning duck pieces over once or twice, about 15 min.

❑ Add wine and bay leaf, cover, and continue to cook until meat is tender and sauce has thickened, about 10-15 min.

Serve with mămăligă or sautéed potatoes and cooked red cabbage or sauerkraut.

PAN-ROASTED GOOSE

Ostropel de Gâscă

Ostropel (or Ostropat) is a poultry dish prepared similarly to what the French call poêlé, or pot-roasting, and is smothered with onion and garlic.

The same basic recipe as that for PAN ROASTED DUCK (see p. 210) can be used to prepare a PAN-ROASTED GOOSE. Goose is the fattest poultry, and therefore it is important to drain off excess fat by puncturing the goose all around during the first steps of heating the bird in the oven. Also be sure to pour off excess fat from the skillet after browning goose.

To serve 8 persons, buy an 8-10 lb. goose. Then proceed following the recipe for pan-roasted duck.

STUFFED TURKEY MOLDAVIAN STYLE

Curcan Umplut Moldovenesc

½ lb. butter, softened
3 eggs, separated
1 loaf bread, crust removed
2 cups milk
1 turkey liver
1 onion, chopped
1 bay leaf
4 oz. raisins
1 tbsp. fresh sage, chopped
1 tbsp. fresh thyme, chopped
2 tbsp. fresh parsley, chopped
2 tsp. salt
1 tsp. fresh ground black pepper
½ cup chicken stock
8 lb. turkey, cleaned and patted dry
salt to taste
melted fat or cooking oil
1 cup red wine
1 cup water
8 apples, pared and cored
4 tsp. granulated sugar

Serves 8

Preparation time: 60 min., Cooking time: 3-3½ hours

❑ Beat egg yolks to a foam. Beat egg whites stiff.

❑ Dip bread in milk, then squeeze excess out.

❑ Preheat oven to 400°F.

❑ In a skillet, heat a small amount of butter over medium-high heat. Sauté liver, onion, and bay leaf about 5 min. Let cool. Then chop liver.

❑ Prepare stuffing as follows:

Whip 3 tbsps. butter until it becomes creamy.

Add egg yolks, liver, bread, raisins, onion, sage, thyme,

parsley, 2 tsps. salt, and pepper. Moisten with stock, mix well,

then blend in egg whites.

❑ Rub turkey cavities with salt. Fill with stuffing, allowing room for expansion.
Sew up cavities or close with small trussing skewers.

❏ Rub the outside of the turkey with 4 tbsps. butter. Sprinkle with salt and pepper. Drape the turkey with a clean cloth or cheesecloth dipped into melted fat or cooking oil.

❏ Place turkey breast side up in a roasting pan. Pour wine and water over it. Cook uncovered for 15 min. Lower temperature to 325°F. Allow 25 min. per pound or 3 to 3½ hours total cooking time. Lift the cloth and baste with pan juices every ½ hour.

❏ While the turkey cooks, place apples in an oven dish. Fill each with ½ tsp. sugar and a pat of butter.

❏ About 45 min. before turkey is done, remove cloth to allow turkey to brown, and put apples in the oven.

Turkey is ready when a meat thermometer reads 170°F, or when drumsticks swivel easily.

Serve with potatoes and sautéed zucchini or broccoli. Use the pan juices as gravy.

PÂRJOALE DE LEGUME AND OTHER VEGETABLE DISHES

VEGETARIAN HAMBURGERS

Pârjoale de Legume

Ingredients for hamburgers
   1 lb. potatoes, peeled and quartered
   1 tsp. salt
   6 oz. carrots, peeled and sliced
   4 oz. celery stalks, cut into small pieces
   ½ large onion, chopped
   4 tbsp. cooking oil
   3 oz. canned peas
   3 oz. canned green beans
   2 garlic cloves, crushed
   2 tsp. salt
   1 tsp. fresh ground black pepper
   2 tbsp. fresh dill, chopped
   2 tbsp. fresh parsley, chopped
   ¼ cup bread crumbs
   ¼ cup flour
   1 egg yolk
   1 recipe tomato sauce
   3 tbsp. sour cream
   1 tbsp. all purpose flour
   ½ lemon, juice

Ingredients for tomato sauce
   1 tbsp. butter
   2 cups canned tomato sauce
   1 tsp. flour
   1 tsp. salt
   ½ tsp. granulated sugar

   Serves 4
   Preparation time: 25 min., Cooking time: 30 min.

Hamburgers
❑ Bring water and salt to a boil in a kettle over medium-high heat. Add potatoes, carrots, and celery. Boil until tender, about 20 min. Strain and let cool.
❑ In the meantime, in a skillet, heat 1 tbsp. oil over medium-high heat. Add onion, and sauté until golden and soft, about 5 min., then cool.

❏ When cool, place potatoes, celery, carrots, onion, peas, and beans in a bowl, mix, then pass mixture through a fine meat grinder. Return mixture to bowl. Add salt, pepper, garlic, flour, bread crumbs, egg yolk, parsley and dill. Mix well with wooden spoon until smooth.

❏ With damp hands, form mixture into patties. If mixture is too soft, add a little flour or bread crumbs.

❏ In a large skillet, heat the rest of the oil over medium-high heat. Fry patties until brown, about 3-4 min. on each side. Add tomato sauce, cover, and let simmer another 3-4 min.

Serve hot with tomato sauce, accompanied by a salad, or refrigerate and eat cold.

Tomato sauce

❏ In a small saucepan, heat butter over medium heat until it melts. Add tomato sauce. Slowly blend in flour, stirring with a wooden spoon. Cook until sauce thickens, about 5 min. Add salt and sugar. Stir, and cook another minute or two.

LEEKS WITH OLIVES

Praz cu Măsline

6 leeks, not too thick
2 tbsp. cooking oil
2 tbsp. butter
1 tbsp. flour
½ cup soup stock (beef, chicken, or vegetable)
2 tsp. salt
1 tbsp. lemon juice
2 oz. Greek Calamate olives

Serves 4
Preparation time: 15 min., Cooking time: 40 min.

❑ Preheat oven to 350°F.

❑ Clean leeks and trim off and discard green tops and outer leaves. Cut the white portion of each leek into pieces about 2½ in. long.

❑ Bring a kettle of water to boiling. Blanch the leek pieces about 2-3 min. Drain well.

❑ In a small skillet, heat oil over medium heat. Sauté the leeks until nicely browned, turning pieces over as they cook, about 6-7 min. Remove leek pieces and place them in a baking dish with lid.

❑ In a small saucepan, heat the butter over medium-low heat. Slowly add flour, stirring continuously with a wooden spoon. Let cook 1-2 min., then stir in soup stock, salt, and lemon juice. Pour the sauce over leeks in the baking dish. Cover tightly and braise in oven for 15 min.

❑ While leeks are cooking, bring the kettle of water to boil again, and blanch olives for 2-3 min. Drain well.

❑ When leeks are cooked, add olives, and continue to cook, uncovered, for another 10 min.

Serve hot.

CAULIFLOWER, TRANSYLVANIAN STYLE

Conopidă Ardelenească

1½ lb. cauliflower
2 tsp. salt
4 tbsp. butter
1 onion, peeled and chopped
2 tbsp. flour
¾ cup hot water*
3 tbsp. sour cream
2 tbsp. salt
2 tsp. fresh ground black pepper
2 tbsp. fresh parsley, chopped

Serves 4
Preparation time: 10 min., Cooking time: 30 min.

❏ Remove all green leaves from cauliflower. Place in a bowl, sprinkle with salt and cover with cold water. Let sit for about 30 min.
❏ Cut cauliflower into small florets.
❏ Heat butter in a large, heavy skillet over medium heat. Add onion and flour. Stir and sauté until onion softens and turns yellow gold, about 4-5 min.
❏ Add cauliflower florets, mix well, and fry with onion another 10 min., mixing and turning with a wooden spoon.
❏ Add hot water little by little, stirring continually, and cook another 5-10 min. until cauliflower is done. Add sour cream, salt, and pepper. Stir well, and cook another 5 min.

Serve, sprinkled with parsley, as a delicious vegetarian dish, or as a vegetable with meat or fish.

This dish is from Ion Negrea's personal portfolio of recipes. Mr. Negrea is at the time of this writing the executive manager of the Inter-Continental Hotel in Bucharest, as well as vice-president of the Romanian Cooks and Pastry-Cooks Association.

---

* If you wish, you may use chicken stock.

CAULIFLOWER WITH CHEESE

Conopidă cu Brânză

1½ lbs. cauliflower
salt to taste
6 oz. caşcaval cheese*, grated
2 tbsp. bread crumbs
2 tbsp. butter, melted

Serves 4
Preparation time: 15 min., Cooking time: 25 min.

❏ Remove all green leaves from the cauliflower. Place in a bowl, sprinkle with salt and cover with cold water. Let sit about 30 min.
❏ Cut cauliflower into small florets.
❏ Preheat oven to 400°F.
❏ In a kettle, bring enough water to cover cauliflower to boil, add cauliflower and salt, and cook uncovered until tender, about 10-15 min. Drain well.
❏ Butter an oven dish. Add cauliflower. Sprinkle with salt to taste. Sprinkle grated cheese over cauliflower, then bread crumbs. Pour melted butter evenly over the top.
❏ Bake in oven until cheese is melted and surface browns, about 15 min.

Serve hot, as a vegetarian dish or as a side dish with meat or fish.

---

* You can use any similar hard ewe cheese with strong flavor. A good substitute is Italian Pecorino Toscano or Pecorino Romano.

POTATOES WITH SOUR CREAM
Cartofi cu Smântână

1½ lbs. new potatoes
salt to taste
¾ cup milk
½ tbsp. butter
4 tbsp. sour cream

Serves 4
Preparation time: 15 min., Cooking time: 35 min.

❏ In a kettle, heat water with salt over high heat. When water boils, add unpeeled potatoes and parboil until they just begin to soften, about 15 min.

❏ Drain potatoes and let cool for a few minutes. Peel and cut into ¼ in. slices. Sprinkle with salt.

❏ In a skillet, heat milk and butter over medium heat. When milk starts to bubble, lower heat to medium-low. Add potatoes gently, and simmer until milk is almost evaporated, shaking skillet from time to time to keep potatoes from sticking to the bottom of the skillet, about 15 min.

❏ Add sour cream, and simmer about 10 more min., shaking the skillet to spread and mix sour cream.

Serve hot, as a vegetarian dish or as a side dish with meat.

POTATOES, COUNTRY STYLE

Cartofi Ţărăneşti

4 potatoes
½ onion
3 oz. lardon*, cut into small pieces**
2 garlic cloves, peeled and chopped
salt and pepper to taste

> *Serves 4*
> *Preparation time: 10 min., Cooking time: 15 min.*

❑ Peel and boil potatoes.

❑ In a heavy skillet, sauté onion and lardon over medium-high heat until onion is golden brown and lardon is crisp, about 6-7 min. Add garlic, and cook another 2 min.

❑ Lower heat to low, add boiled potatoes, break up potatoes with a fork into small, rough pieces. Mix well with onion, lardon, and fat. Add salt and pepper. Cover skillet and let steam another 8-10 min.

These potatoes are delicious, served as a side dish with meats, or with eggs for breakfast.

---

* If you cannot find French lardon, use the same quantity of smoked bacon strips

EGGPLANT AU GRATIN

Vinete au Gratin

Eggplants are said to originate in Western Africa. They are called aubergines in Great Britain, and have also been called Guinea Squash and Mad Apple. The best eggplants for cooking are the large purple ones. When they are stewed, sautéed, or cooked au gratin, it is important to first extract the excess juice, which tends to be bitter, by steeping them in salt for a half hour. For this recipe, cut eggplants lengthwise into ½ in. slices if the eggplant are small. With larger ones, slice crosswise.

2 lbs. eggplant, peeled and sliced
¼ lb. butter
1 medium onion, chopped
4 garlic cloves, chopped
4 tomatoes, sliced
salt and pepper to taste
3 tbsp. fresh parsley, chopped
2 tbsp. fresh fennel sprigs, chopped
1 tbsp. fresh thyme, chopped
¾ cup bread crumbs
¾ cup parmesan cheese, grated

Serves 4
Preparation time: 45 min.(including the 30 min. steeping of eggplant in salt.), Cooking time: 60 min.

❑ Sprinkle eggplant slices with salt on both sides. Place on sheets of kitchen towel, and let stand for 30-40 min.

❑ In a large skillet, heat 5 tbsps. butter over medium heat. Sauté onion and garlic about 3 min. Add eggplant slices, and sauté about 3 min. on each side, until the slices are nicely browned. You might need to use two skillets or repeat process until all the slices have been browned.

❑ Butter the bottom of an earthen or glass oven dish. (It is important to use only non-reactive ovenware). Arrange eggplant slices and tomato slices in alternate layers in the oven dish, starting with a layer of eggplant. Sprinkle each layer of tomatoes with salt, pepper, parsley, fennel, and thyme, ending with a layer of eggplant, and keeping enough tomato slices for the top layer.

❑ Preheat oven to 350°F.

❑ In the same skillet in which you browned eggplant, heat 1 tbsp. butter over medium heat. Add the last layer of tomato slices, and sauté about 2 min. on each side.

❑ In a small bowl, mix bread crumbs with parmesan cheese.

❑ Arrange the top layer of tomato slices on the eggplant. Sprinkle with salt and pepper. Cover with bread crumb mixture. Cut remaining butter into small pieces, and dot bread crumbs with butter. Sprinkle with remaining parsley, fennel, and thyme. Bake about 40-45 min.

Serve alone as a light evening meal, or as a side dish to accompany meat or poultry.

WHIPPED MASHED BEANS

Fasole Bătută

10 oz. dry white beans, navy, kidney, or haricot
1 tbsp. salt
1 onion, peeled and sliced
1 carrot, peeled and sliced
2 tbsp. cooking oil
1 garlic clove, crushed
2 tsp. salt
2 tsp. fresh ground black pepper
½ cup olive oil
juice of 1 lemon

Serves 4
Preparation time: 20 min., Cooking time: 1 hour 30 min.

❑ Wash beans well, even if they look clean. Cover with cold water for a few minutes, drain, and repeat.

❑ Fill a kettle with cold water. Add beans. Heat over high heat. As soon as water starts to boil, drain beans. Refill kettle with cold water, and repeat procedure.

❑ Refill kettle with at least 2 qts. of cold water. Add beans. Heat on high heat. As soon as water begins to boil, add salt, ½ sliced onion, and carrot. Lower temperature to medium. Partially cover and cook for about 1½ hours, or until beans are soft.

❑ While beans are cooking, heat cooking oil in a skillet over medium-high heat. Add rest of onion and sauté until nicely browned, about 4-5 min.

❑ When beans are tender, drain and let cool. Save about a cup of bean stock.

❑ Purée beans in a food processor or pass them through a fine meat grinder. Place the puréed beans in a saucepan.

❑ In a small bowl, mix garlic with salt and pepper. Then add a bit of bean stock, and mix well. Pour over beans.

❑ Dribble 1 tbsp. olive oil over beans. Mix well. Place saucepan over low heat, and with a wooden spoon or fork, beat the mashed beans, adding from time to time a bit of olive oil and lemon juice, until the beans become a smooth, pink paste.

Place mashed beans in a serving dish. Pour sautéed onions with their oil over the top, and serve warm or cold. This is a very rich but tasty dish, usually eaten with marinated vegetables.

BRAISED SAUERKRAUT

Varză Călită

1 lb. sauerkraut, drained
2 tbsp. butter
1 tsp. black peppercorns
1 cup tomato sauce
2 tsp. salt
1 tsp. sweet paprika
¼ cup dry white wine

> *Serves 4*
> *Preparation time: 5 min. (without standing time), Cooking time: 1 hour*

❑ Wash and drain sauerkraut. Save sauerkraut juice for use in sour soups.
❑ Let sauerkraut stand in cold water about 30 min. Then drain well, and squeeze out extra water.
❑ In a saucepan, heat butter over medium-high heat. When melted, add sauerkraut, stir well, and sauté about 5 min., turning with a wooden spoon.
❑ Add peppercorns and ½ cup tomato sauce. Lower heat to low. Stir well, cover, and braise sauerkraut for about 50 min. Add some tomato juice from time to time if sauerkraut gets dry.
❑ Add salt, paprika, and wine. Stir well, cover, and braise another 10 min.

Serve hot with pork, duck, or turkey, as well as grilled fish.

RICE PILAF BALADA

Pilaf Balada

2 tbsp. butter
1 onion, peeled and finely chopped
1 carrot, peeled and finely grated
2 cups chicken stock
1 cup rice
salt and pepper to taste
2 tsp. Delikat[*]
1 bay leaf
2 tbsp. fresh parsley, chopped

Serves 4
Preparation time: 10 min., Cooking time: 35 min.

❑ Preheat oven to 350°F.
❑ In a skillet, heat butter over medium-high heat. Add onion and sauté until onion softens and turns yellow-gold, about 3-4 min. Add carrot, stir, and cook another 2 min.
❑ In a kettle, heat chicken stock over high heat until it begins to boil. Lower heat to medium-low, add onion and carrot, and let simmer about 15 min.
❑ Grease a casserole, add rice and chicken stock. Stir well, add salt, pepper, Delikat, bay leaf, and parsley. Cover and cook in oven about 20 min., or until rice has completely absorbed the chicken stock.

Serve hot as a side dish to meat, poultry, or fish, or as a nutritious vegetarian dish.

If you use bouillon cubes for chicken stock, do not add additional salt.

This recipe was contibuted by the kitchen staff of Hotel Balada in Suceava. (see BEET BORŞ BALADA, p. 93 for story)

---

[*] Delikat is a brand of concentrated soup and stew flavor enhancer in wide usage in Romania. Several brands are available here, such as Aromat by Knorr and Vegeta from Croatia, imported by Jana Foods.

MUSHROOM PATTIES

Piftele (Chiftele) de Ciuperci

This tasty vegetarian dish is based on a recipe contributed by the nuns of the Humor Monastery, one of the beautiful historic Painted Monasteries of southern Bucovina. It is on the nuns' and guests' menu during fasting days before Easter.

> **6 tbsp. cooking oil**
> **1 lb. mushrooms[*], washed and sliced**
> **2 garlic cloves, peeled and sliced**
> **1 onion, peeled and chopped**
> **2 potatoes, peeled and grated**
> **2 tsp. salt**
> **1 tsp. fresh ground black pepper**
> **½ tsp. crushed hot red pepper**
> **3 tsp. Vegeta**^{**}‘
> **4 tbsp. bread crumbs**
> **2 tbsp. fresh dill, chopped**
> **2 cups tomato sauce recipe**^{***}
>
> *Serves 4*
> *Preparation time: 25 min., Cooking time: 35 min.*

❑ In a skillet, heat 2 tbsps. oil over medium-high heat. Add mushrooms and garlic. Sauté, stirring and turning mushrooms with a wooden spoon, about 10 min. Drain water from skillet while cooking. Place mushroom mixture in a bowl, and let cool.

❑ In a separate skillet, heat 2 tbsp. oil over medium-high heat. Add onion, potato, salt, pepper, red pepper, and Vegeta. Stir well. Sauté about 10 min., stirring and turning while cooking. Place in bowl with the mushroom mixture, and let cool.

❑ Pass mixture through a fine meat grinder or food processor, and return to bowl. Add bread crumbs and dill. Mix well.

---

* Use either plain white button mushrooms or Crimini mushrooms.

** Vegeta is a brand of concentrated soup and stew flavor enhancer in wide usage in Romania. Several brands are available, such as Delikat, Aromat by Knorr, and Vegeta, from Croatia, imported by Jana Foods.

*** see chapter on SAUCES, p. 251.

❑ Taking a spoonful of mixture at a time, shape into 1 in. balls, then flatten into patties.

❑ To the skillet in which you sautéed onions and potatoes, add another 2 tbsps. oil. Heat over medium-high heat, and sauté mushroom patties until they are nicely browned on both sides, about 7-8 min. per side.

Pour tomato sauce over patties and serve hot.

MUSHROOM FRICASSE

Fricasse de Ciuperci

2 tbsp. butter
1 oz. scallions, chopped — *ceapā verde*
2 garlic cloves, sliced
½ lb. mushrooms*, diced, with stems
4 eggs, hard boiled
1 tbsp. fennel, chopped
1 tsp. salt
1 tsp. black pepper
1 tsp. crushed hot red pepper
2 tsp. lemon juice
¼ cup beef stock
3 tbsp. sour cream
1 tbsp. flour

Serves 4
Preparation time: 20 min., Cooking time: 25 min.

❏ In a skillet, heat 1 tbsp. butter over medium-high heat. Add scallions and garlic. Stir and sauté until scallions turn a light brown but do not burn, about 4 min.

❏ Add another tbsp. butter and mushrooms, stir and sauté another 4-5 min.

❏ In the meantime, peel and slice hard-boiled eggs lengthwise. Arrange slices side by side to cover the bottom of serving plates, one egg per plate.

❏ To the mushrooms, add fennel, salt, pepper, red pepper, and lemon juice. Stir well. Add beef stock, cover, lower heat to low, and cook slowly until tender, about 10 min.

❏ In a small bowl, mix sour cream with flour. Add mixture slowly to mushrooms, stirring well, and allow to simmer for another few minutes until the sauce thickens. Pour the mushroom sauce over the eggs, and serve.

---

* Any mushrooms will do, but try to choose those with a strong flavor, such as shiitake, crimini, or cepes.

FRENCH TOAST WITH PEAS

Frigănele de Franzelă cu Mazăre

1 egg, slightly beaten
1 tsp. salt
1 tsp. black pepper
½ French baguette, sliced
2 cups cold milk
2 tbsp. butter
1 tsp. butter
2 cups French petits-pois canned peas

Serves 4
Preparation time: 10 min., Cooking time: 12 min.

❑ In a bowl, mix egg with salt and pepper.
❑ Soak bread in milk for about 5 min., then gently dip in egg.
❑ In a skillet, heat 2 tbsps. butter over medium heat. Fry slices of bread until nicely browned, about 5 min. on each side.
❑ In a kettle, heat canned peas over medium heat just to boil. Drain, add another tsp. of butter to the skillet, and sauté peas for about 2-3 min. over medium heat.

Serve hot with the french toast. You can vary this dish by serving the french toast with sautéed mushrooms instead of peas, or by adding a few strips of bacon.

ROMANIAN PROVERBS

© 2/1/97

Illustration by Eve Wilder

*P*roverbs generally refer to common experience and are often expressed using metaphors, alliteration, or rhyme. Nearly every nation has its store of proverbs. Many are common to several nations. Proverbs abound in the Old Testament and in early Greek and Roman literature. Proverbs were extremely popular among the Elizabethans, the most famous collections being those of John Heywood (d. 1580) and Florio (d. 1625). Although the popularity of proverbs declined in the 18th century, they have become a subject for research and classification in more modern times. In the Romanian language, there are innumerable proverbs, dating to uncertain ancient times. Many of them are poignant, some are humorous and indicative of the Romanian's personality and sense of humor.

Some of the proverbs selected for this cookbook involve food, others do not. They were chosen from a Romanian book containing a collection of over 8000 proverbs, which in turn were chosen from an earlier publication of 10 volumes.

Proverbs Associated with Foods

He who steals an egg today
Will steal a cow tomorrow.

Give an egg today
You will receive a cow tomorrow.

He went to the mill and to the grindstone
And returned with the sack full of grains.

He licked the honey from his fingers
Until he ate them too.

Bread as fresh as can be
Wine as old as can be
Wife as young as can be.

ROMANIAN PROVERBS

Brother, brother
But the cheese must be paid for.

Don't get mixed up in everything
Like parsley in every dish.

A sharp vinegar breaks its own bottle.

Big fires are made even in small ovens.

When the chicken sings
The rooster keeps quiet.

Where two eat
A third can eat too.

A good wine and a beautiful wife
Are two sweet poisons.

Cattle is watered with water
Man with sweet words.

Proverbs Not Associated with Foods

Wood that bends is better than wood that breaks.

Even the sea has a bottom.

Justice is where the power is.

Don't laugh at the donkey.
The time will come when you will need
To mount him.

Only one word suffices
For him who wants to understand you.

The husband doesn't know
What the village knows.

A bad person is like charcoal
If it doesn't burn you
It blackens you.

Necessity teaches man
The rod teaches the child.

The needy always answers
That he cannot.

Necessity changes the law.

Water and fire cannot become friends.

You cannot hang on the poor man's justice
It's so thin.

ROMANIAN PROVERBS

A good word puts out a fire faster than
A bucket of water.

No matter how much you caress a snake
It will still bite you.

From the word to the deed
Is like from the earth to the sky.

Don't run after the wagon
That doesn't wait for you.

The story is beautiful
But the lie is big.

Being lazy he shuts his eyes
And opens his mouth.

No one is ever ready
For death and marriage.

PAPANAŞI OTHER DUMPLINGS AND FRITTERS AND ROMANIAN PANCAKES

CHEESE FRITTERS

Papanaşi Prăjiţi

This dish can be served as lunch, a sweet snack, or dessert.

¾ lb. farmers cheese
½ cup flour, sifted
2 eggs
½ tsp. salt
3 tbsp. granulated sugar
1 tsp. lemon rind, grated
1 tsp. baking soda
3 tbsp. cooking oil
1 cup sour cream
½ cup rose petal preserves, or preserves of your choice

Serves 4
Preparation time: 15 min., Cooking time: 10 min.

❑ In a bowl, mix cheese, flour, eggs, salt, sugar, baking soda, and lemon rind. Beat well with a spoon or electric mixer until smooth.

❑ Dip your hands in flour and take a small quantity of batter, enough to make a ball about 2 in. in diameter. Flatten somewhat, and poke a hole in the middle, like a donut. Continue until all batter has been used.

❑ Heat oil in a large skillet over medium high heat. When hot, drop the fritters in the oil, and fry them until they are golden brown and crisp, about 4 min. on each side. Remove with slotted spoon or skimmer.

Sprinkle with granulated sugar, and serve immediately on warmed plates with sour cream and preserves.

This recipe was contributed by Chef Gheorghe Cătană of the Orizont Hotel in Predeal (see p. 117, STUFFED SMOKED SALMON for the story).

CHEESE DUMPLINGS MAGDALENA

Papanași Fierți Magdalena

This dish can be served as lunch, a sweet snack, or dessert.

¾ lb. farmers cheese
3 eggs
3 tbsp. farina
1 tsp. vanilla extract
1 pinch salt
2 tsp. granulated sugar
3 qts. water
3 tbsp. butter
1 cup bread crumbs
1 cup sour cream
½ cup rose petal preserves or preserves of your choice

Serves 4
Preparation time: 15 min., Cooking time: 20 min.

❑ In a bowl, mix cheese, eggs, farina, vanilla extract, salt, and sugar with a spoon or electric mixer until smooth.

❑ Dip hands in flour, then take small amounts of the dough and roll into 1½ in. balls. Poke a hole into center of each, like a doughnut.

❑ In a large kettle, bring water to boil over high heat. Lower heat to medium-low and add some salt.

❑ Drop dumplings into simmering water. They will rise to the surface in 3-4 min., then continue cooking another 10 min.

❑ In the meantime, in a skillet, heat butter over medium heat. Add bread crumbs, and sauté, stirring with wooden spoon, a few minutes until golden, not brown. Have ready before removing dumplings from water.

❑ Remove dumplings gently with slotted spoon and drop directly into bread crumbs; roll around until covered.

Serve hot with granulated sugar, sour cream, and preserves .

DUMPLINGS WITH CAŞCAVAL CHEESE

Găluşte cu Caşcaval

2½ oz. butter
1½ cups chicken stock
2 tsp. salt
1 cup flour
3 eggs
1 tbsp. fresh ground black pepper
2 tsp. salt
4 tbsp. caşcaval cheese, grated*
1 qt. water
1½ cups tomato sauce**
2 tsp. caraway seeds
2 tsp. fennel seeds
4 tbsp. caşcaval cheese, grated***

Serves 4
Preparation time: 30 min., Cooking time: 60 min.

❏ Preheat oven to 375°F.
❏ In a saucepan, melt 2 oz. butter in the chicken stock. Add 2 tsps salt. Bring to a boil.
❏ When liquid is boiling reduce heat to low and add flour all at once. Stir until all liquid is absorbed, the dough separates from the sides of the pan and forms into a ball.
❏ Remove from heat and continue to stir for about 3 min. until the dough cools a little.
❏ Add the eggs slowly, one by one, continuing to stir. Blend in each egg thoroughly before adding the next, and use only two if dough is soft. Add pepper, 2 tsps. salt, and 4 tbsps. of caşcaval cheese. Stir well.
❏ In a large saucepan, bring water to a boil. Lower heat to medium-low. The water should just barely bubble. Drop dough a teaspoonful at a time. The dumplings will sink to the bottom, and then rise to the top.
❏ Let dumplings simmer until they are firm, about 20 min. Then gently drain them, and place in a buttered oven or gratin dish.

---

* Instead of caşcaval, you can use mature cheddar cheese.
** You can use any spaghetti sauce or stewed tomatoes.
*** Instead of caşcaval, you can use parmesan cheese.

❑ In a small saucepan, heat tomato sauce, add caraway seeds, fennel seeds, and remaining butter. Stir to mix well.

❑ Pour sauce over dumplings and sprinkle with 4 tbsps. of caşcaval cheese.

❑ Place in oven for 30 min. Serve.

CRULLERS

Minciunele (Little Lies)

This recipe is made with a French pâte sucrée (sweet flan pastry).

1 cup flour
1 pinch salt
1 egg
1 egg yolk
¼ cup superfine sugar
2 oz. butter, diced, at room temperature
3 tbsp. rum
cooking oil for deep-frying
1 cup granulated sugar

> *Makes about 20 crullers*
> *Preparation time: 15 min. plus chilling time, Cooking time: 6 min. per batch*

❑ Sift flour and salt on to a marble or stone work surface, or into a large bowl. Make a well in the center.

❑ In a small bowl, beat the egg and yolk. Add the sugar and continue to beat with a fork. Add butter little by little and continue to beat until butter is partially blended into mixture. Add rum and beat a few more seconds. Pour mixture into the flour well.

❑ Using finger tips of one hand, pinch and rub the sugar, egg, rum, butter mixture to work in the flour, bit by bit. Use enough of the flour to turn the mixture into an easy to handle ball of dough.

❑ With your hands dry and floured, knead the dough lightly a few times.

❑ Cover the dough with aluminium foil or plastic, and chill 1 to 2 hours, overnight if possible.

❑ Roll out the dough on a floured surface with a floured rolling pin.

❑ Use a dough cutting wheel to make strips 3 in. x 1 in. Cut a long slit in the center of each, and pull both ends through to form a bow or butterfly.

❑ Deep-fry crullers to a golden brown in hot cooking oil. They sink to the bottom and then rise to the top of the oil as they puff up. After 2-3 min., turn crullers and fry them for another 2-3 min.

❑ Lift them out of the oil with a slotted spoon. Cool, and sprinkle with granulated sugar.

These crullers are abolutely delicious, served as a dessert or with afternoon tea or coffee.

ROMANIAN PANCAKES

Clătite

Romanian pancakes are similar to French crêpes but they are more like a light, thin pancake. Like crêpes, they can be prepared with a savory or sweet filling. Unlike French crêpes, they don't get dry. They can be kept in the refrigerator and reheated. Following is a basic recipe.

1¼ cups plain all purpose flour
2 eggs
1 pinch salt
2 tbsp. superfine granulated sugar[*]
1½ cups milk
2 tsp. butter, melted, for batter
1 tbsp. butter, melted, for cooking

Makes 8-10 pancakes
Preparation time: 10 min. (not including the 30 min. standing time),
Cooking time: 8 min.

❑ Sift the flour into a large bowl. Make a well in the center. Break the eggs into the well. Add a pinch of salt and the sugar for sweet pancakes, or 2 tsps. salt for savory pancakes. Beat egg mixture well with a fork. Add the milk and continue to beat, slowly adding the flour, until the batter is smooth. Add the melted butter, while continuing to beat the mixture with the fork. The batter should be the consistency of a light cream.

❑ Let batter stand for 30 minutes.

❑ Butter a medium skillet with a brush. Heat over medium-high heat. Test butter temperature by splashing a few drops of water into the butter. Bubbles will sizzle then evaporate in a few seconds when temperature is correct.

❑ Ladle about 3 tbsps. of batter at a time in the center of the skillet and immediately tilt the skillet in a slow, circular motion so that the batter spreads to cover the entire bottom of the skillet. As soon as one side starts to brown, flip the pancake over, either with a spatula or by a quick jerk of the skillet. Brown the other side, and then place pancake on a warm dish in the oven at low temperature. It should take about 30 seconds a side to make each pancake. Butter the skillet each time before adding the batter.

---

[*] For savory pancakes, substitute 2 tsps. of salt for sugar.

When all the pancakes are made and still warm, fill them according to the specific recipes in this chapter.

PANCAKES WITH MEAT

Clătite cu Carne

A meat grinder makes this recipe easier. If one is not available, buy lean ground beef, chop onion as fine as possible, then mix ingredients well.

1 recipe pancake batter[*]
3 tbsp. cooking oil
2 oz. onion, chopped
1 garlic clove, crushed
½ lb. lean beef, cut into small cubes
2 tbsp. water
2 eggs, beaten, each in a separate dish
2 tsp. salt
1 tsp. fresh ground black pepper
2 tbsp. sour cream

Makes 8-10 pancakes
Preparation time: 25 min. (not including the 30 min. standing time),
Cooking time: 45 min.

❑ Prepare the pancake batter and let stand while you start preparing the meat filling.

❑ Heat 1 tbsp. oil in a skillet over medium heat. Add onion and garlic and sauté, stirring until golden brown, about 3 min. Remove onion mixture and place it in a bowl. Keep skillet with its oil.

❑ Add the meat, stir, and let it cool for a few minutes. Pass meat mixture through the meat grinder using a fine or medium screen.

❑ In the skillet where the onion and garlic were browned, add another tbsp. oil, and heat over medium heat. Add 2 tbsps. water. When water begins to boil, add the ground meat, cover, and cook for 2 min. Stir, cover, and cook for another 2 min. Remove lid and continue to cook, stirring occasionally, for another 2-3 min., or until water has evaporated and meat is nicely browned. Remove meat, return to bowl, and let cool.

❑ When cool, add 1 beaten egg, salt, pepper, and sour cream. Mix well.

❑ Make the pancakes and keep them warm in the oven at low temperature as you finish them.

❑ Place 1-2 tbsps. meat in center of each pancake. Flip two sides over, then the other two.

---

[*] See ROMANIAN PANCAKES, p. 245.

❏ In a deep dish, mix one egg with 1 tsp. oil. Dip each pancake in the egg mixture to coat both sides.

❏ Heat 1 tbsp. oil in a skillet over medium heat, and brown the stuffed pancakes about 5-6 min. per side.

Serve alone, with sour cream, or with vegetables.

PANCAKES WITH CHEESE

Clătite cu Brânză

1 recipe pancake batter*
6 oz. farmers cheese
1 egg, slightly beaten
½ cup granulated sugar
rind of ½ lemon
1 tsp. vanilla extract
1 pinch salt
¼ cup raisins (optional)

> *Makes 8-10 pancakes*
> *Preparation time: 20 min. (not including the 30 min. standing time),*
> *Cooking time: 30 min.*

❑ Prepare the pancakes, and keep them warm in the oven at low temperature.

❑ Beat cheese well, either with a wooden spoon or electric mixer, until smooth. Add the rest of the ingredients except the raisins, and beat a minute or two more. Then, if you wish, add raisins and mix.

❑ Preheat oven to 300°F.

❑ Place one pancake at a time on flat surface. Center a tablespoon of the cheese mixture on each pancake. Flip two sides over, then third side and roll pancake around the cheese.

❑ Place the filled pancakes, one next to the other in an oven dish. Bake for 8-10 min.

Serve warm, sprinkled with sugar, with sour cream on each pancake.

---

* See ROMANIAN PANCAKES, p. 245, and use recipe for sweet pancakes.

PANCAKES WITH PRESERVES

Clătite cu Dulceață

1 recipe batter*
6 oz. strawberry, rasberry or other preserves or jam
Makes 8-10 pancakes
Preparation Time: 20 min. (not including the 30 min. standing time)
Cooking time: 20 min.

❑ Prepare the pancakes, and keep them warm in the oven at low temperature.
❑ Place a pancake at a time on a plate or work surface. Place about 2 tsps. of preserves or jam in the center. Flip two sides over, and then the other sides (or roll pancake over the preserve).
❑ Place the filled pancakes, one next to the other, in an oven dish; cover and warm in oven before serving. If you wish, you can sprinkle with granulated sugar.

---

* See ROMANIAN PANCAKES, p. 245.

MUJDEI AND OTHER SAUCES

COLD GARLIC SAUCE

Mujjdei de Usturoi

3 garlic cloves, peeled and crushed
2 tbsp. olive oil
¾ cup beef stock, hot
1 tsp. salt

Serves 4
Preparation time: 15 min. (plus cooling time)

❏ Place crushed garlic in a bowl.
❏ Add olive oil. Stir well. Add beef stock and salt. Stir, pass through sieve, press with wooden spoon to push garlic through; discard any that remains. Let cool.

Use this sauce in the recipe for CHARCOAL-GRILLED STEAK (see p. 140). The extra flavor is great on any barbecued meats, sausages, or fowl.

GARLIC SAUCE WITH SOUR CREAM

Sos de Usturoi cu Smântână

1 tbsp. butter
1 tbsp. flour
2 garlic cloves, crushed
½ tsp. salt
1 tbsp. fresh parsley, chopped
½ tsp. ground thyme
1 tsp. wine vinegar
¾ cup beef stock
1 tbsp. sour cream

Serves 4
Preparation time : 20 min., Cooking time: 20 min.

❑ In a small saucepan, heat butter over medium heat. When butter has melted, add flour, mix well with wooden spoon, and continue to stir for about 2 min. until flour turns brown, but doesn't burn.

❑ Add garlic, stir, then add salt, parsley, thyme, and vinegar. Stir again, and add bouillon. Lower heat to medium-low, and simmer for about 10 min.

❑ Mix 2-3 tablespoons sauce with sour cream in a small bowl. Add to liquid in saucepan. Simmer another 5 min. Serve in sauceboat.

This sauce is delicious served with roast lamb, or spooned over boiled potatoes, fish, or poached dishes.

HORSERADISH SAUCE

Sos de Hrean

1 horseradish root, peeled and grated
3 tbsp. water
1 tbsp. vinegar
1 tsp. salt
1 pinch granulated sugar

Serves 4
Preparation time: 10 min.

❑ In a non-reactive bowl, mix water and vinegar. Add salt and sugar, and stir to dissolve. Add grated horseradish to your taste.

❑ Keep well covered until ready to serve.

Serve cold with boiled meats or poultry.

HORSERADISH SAUCE WITH SOUR CREAM

Sos de Hrean cu Smântână

1 tbsp. butter
2 tsp. flour
1 horseradish root, peeled and grated
1 tsp. salt
1 pinch granulated sugar
4 tbsp. beef stock
½ cup sour cream

Serves 4
Preparation time: 10 min., Cooking time: 7 min.

❏ In a saucepan, heat butter over medium-high heat. Blend in flour with a wooden spoon. Let cool 2 min. Add horseradish to your taste, salt, and sugar. Stir, lower heat to medium-low. Add beef stock and sour cream. Stir and let simmer about 5 min. Taste, and if it is not strong enough, add a bit more horseradish, stir, and simmer another 2 min.

Serve warm immediately, with boiled meats.

DILL SAUCE WITH SOUR CREAM

Sos de Mărar cu Smântână

1 tbsp. butter
2 tsp. flour
¾ cup beef stock, cold
1 tsp. salt
2 tbsp. fresh dill, chopped
2 tbsp. sour cream
1 tsp. salt

Serves 4
Preparation time: 10 min., Cooking time: 10 min.

❑ In a saucepan, heat butter over medium-high heat. When melted, blend in flour little by little stirring continuously for about 2 min.

❑ Add beef stock, lower heat to medium-low. Add dill and salt, and let simmer about 5 min. Add sour cream, stir well, and cook another 5 min. stirring occasionally.

Serve hot with boiled meats or poultry.

MUSTARD SAUCE

Sos de Muştar

There are as many mustard sauce recipes in Romania as there are regions, and even within regions there are variations. This one is tasty, tangy, yet delicate.

2 tbsp. flour, sifted
1 cup beef stock, cold
2 tbsp. butter, melted
4 tbsp. sour cream
1 tbsp. white wine vinegar
1 tsp. salt
1 tbsp. French Dijon mustard
1 tsp. granulated sugar

Serves 4
Preparation time: 10 min., Cooking time: 10 min.

❑ In a bowl, mix cold beef stock with flour until flour is completely dissolved.

❑ In a saucepan, heat butter over medium heat. Add beef stock mixture, stirring with a wooden spoon. Add sour cream and mix well until sour cream is thoroughly blended into sauce. Then add vinegar and salt. Finally add mustard and sugar. Continue to cook over medium heat until sauce thickens, about 10 min.

Delicious served with rasols (boiled beef, chicken or tongue).

Special thanks to chef Nicolae Turean at the Hotel Împăratul Romanilor in Sibiu, who contributed this recipe for the book. See PORK LOIN AU GRATIN SIBIU STYLE, p. 148, for story.

SAUCE VINAIGRETTE

Sos Vinaigrette

1 tsp. fines herbes[*]
1 tsp. salt
½ tsp. fresh ground black pepper
1 tbsp. white wine vinegar
1 tsp. French Dijon mustard
3 tbsp. olive oil

Serves 4
Preparation time: 10 min.

❑ In a small cup or bowl, combine fines herbes, salt and pepper. Add vinegar and mustard. Mix well until mustard is dissolved. Add olive oil, mix well.

---

[*] parsley, chives, tarragon, chervil

TOMATO SAUCE

Sos de Roşii

2 tbsp. cooking oil
1 onion, peeled and chopped
3 tbsp. tomato paste
2 tsp. Vegeta[*]
2 tsp. flour
1 cup cold water
2 tsp. salt
1 tsp. fresh ground black pepper
½ cup dry white wine

> *Serves 4*
> *Preparation time: 25 min.*

❑ In a skillet, heat oil over medium-high heat. Add onion, and sauté until golden yellow, about 5 min.

❑ Add tomato paste and Vegeta, stir, and cook another 2 min.

❑ Add flour and stir well. Lower heat to medium-low.

❑ Add water little by little, stirring continually, until sauce begins to thicken. Add salt and pepper, and stir. Add wine, and continue to simmer another few minutes.

Serve hot over meatballs, patties, dumplings, or fritters.

---

* Vegeta is a brand of concentrated soup and stew flavor enhancer used in Romania. Several brands are available here, such as Delikat, Aromat by Knorr, and Vegeta from Croatia, imported by Jana Foods.

CAKES, DESSERTS AND COFFEES

CAKES AND DESSERTS

Cake recipes given in this chapter are limited to two festive cakes, Cozonac and Pască, which are served everywhere in Romania on holidays and for religious events. Dessert recipes include Baclava and Cataif, Turkish pastries very popular in Romania, and Lemon Soufflé and Hazelnut Cream.

Romanians love sweets, and Romania's gastronomy includes a great variety. However, most of the cakes and desserts are either Turkish, Austrian, or French. The list is endless, and is better left as the subject for another book.

ROMANIAN PANETONE

Cozonac

Here is a recipe for a yeast coffee cake that you will be happy to feature at any coffee party, enjoy for family breakfast, or celebrate Christmas with.

Similar traditional breads or cakes are baked in most European countries, such as the Norwegian Jule kuge, the Bohemian houska, the Austrian guge-hupf, the German stollen, and the Russian kulich. The cozonac is the Italian panetone of the Romanians.

Before starting preparation of this cake, you might refer to ROMANIAN PANETONE WITH CHEESE, p. 266. You can easily split the dough in two and prepare one round cake of Romanian panetone, and one of Romanian panetone with cheese.

5 tbsp. all purpose flour
1½ cups milk
2 oz. yeast*
½ cup milk
8 egg yolks, for the dough
1½ cups superfine sugar
8 oz. raisins
grated rind of 1 lemon
7 cups all purpose flour
8 oz. butter, melted
2 tbsp. dark rum
1 tsp. vanilla extract
2 tbsp. cooking oil
2 egg yolks, for glaze
2 tbsp. cold water
2 oz. walnuts, chopped (optional)
½ cup powder sugar (optional)

Makes enough for one 9 x 5 x 3 in. loaf pan, and one 9 in. round cake pan.
Preparation time: 1 hour, 45 min., not counting standing time., cooking time: 1 hour

❑ In a small bowl, put 5 tbsps. flour.

---

* Yeast—There are two kinds of yeast available, active dry and moist compressed. Compressed yeast is preferred. You can, however, substitute a package of active dry yeast.

❏ In a small kettle, heat ¾ cup milk to boiling. Stir it into the 5 tbsps. flour, and beat with wooden spoon until the mixture becomes a smooth paste without lumps. Let cool about 10 min.

❏ In the same kettle, heat another ¾ cup milk until it is just lukewarm. If it gets hot, let it cool down, as hot milk will kill yeast. In a small bowl, pour the lukewarm milk over the yeast. Crumble the yeast with a spoon, and stir until it is completely dissolved.

❏ Add the yeast mixture to the flour paste, and beat with a fork or wire whisk until large air bubbles appear. Cover the bowl with a cloth and keep near a source of warmth, such as a radiator or on the stove if other food is cooking. Allow the mixture to rise (at least 15 min.)

❏ In the same kettle, heat the rest of the milk until it is lukewarm. Do not overheat.

❏ Warm a large bowl to room temperature. Pour lukewarm milk into the bowl. While you start the dough, keep the bowl warm. Add, one by one, in this sequence: first the 8 egg yolks; stir with the wooden spoon; then the superfine sugar, and raisins, followed by lemon rind, the yeast mixture, and finally the rest of the flour. At first, continue to use the wooden spoon to stir, pushing the dough inward from the edges of the bowl. Then start kneading the dough with buttered hands.

❏ Keep kneading the dough energetically. From time to time, add a bit of melted butter. After kneading about 15-20 min., the dough will begin to detach itself from your hands and bowl. Use just enough butter to free the dough completely from your hands and form a moist, pliable ball. It will probably take about 6 oz. Save the rest.

❏ Wash your hands to remove the rest of any sticky dough. Then add the rum, vanilla, and oil. Continue to knead the dough for another 2-3 min. Cover the bowl with a cloth and, if possible, also a warm blanket or towel. Keep in a warm area for 2-3 hours. Yeast grows best at a temperature of 80°-85°F. Check after 2 hours. The dough should rise to double the original size.

❏ Punch the dough down with your fist, then, with your hands dipped in melted butter, knead the dough for another 5-10 min.

❏ Pre-heat the oven to 350°F.

❏ Keep your hands lubricated with butter and butter deep baking tins. It doesn't really matter what shape they are. Twist big pieces of the dough several times, and place in the baking pans so to fill them not more than one half of their height. Then cover the tins with a cloth and blanket. Keep in a warm place and let stand another 1-1½ hours. The dough will rise to the top of the pans.

❑ Mix the remaining egg yolks with 2 tbsps. cold water, and brush the top of the dough with a pastry brush. Sprinkle walnuts and a few raisins on the dough. Bake for one hour, or until a knife plunged through the middle of the cake comes out clean and dry.

❑ Remove cakes from the pans, cool on wire racks away from drafts. If you wish, while the cakes are still hot, you can sprinkle them with confectioners sugar or walnuts, or both.

ROMANIAN PANETONE WITH CHEESE

Pască

This is another very popular festive cake in Romania, and it often appears at the Easter table together with the cozonac (Romanian panetone). A good way of preparing this cake is to prepare a dough following the recipe shown for Romanian panetone, and then divide the dough in half, to bake one panetone and one panetone with cheese. Otherwise, make a dough with half the quantities given for the panetone.

1 lb. panetone dough*
1 tsp. butter

Ingredients for the cheese filling:
1 lb. farmers cheese
2 tbsp. butter, soft
¼ cup granulated sugar
3 egg yolks, slightly beaten
1 tbsp. flour
¼ tsp. vanilla extract
1 pinch salt
3 oz. raisins
1 egg yolk

> *Preparation time: 30 min., not counting time for preparation of dough, or standing time. Cooking time: 1 hour*
> *Preheat oven to 350°F.*

❏ Prepare a large, flat cake mold, with edges about 1½-2 in. high. Butter it well. Roll out dough to ¼ in. thickness. Line cake mold, saving a handful of dough.

❏ With the extra dough, form two long, pencil-thin ropes by rolling it between your palms. Twist the two ropes together, and use for border around the top edge of the dough.

❏ Cover cake mold with a damp kitchen towel and let sit an hour or so to allow dough to rise.

❏ While dough is rising, prepare cheese filling. Beat cheese well with wooden spoon or an electric mixer. Add all the ingredients except for the raisins. Beat another few minutes until batter is smooth. Add raisins and mix well.

* See ROMANIAN PANETONE, p. 263.

❑ When dough has risen, turn cheese filling over the dough, making sure it does not go over the edge.
❑ Baste cheese filling and dough border with the egg yolk. Place in oven for about one hour.

Remove cake from oven and cool on wire rack away from any draft. Remove from cake pan.

LEMON SOUFFLÉ

Sufleu de Lămâie

¼ lb. butter
6 eggs, yolks and whites separated
1/3 cup granulated sugar
4 tsp. lemon juice
1 pinch salt
1 tsp. grated lemon rind
1 tsp. vanilla extract

Serves 4
Preparation time: 20 min., Cooking time: 45 min.

❑ Preheat oven to 300°F.
❑ Melt butter, and skim off foam.
❑ Beat egg yolks with wire whip or fork. With a clean whip or fork, beat egg whites to a fluffy foam.
❑ Fill bottom of double-boiler, or substitute, with hot water. Heat to boil, then reduce to simmer over medium-low heat.
❑ Meanwhile, blend sugar and egg yolks well in top of double-boiler, and place over simmering water. Add butter slowly, little by little, stirring continually.
❑ Continue stirring while adding lemon juice, salt, and lemon rind. When all is well blended and begins to thicken, about 10 min., remove from heat and let cool.
❑ When mixture is cool, fold in egg whites, add vanilla extract, and stir well.
❑ Pour mixture into a buttered oven dish or individual custard cups. Place in an oven pan containing about 1 inch of hot water. Bake 10 min. Increase temperature to 350°F and continue baking another 30 min., or until soufflé is a nice golden brown. Baking time depends on containers and oven.

Serve hot.

HAZELNUT CREAM

Cremă de Alune

2 tbsp. butter
2 tbsp. cocoa powder (unsweetened)
2 tbsp. superfine granulated sugar
4 drops vanilla extract
½ cup milk
3 egg yolks
¼ cup finely ground hazelnuts
1 tbsp. butter
¼ cup bread crumbs
whipped cream

Serves 4
Preparation time: 10 min., Cooking time: 15 min.

❏ Heat water in bottom of double-boiler over high heat. In the top of the double-boiler, mix 2 tbsps. butter with cocoa powder and sugar. Add milk and vanilla extract, and stir with wooden spoon until mixture begins to thicken, about 10 min.

❏ Beat egg yolks with wire whip into a froth. Blend into thickened mixture and continue to heat in double-boiler, stirring continually, until it thickens and has a creamy texture, about 5-6 min. Add hazelnuts, and mix well.

❏ Heat 1 tbsp. butter in a small saucepan over medium heat. Add bread crumbs and brown them, stirring to avoid burning, about 3 min.

❏ Put a thin layer of bread crumbs on bottom of dessert cups, and add hazelnut cream. Cover with whipped cream, and serve cold.

BAKLAVA

Baclava

Baklava, the King of the Middle Eastern desserts, has its origins in the Byzantine Empire during the first millennium after Christ. It is equally popular in the Arab lands as in Turkey, Greece, and Romania.

It is a crisp, light and delicately flavored pastry, made of buttery phyllo pastry sheets, chopped nuts, and sticky honey and sugar syrup. Originally, baklava was made with 40 layers of pastry, symbolizing the 40 days of Lent, and it was always part of the Easter dinner menu. You can make it with any number of layers, 12 being common in Romania.

For quantities given, use a 7 x 12 in. baking dish.

Baklava:

½ lb. butter
12 or 16 oz. package frozen phyllo pastry dough*
3 cups chopped walnuts**
¼ cup rum (optional)

Serves 8
Preparation time: 30 min., Cooking time: 1 hour

❏ Preheat oven to 350°F.
❏ Prepare syrup as below.
❏ Melt butter, and skim off foam.
❏ Butter baking dish, then gently lay one sheet of dough on the bottom. Brush with melted butter. Add, one by one, 3 more sheets, brushing each one with butter. Spread a cup of the chopped nuts evenly on top sheet.
❏ Add 2 more sheets of dough, buttering each, then spread another cup of nuts on top.
❏ Repeat procedure with another 2 buttered sheets and the remaining nuts.
❏ Cover with another 4 sheets of dough, each brushed with melted butter, using a generous amount on the last sheet.
❏ With a sharp, serrated and pointed knife, cut through pastry lengthwise into

---

* Phyllo pastry dough is time consuming to prepare, but it is sold frozen in supermarkets, fancy food grocers, or ethnic delis. It is sometimes called fillo, or strudel dough. In Romanian the phillo pastry sheets are called Foi de Plăcintă.

** Baklava is made with walnuts, walnuts and almonds, or walnuts and pistachios. Use whatever combination you like best.

3 equal strips. Then cut across width into 4 equal strips. If you wish, you can then cut each rectangle into two diagonally, making 24 triangles.

❑ Spoon remaining butter along the cut lines to prevent pieces from sticking together when baked.

❑ Bake in oven for 40 min. Pour rum over hot pastry, and then slowly pour sugar and honey syrup over it. Bake another 10-15 min., or until baklava turns a nice golden brown.

❑ Remove from oven. Cover with a clean towel, and keep in cool place, but not in the refrigerator, as the sugar will crystallize.

Before serving, baste baklava with its syrup. Serve 2-3 triangles per person, cold, with Turkish coffee.

Syrup:
   2 cups water
   ¾ cup granulated sugar
   3 tbsp. honey
   1 tbsp. lemon juice
   ½ lemon, rind
   2 tbsp. rose water (optional)

❑ In a heavy, non-reactive, saucepan mix water, sugar, honey, lemon juice, and lemon rind. Heat over medium-high heat. Bring to a boil. Boil, uncovered, for 8-10 min., or until syrup is thick enough to stick to the surface of a spoon. Add rose water, remove from heat, and let cool.

SHREDDED PASTRY WITH NUTS
Cataif

This delicious, crunchy pastry is popular in all of the Near and Middle East. It is also popular in Romania, where it was introduced during the centuries of Turkish Ottoman domination.

In Turkey, where *kadayif* is a generic word for a variety of pastries not made of phyllo dough, this recipe is called Tel Kadayif, tel meaning hair, angel hair, or wire. In Greek it is called Kataifi.

For quantities given, use a 7 x 12 in. baking dish.

<u>Pastry:</u>
½ lb. butter
16 oz. package frozen tel kadayif dough*
2 cups chopped walnuts**

Serves 8-10
Preparation time: 30 min., Cooking time: 45 min.

❑ Preheat oven to 350°F.
❑ Prepare syrup as below.
❑ Melt butter, and skim foam from top.
❑ Butter a baking sheet. Separate shredded dough using a fork, and remove any thick chunks. Using the fork, spread half of the dough over the bottom of the baking dish. Try to work fast as this dough tends to dry very quickly and crumble.
❑ Cover surface with walnuts. Spread the other half of the dough on top. Pour melted butter over the whole pastry.
❑ Bake in oven about 40-45 min., or until pastry turns a nice golden brown.
❑ Remove from oven. Drain off excess butter, and pour hot syrup over pastry. Cover with a clean towel, and keep in cool place, but do not refrigerate, as the sugar will crystalize.
❑ When ready to serve, cut into serving portions, and baste with syrup. Some like it with whipped cream.

---

* Tel Kadayif dough is time consuming and difficult to prepare, but it can be found frozen in Greek ethnic delis (where it is called Kataifi dough), as well as in Turkish, and Middle Eastern ethnic delis.

** Cataif can be prepared without any nuts, with walnuts, or with pistachios.

Syrup:
2 cups water
1 cup granulated sugar
3 tbsp. honey
1 tbsp. lemon juice
1 tsp. vanilla extract

❏ In a heavy, non-reactive, saucepan, mix water, sugar, honey, and lemon juice. Heat over medium-high heat. Bring to a boil. Boil, uncovered, for 8-10 min., or until syrup is thick enough to stick to the surface of a spoon. Add vanilla extract, remove from heat, and keep hot.

COFFEE

Cafea

*T*hese days, it is hard to believe that Romania was once a coffee-drinking country, where in the larger cities there were more coffee and pastry houses than in almost any other European city, and where a variety of excellent brews were available. Today it is difficult to find a decent cup of coffee anywhere, and imported coffee is very expensive. Hopefully all this will change soon.

The traditional coffee in Romania is Turkish. It is not hard to make, and if you cook a Romanian meal for your family or guests, it would be fitting to finish it with a steaming, creamy Cafea Turcească, or just O Turcească, as the Romanians say.

The recipes for this coffee, as well as for two other popular Romanian coffee drinks, follow.

TURKISH COFFEE

Cafea Turcească

To make a good Turkish coffee, you need two items. The best coffee bean to use is the mocha bean. This coffee, named after the ancient Yemeni port of Moka on the Red Sea, will give a creamy brew with a fragrance typical of Turkish coffee. If you cannot find an unblended mocha, buy continental or espresso roast, and have it ground very fine for Turkish coffee. The next item is a brass or copper pot with a long narrow handle, commonly referred to as an ibrik*. You can usually find one in gourmet grocery stores, specialty kitchenware shops, or ethnic Turkish, Greek, or Middle Eastern delis, and it is not expensive.

The coffee is served in small Turkish coffee cups. If you don't have any, use demitasse cups and fill them halfway.

2 Turkish coffee cups cold water
2 lumps sugar
2 heaping tsp. coffee

Serves 2
Preparation time: 2 min., Cooking time: 10 min.

❑ Put water, sugar, and coffee in the ibrik. Don't stir. Place on medium-high heat. As soon as the water starts to boil, stir coffee with a long-handled spoon. Coffee will soon begin to rise to the brim of the pot, and a light-colored froth, called caimac in Romanian, will form on the surface. Remove pot from heat, quickly skim off froth, and distribute in the two Turkish coffee cups.

❑ Place ibrik back on heat, and boil until coffee again rises to the brim. Remove from heat, skim off froth. Repeat three times.

❑ Immediately after the last rise, dribble a few drops of cold water into the pot. The cold water will precipitate the grounds to the bottom.

❑ Divide the coffee between the cups. You should have two cups of creamy, fragrant coffee, with a coating of froth on top. Wait a couple of minutes to let the grounds to settle, and then enjoy it.

---

* The word ibrik, written *ibric* in Romanian, is actually a misnomer. The Turkish word ibrik means teapot, and derives from the Arabic name for the copper or brass pot with a lid and long curved spout used to prepare both Arabic coffee and tea. The pot for Turkish coffee is quite different, and is called Jezve in Turkish.

** Use an extra lump of sugar per cup for those who like their coffee very sweet.

COFFEE MAZAGRAN

Cafea Mazagran

This is a cool, refreshing coffee drink, enjoyed during hot summer evenings at garden and terrace coffee houses. It was named after General Mazagran who apparently first concocted it during the Crimean War in the 1850s.

Prepare coffee ahead of time or the day before serving.

8 cups of French Roast coffee
2 tbsp. chickory
sugar to taste
¼ cup rum
whipped cream

> *Serves 8*
> *Preparation time: 2 min., Cooking time: 10 min.*

❑ Brew a pot of coffee using the French Roast coffee mixed with the chickory. Let cool and place in a bottle in the refrigerator.

❑ When ready to serve, pour cold, black coffee into tall glasses filled with crushed ice. Add sugar to taste, and a bit of rum into each glass. Stir well, and spoon whipped cream on top.

Serve with a straw.

COFFEE FRAPPÉ

Cafe Frape

This is a popular refreshing summer coffee drink. Prepare in advance or the day before.

8 cups of French roast coffee
2 tbsp. chicory
sugar to taste
¼ cup rum
8 scoops vanilla ice cream
whipped cream

Serves 8
Preparation time: 5 min., Cooking time: 10 min.

❏ Brew a pot of coffee using the French roast coffee mixed with the chicory. Let cool and place in a bottle in the refrigerator.
❏ For each serving, in a shake mixer or blender, process one cup of cold coffee, sugar to taste, a little rum, and one scoop of ice cream. Pour into glass filled with cracked ice, and spoon whipped cream on top.

Serve with a straw.

PRESERVES AND FONDANTS

PRESERVES

Dulceaţă

Preparing homemade preserves is very popular in Romania, where home-makers take pride in the excellence and great variety of their creations. Not only are preserves here made from the usual fruits, such as strawberries, raspberries, cherries, apricots, and peaches, but also from rose petals, walnuts, and hazelnuts.

In Romania, it is traditional to welcome guests with a spoonful of homemade preserves and a glass of ice cold water. Sometimes, a cup of sweet, hot, Turkish coffee is also served, to be sipped after the preserves. In the old days, during the intense heat of the Romanian summer days, street vendors offered pre-serves and ice water to thirsty passers-by.

Preparation. The traditional methods of making preserves were handed down from generation to generation, from mother to daughter. Most of the recipes in older Romanian cookbooks have two disadvantages: they use huge quantities of sugar, which is incompatible with today's lifestyle, and the methods described to test for the jelling point, that is the exact point at which the fruit pectin and sugar in the syrup jell, are not accurate.

For each of the preserves included in this chapter, two recipes are given, a traditional Romanian one for those of you who are experienced and don't mind the extra sugar, and another based on a method described by Madelaine Bullwinkel*, which uses about one-third of the sugar and depends less on experience.

Minimum equipment recommended for preserving

1. Jelly jars, 8 or 12oz, with vacuum-seal lids and screw-cap covers.
2. Large, deep pot for sterilizing jars, fitted with a round cake-cooling rack.
3. Heavy, non-reactive 4 to 5 qt. jam pot for preserving. It should be deeper than it is wide, and should preferably not be wider at the base than the burner on which it will heat, in order to distribute the heat evenly.
4. Conical sieve lined with cheesecloth for straining the fruit juice.
5. Sturdy, easy-to-read candy/jelly thermometer, or an instant meat/yeast thermometer.
6. Skimmer.
7. Jar lifter is handy for removing and draining the hot jars after the sterilizing water bath.

---

* Bullwinkel, Madelaine. *Gourmet Preserves Chez Madelaine.*

Final notes. In order to make preserves from other fruits, consider that fruits vary in hardiness, amount of juice, and amount of pectin. Therefore, consult a resource on making preserves about the amount of sugar, addition of other ingredients, and the length of cooking time. Don't get discouraged if you do not have a perfect product the first time. Keep trying. It's worth the effort. Homemade preserves are fun and much more flavorful than commercially produced products. Next time you have guests, surprise them with a Romanian token of hospitality.

Sterilizing equipment. Remember to work under clean conditions. In addition to washing jars, lids and jar caps, you must also sterilze them in boiling water. Use a large kettle with a rack or towel on the bottom to prevent the glasses from breaking. Just before you are ready to fill the jars, lift them out with a jar lifter or tongs and drain them. They will dry quickly because they are so hot. Check the jars for damage or chips before you fill them because the lids will not seal unless the rims are smooth. For the same reason, you must wipe any dribbled jelly off the rims before you place the lids.

RASPBERRY PRESERVES

Dulceaţă de Zmeură

<u>Traditional Method</u>

2 lbs. ripe raspberries
1 pt. water
4 cups granulated sugar
1 lemon, peeled and cut in half

Makes about five 8oz jars
Preparation time: 10 min., Cooking time: 60 min.

❑ Wash raspberries gently in a colander. Remove stems or other debris.

❑ In a jam pot*, add water. Stir in sugar. Mix well. Heat over medium-low heat until sugar is completely dissolved.

❑ Increase heat to medium-high. Cook until syrup begins to thicken. When it reaches this stage, it is very important to immediately start testing for the soft ball stage. The next few steps should be followed quickly, so the sugar does not crystalize and stick to the bottom of the pot.

❑ There are two methods to test for the soft ball stage:

  1. From a spoon dribble into a small cup of very cold water two or three drops of the boiling syrup. If they don't dissolve immediately and adhere in a lump that you can move around with the spoon or your finger, go to the next step. If they dissolve, continue to cook and test again in fresh cold water.

  2. Or, dribble a few drops of boiling syrup onto a chilled plate. The drops should form mounds that don't run.

❑ Add raspberries and continue cooking for 1-2 min. Remove pot from heat and let stand about 10-15 min. This will allow the raspberries to release their juice into the syrup.

❑ Return pot to high heat, add lemon, and allow syrup to boil again. Skim scum from the surface. Test for jell using the same methods as described above. Drops should congeal into firm balls.

❑ When test indicates that preserve will jell, remove from heat. Let cool 5-10 min. Then fill clean, sterilized jam jars to within 1/8 in. of the rim. Wipe rims with damp cloth to make sure they are clean. Put the lids on, and screw caps

---

* ee PRESERVES, p. 280 for a more detailed discussion on preparation of preserves , including recommended equipment.

tight. Turn jars upside down briefly to create a vacuum, and let cool on a wire rack.

<u>Modern method:</u>

2 lbs. ripe raspberries
2 cups granulated sugar
1 tbsp. fresh lemon juice

Makes about five 8 oz. jars
Preparation time: 5 min., Cooking time: 1 hour 45 min.

❑ Preheat oven to 300°F.

❑ Rinse raspberries. Place in a Pyrex or other non-reactive casserole, and bake in oven for about 45-60 min. Remove from oven when berries are floating in their juice, but still retain their shape and texture.

❑ Carefully strain juice through a colander. Place berries in a conical sieve lined with cheesecloth over a bowl, and let them sit about 15 minutes to drain off remaining juice. Set raspberries aside.

❑ Measure the total quantity of juice extracted from the berries. You should have approximately 1½ cups. Use the same quantity of sugar to prepare the syrup.

❑ Heat raspberry juice in a jam pot* over medium-highh heat. Stir in sugar, ½ cup at a time, allowing syrup to return to boiling point each time. Continue cooking until the jell point, which is 8 degrees above the boiling temperature. Work quickly, as this happens in about 5 min.

❑ Remove from heat, and skim foam off surface. Gently stir in raspberries to avoid crushing them, and let them steep in the jelly for 15 min.

❑ Return preserves to a boil, then stir in another ½ cup sugar and lemon juice. Cook preserves, watching thermometer carefully. It should rise to 216°F in about 5 min. Stir preserves frequently, and partly cover pot if it starts to spatter. After the the temperature begins to fall in about 5 min., take pot off the heat. Do not cook longer than 10 min.

❑ Skim surface again and fill hot, sterilized jars to within 1/8 in. of rims. Wipe the rims clean, attach lids, and screw caps on tightly. Invert jars briefly for a quick vacuum seal, and let cool on a wire rack.

---

* See PRESERVES, p. 280 for a more detailed discussion on preparation of preserves, including recommended equipment.

PLUM PRESERVES

Dulceață de Prune

Traditional method:
2 lbs. ripe, but not soft, plums
10 walnuts, shelled
1 pt. water
4 cups granulated sugar
1 lemon, juice

Makes about five 8 oz jars
Preparation time: 10 min., Cooking time: 60 min.

❏ Blanch plums in boiling water for 30 seconds. Drain, dip in cold water, peel skins off and remove pits. Let plums stand in cold water for 15 min.

❏ Break walnut meat into 4 quarters. Stuff each plum with a piece of walnut.

❏ In a jam pot*, stir sugar into water. Heat over medium-low heat until sugar is completely dissolved.

❏ Increase heat to medium-high. Cook until syrup begins to thicken. When it reaches this stage, it is very important to immediately start testing for what is referred to as the soft ball stage. The next few steps should be followed quickly so the sugar does not crystalize and stick to the bottom of the pot. See page 282 for methods of testing for the soft ball stage.

❏ When syrup has reached the soft ball stage, remove from heat, add plums, cover, and let steep for 15 min.

❏ Return pot to hot heat, add lemon juice, and allow syrup to boil again. Skim scum from the surface. Test for jell using the same methods as described above. Drops should congeal into firm mounds.

❏ When test indicates that preserve will jell, remove from heat. Let cool 5-10 min. Then fill clean, sterilized jam jars to within 1/8 in. of the rim. Wipe rims with damp cloth to make sure they are clean. Put the lids on, and screw caps tight. Turn jars upside down briefly to create a vacuum, and let cool on a wire rack.

---

* see PRESERVES, p. 280 for a more detailed discussion on preparation of preserves, including recommended equipment.

Modern method:

3 lbs. ripe, but not soft, plums
1 cup water
2½ cups sugar
½ cup walnut meats, coarsely broken up
1½ tbsp. fresh lemon juice
1 tsp. vanilla extract

Makes about six 8 oz. jars
Preparation time: 5 min., Cooking time: 1 hour, 45 min.

❑ Blanch plums in boiling water for about 30 sec. Drain, pass under cold water, quarter, and remove pits. Let stand in bowl filled with cold water for 15 min.

❑ In a jam pot* mix plums with water. Bring to boil over medium-high heat. Reduce heat to medium-low, cover, and simmer for 20 min.

❑ While plums are cooking, sterilize jars and caps in large kettle for 15 min. Leave jars in water until needed.

❑ Remove plums from heat, strain juices through conical strainer lined with cheesecloth, and set aside for 15 min. to drain off remaining juice. Measure total quantity of juice and use an equal amount of sugar. You should have 1½ cups, or a little more, juice. Set plums aside.

❑ Return juice to jam pot and bring to boil over medium-high heat. Add 1 tsp. lemon juice. Then stir in sugar, ½ cup at a time, waiting for juice to return to boil each time. Boil 5-10 min., watching thermometer. Syrup will reach jell point 8° above boiling point.

❑ Remove from heat, add plums and nuts, cover, and let steep for 15 min.

❑ Return preserves to medium-high heat, add ½ tbsp. lemon juice and vanilla extract, stir, and bring to a boil. Cook preserves , watching thermometer carefully. It will rise to 215°F in about 10 min. Stir preserves frequently, and partially cover pot if it starts to spatter. When the temperature begins to fall after the first 5 min., take pot off heat. Do not cook longer than 10 min.

❑ Skim surface and ladle preserves into hot, sterilized jars to within 1/8 in. of rims. Wipe the rims clean, attach lids, and screw caps on tightly. Invert jars briefly for a quick vacuum seal, and let cool on a wire rack.

---

* see PRESSERVES, p. 280 for a more detailed discussion on preparation of preserves, including recommended equipment.

SOUR CABBAGE IN A BARREL

Varză Acră în Butoi

You can make sour cabbage for sauerkraut or for use in stuffed cabbage.

heads of cabbage
1 qt. water
¼ cup coarse salt or sea salt for each 10 lbs. cabbage
2 cups fresh uncooked corn kernels
1 bunch dill

To make sour cabbage:

❑ Remove all loose outer green leaves from cabbages so heads are tight balls. With a sharp knife, remove hard cores, leaving clean conical holes through the middle of each head of cabbage.

❑ Prepare a brine solution of water and salt.

❑ Use a barrel large enough to hold the cabbage you want to prepare with a little extra space on top. The traditional barrels are made of oak, but you can use any non-reactive material such as glass or plastic. Fill barrel with cabbage.

❑ Add corn kernels and dill, pour brine solution over cabbage, press cabbage down with a flat piece of wood, preferably oak, and weight down with a clean stone or rock on top. Leave barrel open. Fermentation will start immediately, and by the next day, cabbage juices and the brine solution should begin to fill the barrel. Add enough water to cover cabbage. Let stand, open to atmosphere, in a cool place. Temperature should be 60°-70°F. Sour cabbage will be ready in about 3 weeks. However, most Romanians make it in autumn and let it ferment about 2 months for use in Christmas cooking.

To make sauerkraut:

❑ Use the same method as above, but shred cabbage and then place shredded cabbage in barrel. When done, fill sterile preserving jars with sauerkraut and half-fill each jar with the sauerkraut juice. Seal.

FONDANTS

Şerbeturi

Just as a teaspoon of homemade preserves is served with a glass of ice cold water to greet and welcome guests, so may homemade fondant, şerbet (sher-bét), be offered. By custom, a teaspoon of fondant is placed in a glass of ice-cold water. The guest takes it out of the water, eats it, and then drinks the water as a "chaser."

These fondants, of Arabic origin, are sweet, velvety, and butter-like. They are made from a syrup of sugar and clear juice, similar to the way jellies are made. Once the syrup reaches its jell point, or syrup is sufficiently thick, it is removed from heat, and stirred continually in one direction until it thickens, becomes butter-like, and changes color. It is then placed in canning jars. In Romania, şerbets are made with a variety of fruit, as well as with coffee, chocolate, rose petals, or hazelnuts.

RASPBERRY FONDANT

Şerbet de Zmeură

3 lbs. ripe raspberries
2½ cups granulated sugar
4 tbsp. lemon juice

Makes about three 8oz jars
Preparation time: 30 min., Cooking time: 40 min.

❏ Preheat oven to 300°F.

❏ Wash raspberries gently in a colander. Remove stems and debris. Place in a Pyrex or other non-reactive casserole, and bake in oven for about 40 min. Remove from oven.

❏ Strain juice and raspberries in a conical sieve over a bowl. Press raspberries against the sides of the sieve with a wooden spoon to squeeze out as much juice as possible. Let drain for 15 min. Discard solids.

❏ Pass juice again through the conical sieve, now lined with cheesecloth. Let drain 15 min.

❏ Measure the total quantity of juice extracted. You should have approximately 2-2½ cups. Use the same quantity of sugar.

❏ Heat raspberry juice in a jam pot over medium heat. Stir in ½ cup sugar until dissolved. Continue adding ½ cup sugar at a time, stirring until it dissolves before adding more, until all sugar is used up. Add 2 tbsps lemon juice, Increase heat to medium-high. Boil until thermometer reaches 8° above boiling temperature. *

❏ Remove from heat, and skim off foam on surface. Stir in another ½ cup sugar and 1 tbsp. lemon juice.

❏ Return syrup to a boil. Cook another 5-10 min. until temperature reaches about 22° above boiling on a calibrated thermometer. Temperature will stay steady or start dropping. But, cook no more than 10 min.

❏ Skim surface again. Pour hot syrup into a bowl, cover with a damp cloth, and let cool slightly until you can touch the syrup, about 15 min.

❏ Anchor the bowl well. Traditionally, Romanians turn a stool upside down and wedge the bowl between the legs of the stool. Or, you can sit down and squeeze the bowl between your legs. Stir with a melesteu or handle of a

---

* see PRESERVES , p. 280 for a more detailed discussion on preparation of preserves , including recommended equipment. It applies equally to the making of sherbets.

wooden spoon, in one direction only, until color of syrup lightens and syrup starts to thicken. Then add another tbsp. of lemon juice, and continue stirring until syrup becomes velvety and butter-like in consistency.

❑ You may also use an electric mixer, the first few minutes at a very low speed, then at a speed you would use for beating fudge.

❑ Fill hot, sterilized, dry canning jars. Wipe rims clean, attach lids, and screw caps on tightly. Let cool and store in a cool place.

COFFEE FONDANT

Şerbet de Cafea

1 cup water
2½ cups granulated sugar
3 tbsp. lemon juice
1 cup strong brewed French roast coffee

Makes about three 8oz jars
Preparation time: 30 min., Cooking time: 15 min.

❏ Heat water in a jam pot* over medium heat. Stir in ½ cup sugar until dissolved. Continue adding ½ cup sugar at a time, waiting until it dissolves before stirring in the next, until 2 cups sugar is used. Add 1 tbsp. lemon juice and coffee. Increase heat to medium-high. Boil until temperature reaches 8° above boiling point on your calibrated thermometer.

❏ Remove from heat. Stir in the rest of the sugar and 1 tbsp. lemon juice.

❏ Return syrup to a boil. Cook another 5-10 min. until temperature reaches about 22° above boiling and stays steady or starts dropping, but cook no more than 10 min.

❏ Pour hot syrup into a bowl, cover with a damp cloth, and let cool slightly until you can touch it.

❏ Anchor the bowl well. Traditionally, Romanians turn a stool upside down and wedge the bowl between the legs of the stool. Or, you can sit down and squeeze the bowl between your legs. Stir syrup in one direction with a melesteu or handle of a wooden spoon until syrup starts to lighten and thicken. Then add another tbsp. of lemon juice, and continue stirring until syrup becomes velvety and butter-like in consistency.

❏ You may use an electric mixer, first at a very low speed, then at a speed you would use for beating fudge.

❏ Fill hot, sterilized, dry canning jars. Wipe rims clean, attach lids, and screw caps on tightly. Let cool and store in a cool place.

---

* see PRESERVES, p. 280 for a more detailed discussion on preparation of preserves, including recommended equipment. It applies equally to the making of sherbets.

TRADITIONAL MENUS

TRADITIONAL ROMANIAN MENUS

BREAKFAST

The Romanian breakfast is very similar to the Dutch "Coffee Table." It usually consists of a variety of breads and rolls, and a selection cheeses, ham or salami, hard-boiled eggs, sausages, jams and marmalade, tea or coffee.

LUNCH

In the days when the family had time to come home for lunch, it was the main meal of the day, and consisted either of the basic ciorbă and mămăligă, or of an elaborate 5 or 6 course meal for the more affluent, followed by a siesta.

IN-BETWEEN

In cities, a great deal of snacking takes place after work hours. Pastry shops, outdoor and indoor cafés, snack places, and street vendors are busy with passers-by enjoying appetizers with șpriț (white wine mixed with ice-cold soda), ice cream, or pastries with Turkish coffee, beer, or a țuică.

DINNER

Dinner is eaten late, usually after 8PM.

FESTIVE MEALS

Whether rich or poor, on Christmas, St. Basil's (New Year's), and Easter Sunday, every household sits down to a more elaborate dinner of special dishes which are traditional to the particular religious holiday.

CHRISTMAS AND NEW YEAR'S

Romanian winters are cold, the wind often howls across the land, the snow is deep, and windows are etched with intricate ice crystals in kaleidoscopic star-like patterns. The celebration of the Lord's birth is an important event. Homemakers are busy preparing for the Christmas dinner. It is the tradition that each household slaughters a suckling pig. The *pig's cadge* is an old ceremony, starting with the slaughter of the animal, butchering it, and then inviting those who took part in the ritual to partake of the roast, and toast with a glass of wine or țuică. Every part of the pig is used for roasts, stews, sausage, pig's trotters, hams, ribs, bacon, and, of course, those wonderful sarmale, the stuffed cabbage or grape leaves. This is also the time when breads and cakes are baked for dessert and for the children who come caroling, to wish them, according to custom, abundance and health.

At Christmas, children of all ages go caroling in groups of three or four. Each group, by tradition, carries a wooden star, representing the Star of Bethlehem, decorated with colored paper, pictures of the Nativity and bells, mounted on a post. They dress up in fur caps, national holiday costumes, sheepskin jackets and boots. Sometimes they wear masks representing the Three Wise Men. They go from door to door, reciting poems and singing carols, while the leader shakes the star so that the bells ring. The children usually are given some coins or fresh baked cakes and invited to join the families who, after a copious meal, are sitting around a fire. This is the time when parents and grandparents entertain the youngsters with folktales or fables that have been passed on from generation to generation.

A Christmas Dinner Menu

Pork and Rice Sausages
Stuffed Cabbage with Polenta
Roast Pork
Romanian Panetone

New Year's is the celebration of the future, a time of prayer and hope for a bountiful harvest and successful year to come. In the villages around the country, children prepare for a late night house-to-house visit. Groups traditionally make a small decorated replica, plugușor, of the big wooden buffalo-drawn plows of the Romanian farmers, and drag it through the snow with a buffalo made from a small barrel, buhai. One end is open and the other covered by a stretched sheepskin. A few strands of horse hair are pulled through a hole in the center of the skin and when they are tugged, this strange and ancient instrument emits a hair-raising sound, reminiscent of a buffalo's bellow. Another group member carries a whip, which he snaps hard in the air, imitating the farmer urging the buffalo on. All this commotion is usually greeted with a sense of humor, but sometimes an irate family trying to sleep will throw stones after the kids.

The New-Year's dinner often includes rabbit or goose. However, in certain regions of Romania, natives insist that New Year's dinner must include pork because the pig charges forward, and under no circumstances should poultry be part of the feast because when birds dig in the earth, they kick it backwards.

293

Carolers by Leo Glueckselig.

EASTER

Easter is the celebration of Christ's resurrection. After the body has been purified by 40 days of fast, everyone prepares for an Easter Sunday feast. Passers-by, friends, and family greet each other with "Christ has risen," to which the reply is "It is true that He has risen...."

Easter eggs, hard-boiled, and either elaborately handpainted with floral or national motives, or just tinted red, are "knocked." Everyone around the table knocks an egg with that of the next person, and the winner is the one whose egg does not break after all the others are cracked. Then, the eggs are peeled, dipped into salt, and eaten. The main portion of the Easter meal is spring lamb. As is the case with pork at Christmas, all parts of the lamb are made into roasts, stews, haggis, and ciorbă (see DICTIONARY, p 23).

An Easter Dinner Menu

Easter Eggs
Lamb Ciorbă
Romanian Haggis
Braised Lamb with Polenta
Romanian Panetone with Cheese

ROMANIA'S WINES

*J*ust as the Romanians' history goes back some 4000 years[*], so do their wines. The cultivation of the vine in this region started earlier than in most of Western Europe. The abundance and fame of the Dacian[*] wines has been recognized for hundreds of years. To discourage migratory peoples' incursions, one of the drastic steps Dacian king Burebista[*] took was to order all the vineyards destroyed. Some, however, survived, and soon many were replanted. When Dacia[*] was a province of the Roman Empire, coins had a representation of a woman to whom two children were offering grain sheaves and grapes, symbolic of the province's wealth. Over the centuries the wines of Dacia have been popular in the duchies of Venice, Genoa, and later in the Vatican.

Peter the Great, Tzar of Russia, was profoundly impressed by the fine wines of Cotnari, which he drank in Iaşi during an official visit to the Moldavian capital in 1711. These wines have been known since the middle ages as "Pearl of Moldavia" or "Flower of Moldavia."

A hundred years later, Napoleon I appreciated the quality of those same wines during the campaign against Russia in 1812, when he received from the Moldavian horsemen many "big round bottles with narrow necks," as he passed through Poland at the head of the French armies.

Unfortunately, in 1884 an invasion of the grape phylloxera, a North American insect which nearly destroyed the French wine industry in the 1860s, damaged much of the Romanian vine production. Only after great effort and grafting to more resistant vines were the major Romanian vineyards restored.

Many gold medals and grand prix have been won by Romanian vineyards in recent decades. Romania came in third for white wines and second for red wines at the prestigious Wine America '93 International Wine Competition, March 7-9, 1993, at the New York Hilton. If you have not yet experienced Romanian wines, do give them a try. They compare favorably with French, Italian, German, Spanish, Australian and other wines, and prices are still reasonable.

Getting to know Romanian wines.

The vineyards by province and the grape varieties they produce are listed below:

---

[*] see the chapter THE HERITAGE OF ROMANIA AND ITS PEOPLE

Moldavia

The Cotnari vineyards, north of Iaşi, are still producing some of the finest wines today from native grape varieties known as Cotnari (Vitis Vinifera), Grasă, Fetească de Cotnari, Tămâioasa Românească, and Frâncuşa. Cotnari wine was awarded the Merit Diploma at the international exhibitions in Vienna (1873) and in Budapest (1889), and the Grand Prix at the Universal Exhibition in Paris (1889).

There are many other vineyards in Moldavia, including Nicoreşti, Odobeşti, Huşi, Bucium, Copou, and Panciu, which produce excellent varieties such as the Fetească albă, Aligote, Riesling, Muscat Ottonel, Busuioacă de Bohotin, Zghihara, Băbească neagră, and the famous mild white wine labeled Galbenă de Odobeşti.

Transylvania

Archeological discoveries in Transylvania testify to centuries of intense vine-growing activity. There are references to famous vineyards in the northern Carpathian area in writings of Herodotus, Plutarch, Xenophon, and Plato. And, it is known that in the 12th century this area supplied wines for the Republic of Venice, which were held in such high esteem that they were exempted from ceiling prices imposed on other foreign wines.

Nowhere else are better flavored and refined wines produced than in Transylvania. Located in charming regions with picturesque landscapes, vineyards such as Târnave, Jidvei, Crăciunel, Apoldu, Alba Iulia, Lechinţa, Dumitra, Băgaciu and Şimeu Silvaniei, produce a great variety of grapes, such as Traminer, Fetească de Târnave, Fetească regală, Furmint, Sauvignon, Muscat Ottonel, Italian Riesling, Pinot gris, and Neuburger.

Wallachia (Oltenia and Muntenia)

The Wallachia region on the slopes of the sub-Carpathians northeast of Bucharest is Dealul Mare (Big Hill), and includes a number of well-known vineyards such as Valea Călugărească, Urlaţi, and Pietroasa, which produce Cabernet Sauvignon, Merlot, Fetească neagră, Fetească albă, Fetească regală, Riesling, and Tămâioasa.

The vineyards of Drăgăşani, Sâmbureşti, Segarcea, Dăbuleni, Corcova, Vânju Mare, and Dealul Viilor, produce both native varieties—Crâmposia, Gordanul, and Braghina—and imported ones such as Sauvignon, Merlot, Cabernet Sauvignon, Pinot noir, and Muscat Ottonel.

Banat

Wines from the Banat region were sought after for many centuries at the Imperial Court of Vienna.

The vineyards of Teremia Mare, Tomnatec, Recaş, and Miniş produce grape varieties called Majarca, Mutoasă de Maderat, Creaţa, Steinschiller, and Cadarcă. Cadarcă produces a ruby red wine. Velvety, with hints of grass and cloves, it is tannin-free.

Dobrogea

Spread across Dobrogea, from the Bulgarian border to the Black Sea, to the approaches of the Danube Delta region, the vineyards of Oltina, Medgidia, Murfatlar, and Niculiţel produce remarkable wines. Varieties include Cabernet Sauvignon, Merlot, Pinot noir, Italian Riesling, Pinot gris, Aligote, and Muscat Ottonel.

Buying Romanian Wines Today

Here, in the United States, wines under the label of Premiat can be found quite readily. Many wine stores and supermarkets carry them. They are excellent wines at prices anyone can afford. They include Sauvignon Blanc, Dry Riesling, and Târnave Castle Riesling from Transylvania; Chardonnay and Merlot from Dobrogea; Cabernet Sauvignon and Pinot noir from the Dealul Mare region. A Cotnari wine under the label of Dacia is also available. If you cannot locate an outlet in your neighborhood, call the importers at the following address. They will be happy to direct you:

Monsieur Henri Wine Company
803 Jefferson Hwy., New Orleans, LA 70121
Phone: (504) 831-9450, Fax: (504) 831-2383

Many excellent vintage wines are imported under the label of SUVERAN Premier Wines. You will enjoy superb wines at comparably reasonable prices. They include Cabernet Sauvignon, Pinot Noir, Riesling de Târnave, Pinot Gris, Fetească de Târnave, Fetească Albă, Traminer, Fetească de Cotnari, Grasă de Cotnari, Busuioacă de Bohotin, and Tămâioasa

If you cannot readily locate an outlet, contact the importers at the following address. They will be happy to direct you:

VINRO, INC
4405 Valley Forge Drive, Cleveland, Ohio 44126-2826
Phone: (216) 331-7979, Fax: (216) 331-6979

A TASTE OF ROMANIAN-JEWISH COOKING

THE ROMANIAN JEWS AND THEIR CUISINE

If you happen to be a New Yorker, or have visited "The Big Apple," you will know that New York would not be New York without its Jewish Delis—and the delis would not be real delis without pastrami sandwiches—but did you know that a Jewish immigrant from Romania was the first to introduce pastrami to the New World? In his small Lower East Side shop, he prepared this delicacy, and offered it to his clients. It proved an instant success, and became so popular that a pastrami Olympics was held in New York in 1973 to decide on the best pastrami sandwich.

The word "pastrami" comes from the Romanian verb *a păstra*, which means "to keep, to preserve." Originally, Romanian *pastramă* was salted mutton, hung up to dry. Typical New York style pastrami is a highly seasoned cured and smoked beef, made from lean cuts of beef, such as the bottom round. It is usually cured in a brine solution containing herbs and spices such as bay leaves, black and white peppercorns, sugar and garlic. The meat is then lightly smoked, boiled, then rolled in pepper, and finally roasted. It can be eaten cold or hot, thin-sliced, and piled high on rye bread.

Who are the Romanian Jews? When did they settle there? Where did they come from? And how did they acquire their cuisine? According to the Old Testament, Jews are the descendants of Abraham, who was born some 4,000 years ago in the ancient city of Ur, in Sumeria (now Iraq). Jewish tribes migrated to Canaan (Ancient Palestine) and settled there, but we do not know for how long. Nor do we know why, by the 13th century BC they appeared in Goshen, a fertile land in Egypt, where they engaged mainly in farming. However, around 1280 BC, the Jews fled from Egypt, where they suffered severe persecution and bondage under Ramses II. It would seem that the Jewish people have been predestined for travel—as is written in Genesis 12:1: "and God said to Abraham, get out of thy country, and from thy kindred, and from thy father's house, unto a land that I will show you." Led out of Egypt by Moses, they wandered in the desert for years, until, in 1230 BC, they at last recaptured Palestine from the Canaanites—but not for long. Philistines attacked them, and took over Palestine. Once more, about 1000 BC, the Jews succeeded in taking their land back, and a period of peace and prosperity followed. They built their first Temple in Jerusalem.

Over the next millennium, as empires were formed, wars waged, and territories expanded, the Jews were in turn defeated, and their land came under the rule of the Assyrians, then the Egyptians and the Babylonians, followed by the Persians. The Babylonians, in 586 BC, destroyed their Temple and exiled them. The Persians allowed the Jews to return to their land, where they rebuilt their Temple, and during the 2nd century BC, they were given their independence. Finally, around AD 70, the Romans conquered Palestine, burned down the Temple, destroyed Jerusalem, and slaughtered an estimated one million Jews.

From Roman days on, and until the second half of the 20th century, the story of the Jews has been one of a people without their own country; one of many migrations; of establishing and re-establishing communities in diverse lands. They have known periods of peace and prosperity, repeatedly inter- rupted by periods of religious and racial persecutions, massacres, and exile. Wherever they settled, Jews brought with them their religious and cultural traditions, and they adopted and assimilated local customs and traditions as well, including their cuisine.

Claudia Roden writes the following in *The Book of Jewish Food*:

Is there such a thing as Jewish food? After years of researching the subject, I can say that each region or country has its own particular Jewish dishes and these are sometimes quite different from the local cuisine. Jews have adopted the foods of the countries they lived in, but in every country their cooking has had a special touch and taste and characteristic features and some entirely original dishes which have made it distinctive and recognizable...

Food is frequently mentioned in the Old Testament. The dietary code of practice required for choosing and preparing foods, known as kosher cooking, is derived from the Bible and the Talmud. From these beginnings, and as a result of the movement of the Jews from country to country, diverse and yet characteristic Jewish styles emerged. Broadly speaking, their cuisine can be divided into two styles—Sephardi and Ashkenazi. *Sephardi* means *of Spain* in Hebrew. Originally it was applied to those Jews who trace their ancestry to Spain, but commonly includes all those who lived in Spain, Portugal, Italy, North Africa, Syria, Turkey, Greece, Iraq, and Iran. Their cuisine is one of warm and sunny climates; they use peppers, squash, eggplant, tomatoes, rice, salt- water fish, and olive oil. *Ashkenaz* is an old Hebrew word for Germany. In common use *Ashkenazi* Jews are those who trace their ancestry to Christian countries in Europe. Mostly, their cuisine is a cold climate one, using chicken fat, onion and garlic, cabbage, carrots and potatoes, freshwater fish, and salt herring.

In the region that is now Romania, there were very few Jews before the 19th century.

Between 600 BC and 700 BC a small number found their way to Northern Balkans by way of Persia and Asia Minor. They were traders and merchants, who settled in Greek colonies and commercial settlements such as Kallatis (now Mangalia), and later in Tomis (now Constanţa). Others came with the Romans during the 2nd century AD, when Dacia was conquered and turned into a Roman province. A Roman legion from Palestine participated in the conquest, and we have archeological evidence, such as Jewish coins from that period, that certain Jewish merchants and traders came to do business there.

During the 15th and 16th centuries, a few of the Sephardim who emigrated from Spain to Greece and Asia Minor during the crusades and inquisition, ended up in Moldavia and Wallachia. However, not more than 1000 to 5000 Jews are estimated to have settled in that area. A dramatic increase in numbers occurred during the 19th century, particularly in Moldavia, where the Jewish population increased from 12,000 in 1803 to 200,000 in 1899. Many of these Jews, both Ashkenazim and Sephardim, whose families had settled in Russia in the Middle Ages, particularly in the Polish territories and the Ukraine, were now heading West because of persecutions and violent pogroms during the period of the Tsars.

By 1939, at the beginning of World War II, Romania's Jewish population peaked at around 800,000. About half were living in the provinces of Bessarabia, Bucovina, and Transylvania, which were integrated into Romania in 1918, at the end of World War I. It was then the second largest ethnic minority with about 4.5% of the Romanian population. By 1945, at the end of the War, only about half of the Jews were left in Romania. After the War, the communist regime allowed the emigration of ethnic minorities, and most of the remaining Jews did so, especially to Israel. By 1956, the number had dropped to about 136,000; by the census of 1977, to 24,667; and by 1992, only 9107 Jews remained in Romania.

Many Romanian Jews who left their homes behind, brought with them recipes handed down by their parents and grandparents; recipes that originated in Romania, adapted or created by their families, and which have now become a part of the diverse Jewish cuisine. A sampling of these dishes follows.

CHOPPED CHICKEN LIVER

(Jewish Pâté)

This recipe was contributed by **Famous Sammy's Roumanian Steak House** in New York City, and is one of the most popular Jewish appetizer dishes.

3 tbsp. *schmaltz**
1 or 2 large white onions, chopped
1 lb. chicken liver
2 tsp. salt
2 tsp. fresh ground black pepper
1 tsp. granulated sugar
2 eggs, hard-boiled and sliced
1 black radish, peeled and grated on the big side
1 onion, chopped
1 cup *gribenes***

Serves 6 - 8
Preparation time: 15 min. Cooking time: 15 min.

❑ Heat the fat in a heavy skillet over medium heat. Add onion and sauté until soft and golden in color, about 5 min. Add liver and continue cooking, stirring with a wooden spoon, until liver is well done, about 8 min.

❑ Add salt, pepper, and sugar. Stir and cook another minute.

❑ Transfer liver mixture to a bowl, let cool a few minutes, and add sliced egg. Mix well, and pass through fine meat grinder or food processor. Return pâté to bowl. If it is too dry, add more *schmaltz*.

❑ Add grated radish, chopped raw onion, and the *gribenes*. Mix well. Moisten with added *schmaltz* and add salt and pepper to taste, if needed.

❑ Arrange on a flat serving dish and chill in the refrigerator until ready to use. The pâté can be garnished with sieved hard-boiled egg yolk and white, and bordered with parsley. Serve with thin slices of bread.

Schmaltz is rendered chicken or goose fat. See p. 304 for recipe. This gives the chopped liver the traditional old-fashioned taste. However, if cholesterol level is of concern, use non-animal fat or oil instead.
***Gribenes* is chicken or goose skin cracklings. See p. 304 for recipe.

SCHMALTZ AND GRIBENES

1 goose or chicken
1 onion, thin sliced
1 tsp. salt
¼ cup cold water

Makes: 1 cup
Preparation time: 10 min. Cooking time: 35 min.

❑ Remove chicken or goose skin and fat from cavity and outside. Cut skin into small pieces, about 1 in. square. Measure about 1 cup full.

❑ Wash and dry. Place in a heavy skillet, add onion, salt, and water. Heat uncovered over very low heat, letting the fat melt slowly. Cook until the fat has melted and water evaporated, about 35 min.

❑ With a slotted spoon, remove gribenes. Sprinkle with salt to taste, let cool, and then place in a covered storage container. Refrigerate.

❑ Strain schmaltz into a small bowl and refrigerate or freeze for later use. Dispose of onion or use it for other purposes.

Schmaltz gave that special flavor to the dishes of the Ashkenazi Jews. It was also used as a spread instead of butter.

The gribenes is also very tasty when mixed with mashed potatoes, and is often eaten as a snack with drinks or as a lunch with rye bread.

SORREL SOUP

Schav Borscht

8 oz. fresh sorrel*
1 cup fresh watercress, chopped
1 onion, chopped
1 cup celery, chopped
1 lb. potatoes, peeled and cubed
1½ qts. Vegetarian Soup stock**
1 lemon, juice and grated zest
1 tbsp. granulated sugar
1 tsp. salt
½ tsp. fresh ground black pepper
¾ cup sour cream
fresh parsley, chopped

Serves 4-6
Preparation time: 50 min. Cooking time: 45 min.
(does not include cooling time)

❑ Unless the sorrel is very young, it will need to be de-ribbed and stemmed. Wash and dry sorrel, pull off the stem, removing firm center rib, and chop coarsely.

❑ In a large non-stick saucepan, place sorrel, watercress, onion, celery, and potatoes. Pour in vegetable stock. Bring to a boil over high heat. Lower heat to low and cook until potatoes are cooked through, about 20 min. Partially cool soup, lightly mashing potatoes.

❑ Purée, in batches, in a blender or food processor. Return soup to saucepan. Add lemon juice and zest, sugar, salt, and pepper. Let soup cool completely in a glass or ceramic container. Then refrigerate.

Serve cold. When ready to serve, mix in part of the sour cream and stir. Squirt the rest of the sour cream to decorate the top of the soup bowls. Sprinkle with parsley.

---

*If sorrel is not available, use fresh young spinach
**Use recipe for Vegetarian Soup stock, p.74, or use stock cubes. If you use stock cubes, reduce salt quantity.

PEPPERS STUFFED WITH CHEESE

Pipiruchkas Reynadas de Keso

Based on a recipe by Claudia Roden[1], this most wonderful dish from Judeo-Spanish communities of the Balkans, including those in Romania, is a favorite first course. It can also be served as a side dish with the main course.

6 red or yellow peppers
2 tbsp. sunflower oil
2 garlic cloves, chopped
1 lb. tomatoes, peeled and chopped*
1 tsp. salt
½ tsp. fresh ground black pepper
1 tsp. granulated sugar
6 slices *telemea* cheese**

Serves 6
Preparation time: 15 min. Cooking time: 50 min.

❑ Grill peppers over charcoal or about 3" under the broiler (see GRILLED PEPPER SALAD, p.52 for suggestions), peel them, and remove the stems and seeds, trying not to tear them too much.
❑ Make a tomato sauce:***
—In a saucepan, heat oil over medium heat. Add garlic and sauté until it begins to color, about 1 min.
—Add tomatoes, salt, pepper, and sugar. Stir, lower heat to low, and simmer for about 15 min.
❑ Preheat oven to 350°F.
❑ Slip a large slice of cheese inside each pepper. Arrange peppers side by side in a baking dish. Pour sauce over them. Bake in oven for about 20 min., until cheese is soft.

Serve very hot.

---

*You can use an equivalent quantity of canned peeled and chopped tomatoes.
**You can substitute with French goat cheese, halumi, or mozzarella.
***As a variant, omit the tomato sauce and just brush the peppers with a bit of olive oil before baking them.
[1]*The Book of Jewish Food* (see Bibliography)

MUSHROOMS WITH TOMATO SAUCE

Based on a recipe by Claudia Roden[1], this dish was prevalent in Jewish communities in both Hungary and Romania. In Romania it was often accompanied by *mămăligă*, a genuinely Romanian favorite side dish, adopted and well loved by Romanian Jews.

> 1 lb. boletus mushrooms*
> 4 tbsp. light vegetable oil
> 1 large onion, chopped
> 4 garlic cloves, crushed
> 1 tsp. sweet paprika
> 1 lb. tomatoes, peeled and chopped**
> 2 tsp. salt
> 1 tsp. granulated sugar
> ½ lemon, juice
> ¾ cup red wine
> ½ tsp. crushed chilli peppers

> *Serves 6*
> *Preparation time: 10 min. Cooking time: 35 min.*

❑ Wipe mushrooms with damp cloth if needed. Remove stems and leave them whole.

❑ In a large skillet, heat oil over medium heat. Sauté onion until soft but not browned, about 3-4 min.

❑ Add garlic, paprika, and mushrooms. Continue cooking, stirring with a wooden spoon, for about 1 min.

❑ Add tomatoes, salt, sugar, and lemon juice. Stir, lower heat to low, and simmer for about 10 min.

❑ Add wine and chilli peppers, and continue cooking for about 20 min., or until mushrooms are tender and the sauce is reduced.

Remove mushrooms to a warm serving dish, and spoon tomato sauce over each mushroom. Serve hot with *mămăligă,* or as a side dish with chicken. It also makes a delicious hot appetizer.

---

* Chanterelles or shiitake mushrooms make delicious substitutes.
**You can use an equivalent quantity of canned peeled and chopped tomatoes.
[1] *The Book of Jewish Food* (see Bibliography)

CHICKPEAS *TZIMMES**

Tzimmes Nahit

This delicious, nutty, slightly sweet, dish is based on a recipe by Oded Schwartz[1], which was handed down to him by his grandmother, Mania Dostrovsky, née Levinson. It originates in Bessarabia, which, before 1812, was part of the Principality of Moldavia, when it was annexed by Russia. In 1916, it was reunited with Romania but in 1940, Soviet forces invaded Bessarabia, and in 1944, it became Soviet, known as the Moldavian SSR. Upon the collapse of the Soviet Union, Bessarabia chose to remain independent, and is known as the Republic of Moldova.

1 cup dry chickpeas, soaked overnight
3 tbsp. *schmaltz***, vegetable fat or oil
2 tbsp. flour
2 tbsp. honey, brown sugar, or syrup
1 tsp. salt
1 tsp. fresh ground black pepper

Serves 6 - 8
Preparation time: 5 min. Cooking time: 20 min.

❑ In a kettle, bring 3-4 cups water to boil. Cook chickpeas until tender, about 45 min. Drain, and save 1¼ cup of cooking liquid.

❑ In a large skillet, melt the fat over low heat. Add flour and mix well. Add honey and continue cooking, stirring continually until mixture starts to caramelize and turn light brown, about 2 min.

❑ Add the saved liquid. Increase heat to medium-high. Bring to boil while stirring. Fold in chickpeas.

❑ Add salt and pepper, and continue to cook for about 10 min., stirring often to prevent sticking. Stir gently to prevent chickpeas from losing their shape.

Serve hot, as a side dish. This goes well with lamb.

---

* The word *tzimmes* comes from the German word *zusammen* meaning "together"— a meal in a pot. Each country is known for its *tzimmes*. Romanians used chickpeas and pumpkin. All *tzimmes* are flavored with generous amounts of pepper and sweetened with sugar or honey.
** Rendered goose or chicken fat.
[1] *In Search of Plenty* (see Bibliography)

HARICOT BEAN SALAD

Based on a recipe by Claudia Roden[1], this is a delicious summer main-course salad. It was a popular dish with Jews throughout the Balkans and Turkey.

1 cup small dried white haricot beans
1 mild onion, finely chopped*
2 tbsp. white wine vinegar
1 tsp. salt
1 tsp. fresh ground black pepper
1 garlic clove, crushed
3 tbsp. fresh parsley, chopped
4 tbsp. extra virgin olive oil
3 eggs, hard-boiled and sliced
3 tomatoes, sliced or wedged
12 black Greek Calamata olives
6 slices *telemea* cheese(optional)**

Serves 4-6
Preparation time: 15 min. Cooking time: 1 - 1½hrs.

❑ Turn beans into a sieve, pick over and remove any foreign matter or damaged beans. Run cold water over the beans. Place beans in a bowl. Pour 3 cups cold water over them, and let soak overnight.***

❑ Drain soaked beans.

❑ In a kettle add water in an amount of about double the volume of the soaked beans. Bring to boil over high heat. Add beans, and boil vigorously for 10 min. Lower heat and simmer gently until beans are tender, about 1 - 1½ hrs. Drain.

❑ Place beans in a bowl and let cool until they are warm.

❑ While the beans are cooling, prepare a vinaigrette sauce with 3 tbsp. olive oil, vinegar, salt and pepper.

❑ To the warm beans, add onion, garlic, and parsley. Mix well. Then add vinaigrette sauce, and mix well again. Let salad cool completely.

Arrange on a serving platter, garnish with eggs, tomatoes, olives, and cheese (optional). Sprinkle tomatoes with remaining olive oil. Sprinkle with salt and pepper to taste.

*This salad is also delicious with chopped shallots.
**You can substitute with Greek feta cheese.
***If there is not enough time to soak overnight, cover beans with water, bring to boil, simmer for 2 min., then soak beans for 2-3 hours.
[1] *The Book of Jewish Food* (see Bibliography)

SWEET AND SOUR FISH

In Eastern Europe, sweet and sour fish was a very popular Jewish dish. In Romania, carp was generally used.

6 carp steaks, about 1" thick*
salt and pepper
2 tbsp. vegetable fat or oil
1 carrot, peeled and sliced
1 onion, chopped
1½ cups mushrooms, sliced
2 cloves garlic, chopped
4 in. fresh ginger, peeled and chopped
4 cups cold water
2 lemons, thin sliced, seeds removed
1 bay leaf
½ tsp. ground cloves
1 tbsp. black peppercorns, slightly crushed
½ cup cider vinegar
2 tbsp. light brown sugar
½ cup raisins
½ cup gingersnap crumbs
4 tbsp. fresh parsley, chopped

Serves 6
Preparation time: 25 min. Cooking time: 1 hr. 10 min.

❏ Sprinkle fish steaks lightly with salt and pepper. Set aside.

❏ In a large non-stick saucepan, heat fat or oil over low heat. Add carrot, onion, mushrooms, garlic, and ginger. Stir well. Cook, covered, until vegetables are lightly browned, about 25 min., stirring occasionally.

❏ Add water, slices of 1 lemon, bay leaf, cloves, and peppercorns. Increase heat to high and bring to a boil, uncovered. Lower heat to low, cover, and simmer for 15 min.

❏ Add fish, cover, and braise over low heat until fish begins to flake and separates easily from center bone, about 12-15 min.

❏ Using a perforated spoon or skimmer, carefully remove fish steaks and place in a deep glass or ceramic dish. Save the cooking broth.

❏ Bring broth to a boil again and cook until liquid is reduced to half, about 7-

10 min. Strain into a smaller saucepan. To the clear broth, add vinegar, brown sugar, and raisins. Reduce heat and simmer 2-3 min. longer. Stir in crumbs and parsley. Cool slightly, then pour over fish. Cool completely, then refrigerate overnight.

Serve chilled, garnished with remaining lemon slices, and accompanied by *mămăligă* (see POLENTA chapter), or noodles.

---

*You can substitute salmon, swordfish, or catfish for carp.

BROILED SAUSAGES

Carnatzlach

This dish appears to be influenced both by the *Moldavian Breaded Meat Patties* (p.173) and the *Mititei* (p.171), but has its own distinct flavor. The name derives from *cârnaţi*, the Romanian word for sausages. These little sausages are delicious eaten hot or cold, with mustard or topped with sautéed, browned onions, and accompanied by *mămăligă* (see *Polenta* chapter p. 104), or french fried potatoes.

1½ lbs. medium lean ground beef or lamb
1 medium onion, grated
1 carrot, peeled and grated
1 large garlic clove, crushed
3 tbsp. fresh parsley, chopped
1 tsp. sage
½ tsp. fresh ground black pepper
1 tsp. hot Hungarian paprika
½ tsp. crushed hot red pepper
1 egg, slightly beaten
flour

Serves 6 (2 sausages per serving)
Preparation time: 15 min. Cooking time: 10-12 min.

❑ In a bowl, combine all ingredients except the flour. Mix well with a wooden spoon, and then with your hands, until all ingredients are well mixed.
❑ With the help of a tablespoon, take portions of meat mixture and shape into sausages about 3 in. x 1 in. in diameter. Taper the ends, and lightly coat with flour. You should end up with about 12 sausage shaped patties.
❑ Preheat broiler to a moderate temperature*. Broil, turning patties to brown well on all sides, about 10-12 min.

Serve hot or cold.

*Alternatively, grill them on the barbecue.

CORNMEAL KUGEL*

Reminiscent of corn bread and some cheesecakes, this tasty dish is moist, sweet, and slightly tangy.

½ cup yellow cornmeal
½ cup flour
½ tsp. salt
1 tsp. baking powder
¼ cup creamy cottage cheese
¾ cup plain yogurt
¾ cup sour cream
2 tbsp. butter, softened
½ cup granulated sugar
2 eggs, separated

Serves 4-6
Preparation time: 30 min. Cooking time: 45 min.

❑ Sift cornmeal, flour, salt, and baking powder into a bowl.
❑ In a separate bowl, mix cottage cheese, yogurt and sour cream together.
❑ Mix ¼ cup sugar with butter. Add egg yolks and beat to a smooth cream.
❑ Transfer the creamed mixture into a large bowl. Stir in cheese mixture and dry ingredients, little by little, alternating each time. Mix until batter is smooth.
❑ Grease a 9" pie oven dish. Preheat oven to 375°F.
❑ In a mixer bowl, mix remaining sugar with egg whites. Whip mixture until stiff. Then fold egg white mixture into batter.
❑ Pour batter into oven dish and bake about 45 min. or until kugel is nicely browned and a knife inserted in the center comes out clean.

Serve warm, spooning some sour cream on it, or cold, with fruit salad. It is also delicious as a coffee cake.

---

*The word *kugel* generally means a pudding, *either* sweet or savory. In German, *kugel* means 'ball'. This possibly indicates the shape of the special pot (*kugel-topf*) in which it was baked.

Bibliography

Algar, Ayla. *Classical Turkish Cooking*. New York: Harper Collins, 1991 (Stamford, CT PL 641.59561A394c).

Bachman, Ronald D. (ed.). *Romania, A Country Study*. Washington, DC: Federal Research Division, Library of Congress, 1991. (Stamford, CT PL 914.98R758cs).

Baerlein, Henry (ed.). *Romanian Oasis*. London, England: Frederick Muller Ltd., 1948. (NY PL 42nd. St.).

Balmez, Didi. *Carte de Bucate*. Bucharest, Romania: Editura Technică, 1978 (NY PL 42nd St. JBE94-10014).

Balmez, Didi. *Carte de Bucate Alese*. Bucharest, Romania: Editura Technică, 1981 (NY PL 42nd St. JFE93-3652).

Balmez, Didi. *Reţete Culinare*. Bucharest, Romania: Editura Technică, 1985.

Battistotti, Bruno, et.al. *Cheese: A Guide to the World of Cheese and Cheesemaking*. Sara Harris (tr.) New York: Facts On File Publications, 1983. (Stamford, CT PL 641.373C515c1).

Bridgewater, William and Kurtz, Seymour (ed.). *The Columbia Encyclopedia, (3rd ed.)*. New York: Columbia University Press, 1963.

Bullwinkel, Madelaine. *Gourmet Preserves Ches Madelaine*. Chicago: Contemporary Books, 1984 (Stamford, CT PL 641.852B938g).

Chamberlain, Lesley. *The Food and Cooking of Eastern Europe*. London, England: Penguin Books Ltd., 1989. (Stamford, CT PL 641.5947C443f).

Claiborne, Craig. *Craig Claiborne's The New York Times Food Encyclopedia*. Whitman, Joan (comp.). New York: Times Books, 1985. (Stamford, CT PL 641.0321C585c).

Creangă, Ion. *Folk Tales from Roumania*. Mabel Nadriş (tr.). New York: Roy Publishers, 1953. (NY PL 42nd. St., NQYE).

315

Davidson, Aloa and Jane. *Dumas on Food*. London, England:The Folio Society, 1978 (NY PL Mid Manhattan 641,3032D).

Eliade, Mircea. *The Romanians—A Concise History*. Rodica Michaela Scafeş (tr.). Bucharest: Roza Vânturilor Publishing House, 1992.

Eminescu, Mihai. *Poems*. Corneliu M. Popescu (tr.). Romania: Editura Cartea Românească, 1989 (Biblioteca Română, NY 850.0 E-48).

Enache, Dumitru. *Bucătărie Pentru Toţi*. Bucharest, Romania: Editura Technica, 1990.

Giacosa, Ilaria Gozzini. *A Taste of Ancient Rome*. Herklotz, Anna (tr.). Chicago: The University of Chicago Press, 1992. (Greenwich, CT PL 641.5937GOZZI).

Grigson, Jane. *Food with the Famous*. New York: Atheneum, 1980. (NY PL Mid Manhattan 641.5G)

Hall, D. J. *Romanian Furrow*. London, England: Methuen & Co., Ltd., 1933 (NY PL 42nd. St., GIVB).

Hoffman, Eva. *Exit into History*. London, England: William Heinemann, 1993.

Ianco, Ana. *175 Recettes de Cuisine Roumaine*. Paris, France: Jacques Grancher, Editor, 1990.

Kramarz, Inge. *The Balkan Cookbook*. New York: Crown Publishers, Inc., 1972. (NY PL 42nd St. JFD94-16462).

Lang, George. *The Cuisine of Hungary*. Atheneum, USA, 1971. Harmondsworth, Middlesex, England: Penguin Books Ltd., 1985.

Liess, Martha. *Kochbuch*. Bucharest, Romania: Verlag für Fremdssprachige Literatur, 1959. (NY PL 42nd St. D-12 3741).

Louard, Elisabeth. *Old World Kitchen: The Rich Tradition of European Peasant Cooking*. New York: Bantam Books, 1987. (Stamford, CT PL 641.594L9260).

McNally, Raymond T. and Radu Florescu. *In Search of Dracula*. New York: Galahad Books, 1972. (Stamford, CT PL 809.933M1691).

McKenzie, Andrew. *Romanian Journey*. London, England: Robert Hale, 1983. (Edinburgh Central Library).

Madeleine, B. *Savoury Rumanian Dishes and Choice Wines*. Bucharest, Romania: Publisher unknown, 1939. (NY PL 42nd St. Annex).

Marian, Simeon Florea. *Legendele Păsărilor*. Iaşi, Romania: Editura Junimea, 1975. (NY PL Donnell, Rom398.245M).

Marin, Sanda. *Carte de Bucate Ed.IV.* Bucharest, Romania: Editura Technică, 1959. (NY PL 42nd St. D-12 5991).

Mirodan, Vladimir. *The Balkan Cookbook.* Gretna, USA: Pelican Publishing Company, 1989.

Marquis, Vivienne & Haskell, Patricia. *The Cheese Book.* New York: Simon and Schuster, 1964, 1965. (Stamford, CT PL 641.373M357c).

Munteanu, George (Ed.). *Proverbe Româneşti.* Bucharest, Romania: Editura Minerva, 1984.

Nelson, Kay Shaw. *The Eastern European Cookbook.* New York: Dover Publications, Inc., 1973. (NY PL 42nd St.).

Niculescu-Mizil, George. *Fata din Împărăţia Curcubeului.* Romania: Editura *Creangă, 1970. (NY PL Donnell, Rom398.2N).*

Pann, Anton. *Povestea Vorbii.* Bucharest, Romania: Editura de Stat pentru Literatură şi Artă, 1957. This edition followed the edition *Culegere de Proverbi sau Povestea Vorbii— de prin Lume Adunate şi Iarăşi la Lume Date* by Anton Pann (3 volumes), Bucharest (1852-1853). (NY PL Donnell Rom398.2049P)

Perl, Lila. *Foods and Festivals of the Danube Lands.* Cleveland, Ohio: The World Publishing Company, 1969. (NY PL 53rd St).

Podoleanu, Liliana & Luca, Thea. *Carte de Bucate.* Bucharest, Romania: Editura Ceres, 1980. (NY PL 42nd St. JFD94-10578).

Polvay, Marina. *All Along the Danube.* Englewood Cliffs, NJ: Prentice-Hall, Inc., 1979.

Popescu, Julian. *Let's Visit Romania.* London: Burke Publishing Company, Ltd., 1984.(Stamford, CT PL J914.98P).

Root, Waverly. *The Food of Italy.* New York: Atheneum, 1971.

Sburlan, Smaranda. *Reţete Culinare Pentru Familia Mea.* Bucharest, Romania: Editura Ceres, 1995.

Septilici, Georgetta. *Gustări Reci...Calde...Salate.* Bucharest, Romania: Editura Ceres, 1994.

Slăvescu, Micaela. *Cuisine de Roumanie.* Paris, France: Syros-Alternatives, 9bis rue Abel Hovelacque, 1992.

Stan, Anişoara. *The Romanian Cook Book.* New York: The Citadel Press, 1951. (NY PL 42nd ST., VTI).

Strătilescu, Tereza. *From Carpathians to Pindus.* Boston, USA: John W. Luce & Company, 1907. (NY PL 42nd St., GIVB).

Sunset (Ed.). *Fish & Shellfish*. Menlo Park, CA., USA: Sunset Publishing Corp., 1991.

Toussaint-Samat, Maguelonne. *A History of Food*. Bell, Anthea (tr.). Original French: Bordas, 1987. Cambridge, MA: Blackwell Publishers, 238 Main Street, Ste. 501, Cambridge, 1992.

Treptow, Kurt W. (ed.). *Classics of Roumanian Literature, Vol I, Selected Works of Ion Creangă and Mihai Eminescu*. New York: Columbia University Press, 1991.

Waldo, Myra. *The Complete Round-the-World Cookbook*. New York: Doubleday & Co., 1967.

Willinger, Faith Heller. *Eating in Italy*. New York: Hearst Books, 1989. (Stamford, CT PL 641,09451W733e)

Additional sources for Romanian-Jewish recipes:

Cohen, Elizabeth Wolf. *New Jewish Cooking*. London: Quintet Publishishing Ltd., 1993.

Marks, Gil. *The World of Jewish Cooking*. New York: Simon and Schuster, 1996.

Roden, Claudia. *The Book of Jewish Food*. London: Penguin Books, Ltd., 1997.

Schwartz, Oded. *In Search of Plenty: A History of Jewish Food*. London: Kyle Cathie, Ltd., 1992.

Wasserstein, Bernard. *Vanishing Disapora*. London: Penguin Books, Ltd., 1996.

INDEX BY NAMES AND PLACES

INDEX OF RECIPES BY CHAPTER

INDEX OF RECIPES

A TASTE OF ROMANIAN-JEWISH COOKING

INDEX DE REŢETE DUPA CAPITOLE

INDEX

ALPHABETICAL INDEX OF RECIPES

INDEX

INDEX

INDEX OF RECIPES

A TASTE OF ROMANIAN-JEWISH COOKING

Romanian interest titles from Hippocrene . . .

Beginner's Romanian

Designed to meet the bilingual needs of the businessperson, tourist or student traveling in Romania. First learn about Romanian history and culture, driving tips, social customs, restaurant practices and other daily tasks. Then learn basic language skills, including vocabulary, grammar and phrases to move about freely in Romania.

200 pages • 5½ x 8½ • 0-7818-0208-3 • $7.95pb • (79)

Romanian Conversation Guide

Perfect for travelers, this is one of the best learner's guides to Romanian available. With easy to follow phonetic transcriptions and a handy index to look up appropriate phrases quickly and easily, this book will help you get around and converse with native speakers with ease.

200 pages • 5 ½ x 8 ½ • 0-87052-803-3 • $9.95pb • (153)

Romanian Grammar

This primer of the Romanian language is an invaluable reference guide for English speakers. Conjugations and declensions are clearly presented in tabular form, and the functions of all parts of speech are demonstrated through illustrative sentences. Providing a comprehensive, and easily understandable introduction to the basic grammatical structure of Romanian, the book can be used both with self-taught courses, and in classroom instruction.

108 pages • 5 ½ x 8 ½ • 0-87052-892-0 • $6.95pb • (232)

Romanian-English/ English-Romanian Standard Dictionary

Including over 18,000 entries with multiple definitions and a guide to Romanian and English pronunciation, this dictionary is perfect for the traveler, businessperson or student. Also includes an appendix of geographical names.

800 pages • 4³/₈ x 7 • 0-7818-0444-2 • $17.95pb • (99)

Prices subject to change without prior notice. **To purchase Hippocrene Books** contact your local bookstore, call (718) 454-2366, or write to: HIPPOCRENE BOOKS, 171 Madison Avenue, New York, NY 10016. Please enclose check or money order, adding $5.00 shipping (UPS) for the first book and $.50 for each additional book.